NEVER TRUST A LIBERAL OVER 3

—ESPECIALLY A REPUBLICAN

NEVER TRUST A LIBERAL OVER 3

—ESPECIALLY A REPUBLICAN

ANN COULTER

REGNERY
Publishing, Inc.
An Eagle Publishing Company • Washington, DC

Copyright © 2013 by Ann Coulter

Cataloging-in-Publication data on file with the Library of Congress

ISBN 978-1-62157-191-9

Published in the United States by
Regnery Publishing, Inc.
One Massachusetts Avenue NW
Washington, DC 20001
www.Regnery.com

Manufactured in the United States of America

10 9 8 7 6 5 4 3 2 1

The interview on pp. 353–62 is reprinted with the permission of Beliefnet, where it originally appeared.

Books are available in quantity for promotional or premium use. Write to Director of Special Sales, Regnery Publishing, Inc., One Massachusetts Avenue NW, Washington, DC 20001, for information on discounts and terms, or call (202) 216-0600.

Distributed to the trade by
Perseus Distribution
250 West 57th Street
New York, NY 10107

For my brothers, John and Jim, who inspired,
directly and indirectly, many of the columns in this book

Contents

CHAPTER ONE

Will This Be on the Midterms?

L IBERALS NEVER GIVE UP. Nothing is ever over until they get their way, much like two-year-olds. That's why we have to go back every few years and remind everyone that we already had this argument, and liberals lost. There's a reason our Party's symbol is the elephant—we never forget—and the Democrats' is a jackass.

Hey—anyone remember when liberals told us in the 1970s that Earth was going to freeze in two years? Now they tell us it's going to overheat in two years.

Remember when Hubert Humphrey said he'd eat his hat if civil rights laws ever led to racial quotas? Now they call us "racist" for opposing racial quotas.

Remember when Teddy Kennedy assured us his immigration bill would not alter the country's ethnic mix? Since the bill passed, immigration has changed the nation's ethnicity from nearly 90 percent white in 1965 to about 63 percent white in 2013.

Remember when they called President Ronald Reagan a dangerous cowboy threatening world peace? Now they act like he was a good partner with liberals in winning the Cold War.

Remember when the media howled that President Bush LIED in his State of the Union address about Saddam Hussein seeking uranium from Niger? Then two investigative committees, here and in Britain, established that he was telling the truth and liberal darling Joe Wilson was the liar.

If you do remember any of that, then Aaron Sorkin's TV show *The Newsroom* will make no sense to you. Conservatives win an argument in real life and then, a year later, Sorkin writes a little teleplay reversing the facts so that liberals get to win.

Most people barely pay attention to what's happening *now*, much less two years ago—and much, much less a few decades ago. That's how the liberal version of history becomes accepted fact. It's not that history is written by the victors. History is written by the pushy. When one side cares MUCH more about the historical record, there's not a lot you can do about it. Especially when the pushy have tenure.

I've often said that I could rewrite the same columns every year because liberals keep telling the same lies. But there's a limit to how many times a person can point out that Valerie Plame wasn't an undercover agent, the August 6, 2001, Presidential Daily Briefing titled "Bin Laden Determined to Strike in US" was irrelevant to the 9/11 attacks, Joe McCarthy was right, the teenagers convicted of the attack on the Central Park jogger were guilty, executed murderer Troy Davis was guilty, armed citizens reduce crime, modern science has proved Darwin wrong, waterboarding as practiced at Guantanamo was never considered a "war crime"—and so on.

(One victory: at least Keith Olbermann has stopped telling people he went to an Ivy League school!)

You think you've finally defeated liberals on some issue, but they're just waiting impatiently to repeat the same thing they said last time. There are entire Hollywood movies about the innocence of Ethel and Julius Rosenberg. The Left never thought the Soviet Union would fall. When it did collapse and all the proof came tumbling out, establishing that Joe McCarthy was right and all the liberal martyrs had been Soviet spies, the natural thing would be for them to shut up for the rest of their lives, hunker down, and hope no one brought it up. Au contraire! They never quit. *You know what, we're going to make* another *movie about the horrors of the Red Scare.* More astonishing than the range of issues liberals got wrong is the fact that they're the ones who won't let it go.

The magnificently successful Iraq War has been rewritten as a failure, the Vietnam War is said to have been "unwinnable" from the start, and liberals claim Ronald Reagan didn't win the Cold War, it just ended. Or maybe Gorbachev ended it. In any event, Reagan merely continued the policies of his predecessors—just like Rudy Giuliani continued Dinkins's crime policies.

The *New York Times'* treatment of any subject will be the same until the end of time, only more so. Every once in awhile, you have to go back and set the record straight. That's what this book does.

Liberal pushiness prevails not only in history but in actual public policy. We vote and vote and vote and vote until they win, and then we never vote again. Or we'll have a big national debate about one of their kooky ideas, the people vote, liberals lose—and they bring a lawsuit to get what they want by judicial decree. Even when we win, we can't win.

In California alone, multiple lawsuits were brought to block popular initiatives banning: racial quotas at state schools, welfare for illegal aliens, and gay marriage. Liberals got a court to overturn the people's will in all these cases, except the prohibition of racial quotas. But they won't stop trying! A federal appeals court first upheld Proposition 209's ban on race discrimination in college admissions in 1997, one year after the initiative passed. In 2012, another lawsuit was brought, again demanding that the same law be overturned—with support from Governor Jerry Brown, who I believe is supposed to defend California's laws.

Proposition 187, denying illegal aliens welfare, passed overwhelmingly in California, with the support of 64 percent of whites, 56 percent of African Americans, and 31 percent of Hispanics. This was in the face of a massive PR campaign portraying the proposition as a piece of anti-Hispanic racism. Forty percent of voters said the only reason they went to the polls that day was to vote on Proposition 187. (The reaction of most Californians to the initiative was: *THAT'S NOT ALREADY THE LAW?*)

Liberal groups instantly challenged the measure in court. Three days after California voters approved it, a federal judge issued a restraining order to prevent the law's implementation, and later declared it "unconstitutional." That ruling was being appealed when Democrat Gray Davis was elected governor and dropped the appeal. A law denying welfare to illegal aliens, approved by nearly 60 percent of California voters, never became law because liberals didn't like it. *I came here illegally, but you know what? I can't make it in this economy. Would you guys mind cutting me a check once a month?* The voters can't stop that.

The entire country jawboned gay marriage for a few years after the Massachusetts Supreme Court foisted the issue on us in 2003 by discovering a right to this novel idea in the state constitution—written in 1779 by the very Christian John Adams. Americans responded by adopting constitutional amendments in thirty-one states explicitly prohibiting gay marriage. Other states banned it by statute. Everywhere gay marriage was put on the ballot, including liberal states like Oregon and California, it lost. (One state briefly seemed to approve of gay marriage—Arizona—but that was apparently a mistake because two years later the voters overwhelmingly approved a constitutional amendment banning it.)

The people hadn't started the argument about gay marriage, but they ended it. The public didn't want gay marriage.

Or at least the people thought they had ended it. When allowing people to vote resulted in a resounding "NO!" liberals sued and got the courts to give them gay marriage. A few years later, voters in three states finally approved gay marriage. The Left's philosophy is: wanting something more than someone else gives us the right to win.

When conservatives win a favorable Supreme Court opinion, it's not a back-door ruling by judges vindicating some nutty theory believed by 20 percent of the people. And when they bring lawsuits it's only to enforce real rights, actually mentioned in the Constitution. Conservative court victories tend to confirm public opinion, not upend it.

The Supreme Court finally acknowledged the right to bear arms, for example, in the 2008 case, *District of Columbia v. Heller*. But by then, thirty-nine states had already adopted concealed-carry laws. Not only that, but even law professors not inclined to agree with the National Rifle Association, such as Akil Amar at Yale, Alan Dershowitz at Harvard, and Sanford Levinson at the University of Texas, had concluded that the Second Amendment guaranteed an individual right to bear arms. After all that, the Court finally admitted what every serious person already knew: the Constitution grants the people a right to bear arms.

But there's no permanent victory on any issue with liberals. Maybe they can't ban guns at the moment, but they'll wait, hoping for a switch in the Supreme Court's membership so they can start grabbing everyone's guns.

After the Newtown, Connecticut, school shooting at the end of 2012, liberals turned on a dime from vein-popping, angry self-righteousness about guns to sneering at gun rights supporters: *no one wants to take your guns away!*

Really? Are you sure, because I think *you* do.

- In March 2013, Illinois congresswoman Jan Schakowsky warned, "An assault weapons ban is just the beginning," adding that "a complete ban on handguns could be possible through state and local action."
- In December 2012, New York governor Andrew Cuomo said, "Confiscation could be an option…mandatory sale to the state could be an option."
- In a 1995 interview about the so-called assault weapons ban, Senator Dianne Feinstein said, "If I could have banned them all—'Mr. and Mrs. America turn in your guns'—I would have!"
- Running for president in 1988, Jesse Jackson described his position on gun control to the *New York Times*, saying, "I would struggle to ban them."

So maybe it's not just right-wing paranoia that leads people to believe Democrats want to take our guns.

In the midst of all these Democratic demands for gun confiscation, on January 11, 2012, MSNBC's Alex Wagner smirked, "No one, anywhere, is talking about doing away with the Second Amendment, and no one, anywhere, is advocating stripping away gun ownership."

Yes, yes, last month Democrats wanted to take your guns away—but that was a whole month ago. They've learned! It's like the guy who tried to rape you last week getting indignant at you for imagining he wants to rape you this week. *You act like I'm trying to rape you! Cuckoo, cuckoo!… What? That was a WEEK ago!* Except that Jan Schakowsky announced her desire for gun confiscation two months after MSNBC's Wagner laughingly assured us, eyes rolling merrily, that "no one, anywhere is advocating stripping away gun ownership."

The question is not, "Would Democrats like to confiscate our guns?" Yes, obviously—that much we know. We can discuss whether they have the power to do it, but don't dare tell us it never crossed their minds.

And by the way, it's sort of suspicious when Democrats say, "We don't want to ban guns, we just want a list of all the people who own them." That was the position of the "Million Mom March" in 2000. They demanded licensing of handgun owners and the national registration of all handguns.

For liberal ideas to work, it's important that no one remember what happened yesterday. Back in 1967, New York mayor John V. Lindsay signed a law requiring all long guns to be registered. Everyone swore up and down that the list of gun owners would never be used to take guns away. Then on August 16, 1991, New York City mayor David Dinkins dusted off Lindsay's list and confiscated all registered rifles and shotguns in the city. Apparently, it was easier to take trap-shooting guns from seventy-year-old guys on Sutton Place than to go to the South Bronx and take Saturday night specials off of criminals.

And that's what made New York City the fun, crime-free, livable city that it was under Dinkins. (Motto: "No Radio.")

Crime hasn't been a major political issue for a while—thanks to Republican crime policies. If there's anything you'd think even liberals wouldn't touch, it would be the policing programs that have pushed crime rates to historic lows. Do not relax, readers: liberals are dying to get their hands on the levers of power so they can start releasing criminals again.

The Democrats' ideas on crime were tested in the 1960s, 1970s, and 1980s, and the result was: mindboggling crime rates. Countless Americans were murdered, robbed, raped, and left permanently disfigured—and not just by Kennedys!—so that liberals could try out ideas dreamed up in all-night college bull sessions. The madness was finally broken in the 1990s, and we saw how quickly crime could drop in places that adopted sane crime policies, especially in New York City under Mayor Rudy Giuliani.

Liberals deny the facts right in front of everyone's eyes, insistently claiming that the crime rate actually began to decline under Mayor David Dinkins. That idea is so preposterous, it is repeated nightly on MSNBC. It's like saying: *The decline in Jew-killing actually began under the Nazis. In fact, the slowdown from 1944 to 1945 was much bigger than from 1945 to 1946. So don't be telling me the Allies did a better job at stopping the Holocaust. That's a calumny against the record of the Führer.*

Yes, Dinkins did such a phenomenal job running the city into the ground during the first three years of his administration that, by his last year, the crime rate had no place else to go but down. The number of murders fell that year from an astronomical 2,154 to an astronomical 1,995.

The first year of the Giuliani administration, crime fell 20 percent—from Dinkins's heroic final year—and continued to fall. By his last year in office there were only 714 murders in the city. By continuing Giuliani's crime policies, Bloomberg has kept the murder rate at historic lows. But as New Yorkers may soon find out, that could change overnight.

The few cities hermetically sealed from logic by Democratic leadership, such as Detroit and Chicago, did not share in the nation's bounty of low crime rates. It's probably good to keep these places around as examples for the next time liberals start rolling their eyes and telling us that incarceration doesn't work. And they will. The arguments may change, but the F-You arrogance remains the same.

Liberals just can't grasp the concept of punishment—except in the narrow cases of gun ownership, smoking, and hate speech, but never for real crimes like, say, murder.

Obama used the excuse of the sequester to release criminal aliens, Massachusetts governor Michael Dukakis released Willie Horton, the Ninth Circuit issued four stays in a single night in an attempt to stop the execution of child-murderer Robert Alton Harris, and six justices of the Supreme Court have been trying since 2011 to force California to release thirty thousand dangerous criminals from prison to relieve overcrowding. (California had no money to build prisons because it had to pay government workers' pensions.)

To advance their policy agenda, liberals depend on people forgetting. Forget what New York was like under David Dinkins. Forget what the nation was like in the 1970s. Forget the prosperity unleashed by Reagan's tax cuts. Forget that every government program always ends up costing six thousand times more than Democrats' original estimate. They need you to forget because they plan to bring the same policies back with an extra dollop of self-righteousness next time.

Republicans win a big policy victory, it works, and the liberal naysayers are proved wrong—then Democrats roll it back the next chance they get. In the 1990s, the Republican Congress reformed welfare and the result was not starving children in the streets—as liberals had predicted—but millions of Americans leaving the welfare rolls and getting jobs. Welfare reform was such a smashing success that Bill Clinton started claiming full credit for it—though he couldn't seem to pass it with a Democratic Congress.

But then the Obama administration came in and eviscerated the crucial work requirements of welfare reform. We went right back to the government not worrying about paying able-bodied Americans not to work. (And not just Obama!)

Reagan's tax cuts gave a huge boost to the U.S. economy—as did tax cuts under John F. Kennedy and Calvin Coolidge. So naturally, a perennial item on Democrats' wish list is to raise taxes. You can't win with these people. Facts and evidence are useless.

The implementation of left-wing policies is especially impressive when you consider that the Democrats' ideas are both insane and hated by most Americans. I believe the citizenry was reasonably clear about not wanting national healthcare back in the 1990s when Bill and Hillary Clinton tried it. The public forced Democrats to abandon their healthcare bill and then punished them for even thinking about it. The next election produced the first Republican Congress in forty years.

But as soon as Democrats controlled the presidency and both houses of Congress again, item no. 1 on the agenda was: universal healthcare. (By "universal," Democrats meant "provided by the government." And by "provided by the government" they meant, "crap that will continuously get worse.")

When have Republicans ever shown the steely-eyed determination of Democrats to rush through a checklist of items the moment they get control of the government? What did Bush get done his first four years as president when he had a Republican House and Senate? Reagan implemented nation-saving tax cuts and ended the Soviet Union, but he couldn't even get rid of the Department of Education, created a few years earlier by Jimmy Carter as a sop to the teachers' unions.

The only policy Republicans have ever pushed with the tenacity of a liberal is amnesty for illegal aliens. So we know Republicans are capable of the Democrats' stick-to-itiveness, but only for something most Americans hate.

Conservatives, we need to adopt the *smart* things Democrats do, not the stupid ones. We like their persistence, but not their plans to wreck the country. We like the part about winning elections, not the part about jamming execrable policies down the nation's throat.

Democrats do not lose any close elections—and not only because they steal the ones that aren't called on Election Day. Of the seven Senate races rated toss-ups by Charlie Cook's Political Report in 2010, Republicans lost 5 of 7. Out of ten Senate races rated toss-ups in 2012, Republicans lost 8 of 10. That is not a Party overly concerned with its electoral success.

Unless Republicans are trying to eliminate themselves as a political party, they've got to stop lunging at easy solutions and imaginary scapegoats. We have to know what keeps going wrong in order to stop it from going wrong again. It's one thing to be hit by lightning and it's another to stand in an open field holding an iron rod during a lightning storm.

Amnesty for illegals is no silver bullet—except to the heart of the Republican Party. The fact that the Democrats need 30 million new voters is just not a good enough reason to legalize 11 million illegal aliens and all their relatives.

Nor is the Tea Party or the "Establishment" responsible for our losses. Those are maledictions, not analyses. (Though it is the "Establishment" pushing that idiotic idea about amnesty.) The Tea Party gets blamed for all the Republican Party's woes, but the problem with those candidates wasn't that that they were too budget-cutty. The problem was they were too into musing about rape. In any event, the Tea Party candidates add up to only four blown Senate races out of thirteen "toss-ups" the Republicans lost.

A third party is not the answer. How do you plan to keep mountebanks out of your third party? Twenty percent of you leapt at Ross Perot as the authentic conservative in 1992. Then his campaign manager turned around and endorsed Bill Clinton.

The Republican Party has no natural defense mechanism against charlatans and saboteurs because politics is not what Republicans think about every second. Democrats love government. They spend their lives trying to maneuver themselves into a position to run other people's lives. Republicans don't want careers in government and give little thought to how to get there. Often they run for president only because they hope it will lead to more speaking gigs and TV appearances.

That may explain why Republicans seem to attract the sort of candidate who enjoys startling people at cocktail parties with outlandish remarks. There's a great living to be made by appealing to rubes and hotheads. Even if you lose, you'll get a talk show. *At that last debate, I was king of the badasses.* That's great, now six Republican congressmen will lose because of you. For the pettiest reasons—ego gratification, revenge, money—some people are perfectly willing to screw over Republicans.

Luckily for the Democrats, there's no shortage of left-wing people to put on TV. If a TV producer wants a spokesman for partial-birth abortion, he can just ask his wife for one of her friends. To attract the attention of TV bookers, apparently a lot of conservatives think they need to run for president.

You have to know you can't win!

Yes, but running will increase my speaking fees.

With the most influential conservative spokesmen in entertainment themselves, there's no one to say, "Let's keep our eye on the ball. All that matters is beating the Democrats." Cheap shot, grandstandy moves are fun, but lead to landslide losses in actual political campaigns. Republicans can't keep sanctioning these publicity stunts. We need to concentrate on winning elections.

What was the point of holding twenty-six Republican primary debates or forums before the end of February 2012? The hucksters are well served by endless primary debates. The TV networks love them. Conservative talk radio thrives on them. It's great for the Ron Paul's Menswear Collection at Macy's. You know who twenty-six debates doesn't help? The Republican Party.

And why are *any* congressmen or businessmen showing up in our presidential primaries? They're never going to get the nomination, so they're just wasting our time and weakening our eventual nominee. In 1988, the Democratic candidates for president were derided as "the Seven Dwarfs." But even that pathetic lineup consisted of three governors, three senators, and Jesse Jackson.

I don't care if it makes you feel good, conservatives: do not ever, ever consider running a presidential candidate who has not been a senator or preferably a governor. No, not even our beloved Ben Carson. What are we concentrating on? That's right: winning. Conservatives who think, "Well, it's never happened before, but that doesn't mean it couldn't happen," are as delusional as liberals who think they've finally found a government program that will save money.

Passion is great, but in politics what matters is scoring. Getting applause from a small slice of enthusiasts while alienating independents accomplishes nothing. I, too, enjoy those who tick off the right people. I *am* someone who ticks off the right people. But we're talking about elections. About half of the Republican presidential candidates in the last two election cycles would have inspired every stupid woman in America to drive to the polls, sobbing, in order to vote against them. (I sobbed on the way to the polls when McCain was running but for a different reason.)

Anyone who hurts the Democrats' electoral prospects is dead. Not so, the Republicans. If John Edwards, Ned Lamont, and Bill Bradley were Republicans, they'd have radio shows, TV gigs, and bestselling books. What ever happened to Wesley Clark? Where's Mike Gravel? Mike Huckabee has a TV show. If you want to know what the other former Republican presidential candidates are doing these days, just turn on the radio or TV.

Democrats rule their base with an iron fist, which is especially impressive when you consider that their base is composed of drama queens and attention seekers who specialize in taking positions that appall most Americans. *Wait until the public finds out the CIA is sleep-depriving al Qaeda terrorists!*

Those are their voters, but the Democratic Party operates like an old communist cadre. Single-mindedly focused on winning elections, the Democrats don't run candidates like Henry Waxman or Sheila Jackson Lee for the United States Senate. They don't run abortion zealot Barbara Boxer in Pennsylvania, abrasive New York senator Chuck Schumer in

Montana, or Montana's phony hayseed Brian Schweitzer in New York. Internet letchario Anthony Weiner isn't allowed out of New York City. They keep Patty Murray locked in her office at all times.

Democratic candidates who have to get elected in places other than New York invariably project a *Leave It to Beaver* normalcy. Running for the U.S. Senate from Arkansas in 2002, for example, Democrat Mark Pryor ran campaign ads showing him reading the Bible and praying at the dinner table with his family. He claimed to be pro-life, pro-Second Amendment, pro-military spending, and pro-Iraq war. *Don't let Emily's List know!*

That's why they win elections.

Democrats are perfectly open about their playbook. Republicans could easily steal it. As Democratic senator Jon Tester of Montana explained in the pages of the *New York Times*, "You don't put a point guard under the basket and tell him to rebound." So the Democrats run a prototypical, fake American like himself in Montana and far-left Barbara Boxer in California.

The *Times* summarized the difference in the parties this way: the Democrats "tailor each campaign to the particular candidates and the states they are running in"—i.e., they run fake Americans in the red states and crusading, self-righteous liberals in the blue states—whereas "Republican campaigns tend to ride national waves, running on broad national issues like the size and scope of government"—i.e., they give no thought whatsoever to winning elections, but Americans sometimes vote them in anyway.

Let's consider just one example of how Republicans lose winnable elections. In four separate Senate races, Republicans were screwed by campaign consultants fleecing deep-pocketed candidates rather than doing the hard work of electing Republicans. I salute anyone who runs for office as a Republican, but Linda McMahon in Connecticut and John

Raese in West Virginia were lied to by campaign consultants who told them they had a shot.

Raese has lost four statewide elections in conservative West Virginia, including the 2010 and 2012 U.S. Senate elections. Republican wiz-kid consultants couldn't learn after the first two? It's great that they can afford Jaguars now, but because of their greed Republicans gave up two Senate seats from a state so conservative that even Democrats have to pretend to love guns and oppose Obamacare. (Let me introduce you to Senator Joe Manchin.)

In a textbook case of Republican malfeasance, Raese was mortally wounded by the National Republican Senatorial Committee's "hickey" campaign commercial. The fact that everyone reading this does not instantly know what I'm talking about proves that Republicans do not punish the people who hurt them.

In 2010, the NRSC hired a Philadelphia ad agency to produce a TV ad for Raese. Knowing nothing about West Virginia, the Philadel phia firm ended up using actors who were like something out of *The Sopranos*. Then it leaked that the Republicans' ad agency had requested "hickey" actors for the West Virginia ad. Raese's lead evaporated overnight.

Why don't we know the names of the moron Republicans who blew West Virginia? Who told Raese he could win? What genius at the NRSC came up with the idea to go to a *Philadelphia* advertising agency for a West Virginia political campaign? (And is his brother-in-law still work-ing there?) I promise you, the Obama campaign organization in West Virginia was not being run out of Philadelphia.

Republicans should refuse to give money to the Party until we have the names of these people and a blood oath that they will never be hired again. Instead, Raese and McMahon's consultants will be probably wrecking the campaigns of five new Republican candidates in 2014.

No one gets rich by sabotaging the Democratic Party. But a lot of people get rich off losing races for the Republican Party. Those races alone amount to at least three and maybe four more Senate seats Republicans should have picked up but lost for no good reason. (In West Virginia, Republicans could easily have won twice; in Connecticut at least once.)

Add those three seats to the races where Republicans had a sudden compulsion to talk about rape during their campaigns (Todd Akin, Richard Mourdock, and Sharon Angle) and a kamikaze candidate in Delaware (Christine O'Donnell); without these unforced errors, Republicans would have a fifty-three-seat majority in the U.S. Senate.

We need to adopt the Democrats' merciless enforcement techniques without the ideology. Is that so hard? Instead, we keep getting all the passion with none of the discipline.

Besides putting liberals in a position to run the country, which is always a mistake, the worst thing about these losses is that they allow the media to roll out the old chestnut about social issues being death for Republicans. That claim is disproved by all recent political history. The Defense of Marriage Act passed the U.S. Senate 85–14. It was signed into law by Clinton, who ran campaign commercials claiming all credit for it. How did Bush's privatization of Social Security go?

Polls going back to 1996 show that large majorities of Americans oppose abortion after the first trimester—by more than 70 percent in recent polls. Reagan wasn't hurt even in states like New York and Connecticut for being pro-life. Nor, more recently, was Chris Christie in New Jersey. How's Paul Ryan's reform of entitlements going?

In fact and to the contrary, it was President Bush *betraying* conservatives that triggered Republicans' latest losing streak. Contrary to liberals' bizarro-world alternative history, Americans didn't turn against Bush over the Iraq War. We had won, executed a dictator, presided over democratic elections, and killed loads of al Qaeda fighters. How was the Iraq War bothering anyone? The conservative base turned against Bush for his years of big spending, followed by his pushing amnesty for illegal aliens, after getting reelected in 2004 with a Republican House and Senate.

Why are social conservatives always being told to shut up when their issues are quite popular with voters? The lesson of Todd Akin and the other unfortunate choices is not to stop being conservative, it's to stop being stupid. True, none of these candidates were as stupid as Senator Patty Murray or as gaffe-prone as Vice President Joe Biden. But we're not Democrats. We don't get protected by the media. Any Republican running for office should know that.

There are no prizes in politics for caring the most, only for scoring the most. Devotion to the cause isn't better than having a modicum of political savvy. If we're serious about improving the country, we need candidates to be brutally honest about their own appeal. That's if they really care about the team. If they just want to score a few points while their team loses, then we need to call in Luca Brasi.

This isn't a game. We aren't picking basketball brackets. Bad things happen when Republicans lose elections and Democrats have veto-proof majorities.

After the Goldwater debacle in 1964, we got the full flowering of Lyndon Johnson's pernicious Great Society programs, responsible for destroying the black family. (And not doing a half-bad job with white families these days, either.) We got Teddy Kennedy's immigration law banning European immigrants and replacing them with a million immigrants a year from the Third World.

After Watergate, we got an off-the-charts left-wing Congress that came just short of outlawing the Republican Party. Among its legislative accomplishments, this overwhelming Democratic Congress:

- systematically dismantled our national intelligence (as Democratic congressman Ron Dellums vowed to do, "brick by brick");
- passed egregiously expensive environmental legislation (estimated to cost more than $100 billion per year as early as the late 1970s);
- established the Legal Services Corporation (which pays lawyers to bring class action lawsuits to increase welfare payments);
- slashed defense spending; and, for the cherry on top...
- betrayed our ally, South Vietnam, by refusing to give them arms after the North invaded, resulting in a total communist takeover of Vietnam and Cambodia.

A few decades later, Democrats on the 9/11 Commission would be on their high horses, railing about the failure of our intelligence. *Huh. I wonder how that happened?* It happened when the overwhelmingly left-wing post-Watergate Congress deliberately hamstrung our intelligence agencies in the 1970s, over the vigorous protests of Republicans.

The country wasn't moving Left. This was just a few years after Richard Nixon crushed George McGovern in the 1972 election and a decade before Reagan won the largest electoral landslide in history. But the media had taken out Nixon with Watergate, allowing far-left liberals to sweep Congress and whip out their dream journals.

The reason we have Obamacare is not because the public was clamoring for the federal government to take over healthcare. It's because the Democrats had sixty senators. They had been waiting around for fifty years to check off the "national healthcare" box on their "FDR's Unfinished Business" list. Not a single Republican in either the House or Senate voted for it. Nationalizing one-sixth of the economy was passed by one party sneering, *Ha, ha—we have sixty votes!*

Elections matter. We're trying to make the country a better place. But if our candidates don't win, we can't do that. As the rest of this book shows, life is a horror when liberals are running things.

CHAPTER TWO

If Chuck Schumer Is Smiling, Vote *Nay!*—and Other Good Advice for Conservatives

have loads of good advice in this chapter. Always get enough sleep, drink plenty of water, and stop losing elections.

Here are my tips for elected Republicans:

1. Do not get elected by patriotic middle class Americans then get to Washington and start doing the bidding of the media and your rich friends from Wall Street and Silicon Valley by pushing amnesty.

2. With the free time you'll have by not lobbying for amnesty, repeal the campaign finance laws so we can get better candidates than you. The reason we have no Reagans anymore is that Reagan wouldn't run for office today with the fundraising hell required by our

campaign finance laws. (After the 2012 elections, the Democratic Party instructed its freshmen congressmen to spend five hours a day on fundraising, according to the *New York Times*.) That's why the country ends up with narcissists like Marco Rubio and sociopaths like Anthony Weiner.

3. Remember that the Non-Fox Media (NFM) is your sworn enemy. If they start lavishing you with praise, you have become the enemy of mankind, or worse, John McCain.

Here are my tips for Republican voters:

1. No elected Republican will do everything you want. Don't run off and instigate an ugly, rancorous, and expensive primary against an incumbent Republican in order to modestly improve the candidate, and very possibly lose the seat.

2. The only exception to Tip No. 1 is that you must destroy any elected Republican who pretends to be a Republican, but then tries to lose every single issue, across the board, by giving the Democrats 30 million new voters with amnesty.

3. Learn to rely on facts and don't get swept up in group-think slogans about "Establishment Republicans." Otherwise, boy will your face be red when you realize you were the one fighting for the Establishment Republicans! (Gingrich, Perry, Santorum, and Paul Ryan—all of whom support amnesty).

BONUS! Tips for Democrats:

1. Be sure your primaries include lots of candidates who will never be the nominee—congressmen, businessmen, and inspirational individuals who have never held elective office. You don't want your base getting too focused on the actual purpose of the exercise.
2. Hold 312 primary debates. We Republicans find that having lots of debates encourages professional attention-seekers to throw their hats in the ring.
3. Extend your primaries through July, or at least June, especially when running against an incumbent. It really keeps the nominee on his toes to have only three months to challenge a candidate who's been campaigning for four years.

Conservatives Need Twelve-Step Program to Manhood
May 10, 2006

It's pretty pathetic when a Kennedy is too drunk to drive into the Potomac. After the visibly intoxicated Representative Patrick Kennedy crashed his car into a police barrier near the Capitol just before 3:00 a.m. last Thursday morning, he explained to the police he was rushing to the Capitol for a vote, a procedure known on the Hill as "last call." (It could have been worse: Patrick's designated driver that night was his uncle Ted.)

At some point in his scrolling list of excuses, Kennedy eventually claimed he was addicted to prescription drugs and checked himself into the newly opened Kennedy Wing of the Mayo Clinic. He explained he had been "sleep driving." If people fall for that, his father, Ted, plans to attribute his 1965 immigration bill to "sleep legislating."

Coming right on the heels of a three-year witch hunt directed at Rush Limbaugh for an addiction to prescription drugs (because of his politics), as well as the continuing threat to put Tom DeLay in prison (because of his politics), you would think there would be at least some discussion of prosecuting the young Kennedy for his addiction to prescription drugs, too.

Perhaps the Republican attorney general in Washington needs to interview Palm Beach's Democratic prosecutor Barry Krischer, who wasted three years and untold taxpayer dollars trying to get Limbaugh, about the danger to society of prescription drug addiction.

Baseball has a system to protect batters from being hit: if your pitcher hits one of our guys, our pitcher will hit one of your guys. This is also the only argument that ever works with Democrats.

Democrats adored the independent counsel statute—until it was used to catch an actual felon in the Oval Office, Bill Clinton. Suddenly they noticed all sorts of problems with the law.

Democrats swore up and down that women never lie about rape—until that same felon was credibly accused of rape by Juanita Broaddrick on NBC News, as well as four other women, all card-carrying Democrats, who described being raped by Clinton in strikingly similar detail (stories told in Christopher Hitchens's book *No One Left to Lie To*).

Conservatives will continue to be threatened with prison on trumped-up charges until Democrats start having to worry about being prosecuted for minor offenses, too. Representative Kennedy's case is not as minor as Rush Limbaugh's offense, which never involved smashing his car into a police barrier. (In the young Kennedy's defense, at least he didn't drown the woman in his car and then hide for nine hours.)

Democrats have declared war against Republicans, and Republicans are wandering around like a bunch of ninny Neville Chamberlains, congratulating themselves on their excellent behavior. They'll have some terrific stories to tell about their Gandhi-like passivity while sitting in cells at Guantanamo after Hillary is elected president.

For a political party that favors defeating foreign enemies, Republicans can't seem to grasp that concept when it comes to domestic enemies. When battling liberals, instead of taking a page from Sun Tzu's *The Art of War*, American conservatives prefer the Jimmy Carter unconditional surrender strategy. Republicans don't have to become dangerous psychotics like liberals, but they could at least act like men.

According to Hollywood, this nation is a cauldron of ethnic hatreds positively brimming with violent skinheads. So why hasn't the former spokesman for the Taliban matriculating at Yale been beaten even more senseless than he already is? Where are the skinheads when you need them? What does a girl have to do to get an angry, club- and torch-wielding mob on its feet? There is not the remotest possibility that a man who was recently defending shooting women in the head for wearing nail polish will so much as be snubbed on the Yale campus.

The only violence on college campuses these days occurs when people like me and David Horowitz show up to give a speech in defense of America. Then we need bomb-sniffing dogs and a lecture hall lined with armed police. But a Talibanist goes about his day at Yale unmolested.

Conservatives may shrink from confrontation with howling, violent liberals, but as General "Buck" Turgidson in *Dr. Strangelove* informed the milquetoast president still hoping to avert a nuclear confrontation with the Russkies: "Well, Mr. President, I would say that General Ripper has already invalidated that policy." I would say liberals have already invalidated conservatives' "Let's all just get along" policy.

The political violence and threats of imprisonment have already begun. Now the only question is whether conservatives will choose victory.

Free the Fitzgerald One!
January 31, 2007

Conservatives often ask why so many Republicans go native when they get to Washington, D.C. The answer is: because you don't defend them when they come under relentless attack from liberal hatchet men.

Lewis Libby did what you wanted. He didn't place secret phone calls to reporters revealing classified intelligence programs. He supported the war on Islamic fascists. He didn't try to raise your taxes like James Baker III. And he has loyally served Dick Cheney, the man conservatives secretly wish were president.

And now he's on trial for—at worst—misremembering who first told him that future reality show contestant Joseph Wilson was sent on a boondoggle to Niger by his wife, Valerie Plame. The way Libby remembered it, NBC's Tim Russert was the first one to tell him. But the way Russert remembers it, he didn't tell Libby about Wilson's wife. (And the way Wilson remembers it, he was sent to Niger by Captain Kirk of the starship *Enterprise*!)

Try this: Who was the first person who told *you* Wilson was sent to Niger by his wife? Who told you a bipartisan Senate panel concluded that Joe Wilson was lying when he denied that his wife had sent him to Niger? While we're at it, who was the first person to correct you on your pronunciation of "Niger"? I don't remember, either—and I'm not running a war.

The exact same people who are now demanding prison for Libby for not remembering who told him about Plame are the ones who told us it was perfectly plausible for Bill Clinton to forget that Monica Lewinsky repeatedly performed oral sex on him in the Oval Office. Even if chubby Jewish brunettes aren't your type, be honest: Which of the two events would stand out more in your memory?

Perjury is intentionally swearing to something you know to be untrue—not misremembering something that later appears, on balance, to be inaccurate.

Here are some simple illustrations. If Clinton had been asked how many sexual encounters it took for him to remember Monica's name (six) and he got the answer wrong, it would not be perjury since, like Monica's name, it's an easy thing to forget and not material.

If Clinton had been asked whether he talked to Representative Jim Chapman and *then* to Representative John Tanner, or to Representative Tanner and *then* to Representative Chapman while Monica was performing oral sex on him in the Oval Office and he got the answer wrong, that also would not be perjury because it's not relevant to the investigation. (Correct answer: Chapman, then Tanner.)

But when Clinton was asked under oath—in a case brought by Paula Jones under the law liberals consider more sacrosanct than any passed in the twentieth century (Section 1983 of the Civil Rights Act): "Mr. President . . . at any time were you and Monica Lewinsky alone together in the Oval Office?" and he answered, "I don't recall," *that* was perjury.

Now take the question: "Who first told you fantasist Wilson was sent to Niger by his wife?" Unless it actually was Captain Kirk of the starship *Enterprise*—the answer to that question is not going to be perjurious. No matter how many witnesses swear they told Libby first, if Libby honestly believed it was Russert, he didn't commit perjury.

So why is there a trial? Because there is no penalty for using the threat of imprisonment as a political weapon against conservatives. Ask Ed Meese, Tom DeLay, or Rush Limbaugh.

If Libby were a Democrat, we would know the sexual proclivities of everyone in Special Prosecutor Patrick Fitzgerald's office, Fitzgerald would be portrayed as a "stalker," Tim Russert's cat would be dead, and the public would know about every toupée at MSNBC.

Republicans don't have to go around killing cats. They just need to bestir themselves to defend their own from rank partisan persecution. But they never do. People who attack conservatives do not have to worry about their own dirty laundry coming out. All they have to worry about is whether *People* magazine will use a good picture of them in its "Sexiest Man Alive" issue.

When Secret Service officers innocently told Monica she couldn't see Clinton because Eleanor Mondale was "visiting" the president, Bill Clinton immediately threatened to fire the officers responsible. (They say Clinton was so mad it took him an extra couple of minutes to "finish off" in the sink.)

Compare that to how the Bush administration treats a federal employee actually violating a citizen's rights. An officer with Bush's own customs office held Rush Limbaugh for three hours at a private airport, mauling his belongings and calling the media about his Viagra prescription before Rush had left the airport. We don't even know her name.

No one has bothered to investigate what prescriptions *she* takes or whether she has any angry relatives willing to badmouth her. She certainly has not been fired for this egregious violation of an American citizen's rights. No worries—it was just a conservative.

You want to protect the borders, cut taxes, fight Islamic fascists, and put up Ten Commandments monuments? Get her name. Find out about Patrick Fitzgerald everything we'd know if he were Ken Starr. If you won't defend your own champions, conservatives, then don't sit back and wonder why so few people want to be your champions.

NOTE: On March 6, 2007, Libby was convicted of obstruction of justice, two counts of perjury, and one count of making false statements. Bush did not pardon Libby, in keeping with the Bush family motto, "F-ck you—I'm out for myself."

With Friends like These, Who Needs Keith Olbermann?
July 28, 2010

W hile engaging in astonishing viciousness toward Republicans, liberals accuse cheerful, law-abiding Tea Party activists of being violent racists. Responding to these vile charges, conservative television pundits apparently think it's a great comeback to say: "There is the fringe on both sides."

Both sides? Really? How about: "That's a despicable lie"? Did that occur to you simpering morons as a possible reply to the slanderous claim that conservatives are bigots?

All the accusations of "racism" at anti-Obama rallies so far have turned out to be completely false. The most notorious was the allegation that one black congressman was spat on and another called the N-word fifteen times at an anti-Obamacare rally on Capitol Hill last March.

The particularly sensitive Representative Emmanuel Cleaver, D-MO, perhaps walking too closely to a protester chanting "Kill the Bill," was hit with some spittle and briefly thought he was a Freedom Rider! When observers contested Cleaver's account—with massive video evidence—he walked back his claim of being spat upon.

The contemptible claim that a protester called civil rights hero John Lewis the N-word fifteen times was an outrageous lie—never made by Lewis himself—but promoted endlessly by teary-eyed reporters.

The media never retracted it, even after the N-word allegation was proved false with a still-uncollected $100,000 reward for video proof taken from a protest crawling with video cameras and reporters hungry for an act of racism.

When St. Louis Tea Party co-founder Dana Loesch said on CNN that no one spat on any black congressmen at the anti-Obamacare rally, a liberal on the panel, Nancy Giles, told her to "shut your mouth," while alleged "comedian" Stephanie Miller repeatedly called Tea Party activists "tea baggers."

It's like watching Hitler hysterically denounce Poland for being mean to Nazi Germany while Polish TV commentators defend Poland by saying, "There are mistakes on both sides."

Meanwhile, we do have video proof of the New Black Panthers standing outside a polling station in Philadelphia in 2008 with billy clubs threatening whites who tried to vote. And there is video footage of Sarah Palin, Karl Rove, Condoleezza Rice, as well as a slew of conservative college speakers, being physically assaulted by crazed liberals.

We also have evidence of liberals' proclivity for violence in the form of mountains of arrest records. Liberal protesters at the 2008 Republican National Convention were arrested for smashing police cars, slashing tires, breaking store windows, and for possessing Molotov cocktails, napalm bombs, and assorted firearms. (If only they could muster up that kind of fighting spirit on foreign battlefields!)

There were no arrests of any conservatives at the Democratic National Convention.

Over the past couple of election cycles, Bush and McCain election headquarters around the country have been repeatedly vandalized, ransacked, burglarized, and shot at (by staunch gun-control advocates, no doubt); Bush and McCain campaign signs have been torched; and Republican campaign volunteers have been physically attacked.

It was a good day when George Bush was merely burned in effigy, compared to Hitler or, most innocuously, portrayed as a monkey.

In the fall of 2008, Obama supporters Maced elderly volunteers in a McCain campaign office in Galax, Virginia. In separate attacks, a half dozen liberals threw Molotov cocktails at, stomped, and shredded McCain signs on families' front yards around Portland, Oregon. One Obama supporter broke a McCain sign being held by a small middle-aged woman in midtown Manhattan before hitting her in the face with the stick. These are just a few acts of violence from the Left too numerous to catalog.

There were arrests in all these cases. And yet, not one of the violent attacks committed by Obama supporters became a national news story. *Obama is in danger from the Tea Partiers! The Poles are mobilizing on the border!*

Since Obama became president, the only recorded violence at Tea Parties or Town Halls was that committed by liberals. Last fall, a conservative had his finger bitten off by a man from a MoveOn.org crowd in Thousand Oaks, California. Two Service Employees International Union thugs have been charged with beating up an African American selling anti-Obama bumper stickers at a St. Louis Tea Party in August 2009.

Respected elder statesmen of the Democratic Party have referred to Obama's "Negro dialect" (Harry Reid), said that, a few years ago, Obama would have been getting them coffee (Bill Clinton), and called him "clean" (Joe Biden). And none of these were said by the Democratic senator who used to be a member of the Ku Klux Klan, the late Bob Byrd.

So I'm thinking that maybe when conservatives are called racists on TV, instead of saying, "There are fringe elements on both sides," conservative commentators might want to think about saying, "That is a complete lie."

Liberals explode in rage when we accuse them of being unpatriotic based on fifty years of their treasonous behavior. They have zero examples of conservative racism, but the best our spokesmen can think to say when accused of racism is: "Man is imperfect."

Conservatives who prefer to come across on TV as wonderfully moderate than to speak the truth should find another line of work and stop defaming conservatives with their "both sides" pabulum.

I hear BP is looking for a new spokesman.

On This Aborted Fetus, the Democrats Plant Their Flag
April 13, 2011

Back in February, Obama's director of the Office of Management and Budget, Jacob Lew, promoted the White House's allegedly draconian budget cuts in the *New York Times*. Saying Obama was going to cut the 2012 budget to the bone, Lew droned on about the "difficult" cuts to "important" programs and the "many tough choices and deep cuts" in the proposed budget.

All told, the White House's brutal, Depression-era austerity plan would have snipped a couple of billion from our multi-trillion-dollar federal budget. When the Republicans proposed that, instead of cutting a few billion, the government chop $60 billion from the budget, Democrats went ballistic. They said it was madness. Republicans were proposing to bring back the miserly federal budget of 2008!

You heard me right: those lunatics were going to roll back federal spending…almost three years! You remember the hellish *Lord of the Flies* days of 2008 when veterans hospitals were shuttered, Social Security checks ceased to be issued, our military was stripped of ammunition, national parks were closed, and stoplights went dark.

Wait, no—none of that happened.

But Democrats control the Senate and the White House, and the media were gearing up to blame Republicans for any government shutdown. The Republicans seemed to be cornered. Between their $60 billion in cuts and the Democrats' proposed cuts of a few billion, it looked as if Democrats were going to succeed in putting the country on a high-speed bullet train to Zimbabwe.

And then, totally by accident, Republicans stumbled onto the Democrats' Achilles heel. Among their specific defunding proposals, Republicans had suggested taking mere peanuts away from Planned Parenthood. The Democrats responded: NO! WE'LL CUT $40 BILLION! JUST DON'T TOUCH PLANNED PARENTHOOD!

All the Republicans had to do was threaten to cut federal funding for abortion, and they got $40 billion in spending cuts overnight. I don't think Republicans did it deliberately. I'm pretty sure they just wanted to cut funding for Planned Parenthood. But, holy cow, did they find the Democrats' weak spot!

Senate Majority Leader Harry Reid threatened to shut down the government to save abortions in the District of Columbia. Reid, who is known as a "pro-life Democrat," said cutting Planned Parenthood's funding was the "one issue" on which he would not budge.

Reid also said that Planned Parenthood had nothing to do with abortion, but mostly provided things like cholesterol screening. In response, Senator Jon Kyl made the obvious point: "You don't have to go to Planned Parenthood to get your cholesterol or your blood pressure checked. If you want an abortion, you go to Planned Parenthood. That's well over 90 percent of what Planned Parenthood does."

The entire mainstream media immediately rose in opposition to Kyl. They indignantly cited Planned Parenthood's claim that abortion constitutes less than 3 percent of the services it provides. Comedy Central's allegedly serious Catholic, Stephen Colbert, spent a week ridiculing Senator Kyl's response to Reid's preposterous claim.

Apparently, it depends on the meaning of "services it provides." If taking thirty seconds to write a prescription for birth control pills is considered the equivalent of a two-hour, multiple-visit $450 abortion, then perhaps abortion does constitute only 3 percent of Planned Parenthood's work.

But according to Planned Parenthood itself, when it comes to services for pregnant women, abortion constituted 97.6 percent of the services Planned Parenthood provided in 2009. Only 2.4 percent of the organization's services for pregnant women involved prenatal care or adoption referrals. Again, according to its own reports, Planned Parenthood performed 332,278 abortions in 2009—or more than a quarter of all abortions in the entire country. It receives about 37 percent of its total revenue from performing abortions. (Nearly 50 percent of its revenue comes from the taxpayers, which Democrats won't allow us to cut.)

Reid and Colbert must be getting a lot of cholesterol tests at Planned Parenthood if they think abortion constitutes only 3 percent of its services. (Contrary to Senator Reid's claim that Planned Parenthood administers important cancer screening tests, none of its affiliates even offer mammograms.)

In any event, the Democrats didn't suddenly agree to $40 billion in budget cuts to save Planned Parenthood's cholesterol screening. If Republicans keep threatening to defund Planned Parenthood, they can probably get Democrats to repeal Obamacare, pass a flat tax, and get a capital sentence for Khalid Sheik Mohammed.

Now we know: Democrats absolutely will not cross the abortion ladies.

Blue-collar workers don't like abortion? Democrats say, "Oh well."

Abortion disproportionately targets black babies? Democrats say, "Who cares?"

A majority of women dislike abortion? Democrats say, "Yes, but we're going to lie about that."

The only members of their base the Democrats will never, ever cross are government workers and abortion-crazed feminists.

CHAPTER THREE

Thou Shalt Not Speak Ill of a Fellow Republican—with the Following Exceptions

"Against stupidity, the gods themselves contend in vain."
—*Friedrich Schiller*

The astute observer will note that the main recommendation of the last chapter is for conservatives to be more like Democrats, except not the sleazy parts. Fight like a Democrat, but with your pants on. Take a page from the Democrat strategy book that's not stuck together.

But instead of imitating the Democrats' good points—winning elections—sometimes it seems as if Republicans have adopted only their bad traits, such as mob action. We don't want slogans and catchphrases. What we're looking for is facts.

It's supposed to be liberals who are driven by envy, running off on wild enthusiasms, pushing causes that appall most Americans, and making decisions based on notions rather than evidence. Republicans don't vote for a bill just because the media call it an "anti-rape bill." We read the bill to see that it's actually a "trial lawyers' full employment bill." (See

Chapter 15.) Conservatives aren't cowed by the argument that "all scientists" (i.e., lawyers and actresses) believe in global warming. We look at the facts. (See Chapter 16.) We don't think shibboleths—"academic freedom," "free speech," "torture," "extremist," and "diversity"—are trump cards. (See Chapters 5, 9, 15, and 16). We don't engage in politics in order to feel like we belong to something larger. (Environmentalism, Obama, Occupy Wall Street—see Chapters 4, 5, and 16.)

So why do so many conservatives suddenly adopt all these liberal behavioral patterns during presidential primaries? There are the shibboleths ("Romneycare!," "Bain Capital," "GOP Establishment"), appeals to status (I'm the true Reaganite!), and maledictions ("looter," "profiteer," "vulture capitalist," "tool of Wall Street"), and the politics of belonging ("true conservatives" vs. "the Establishment").

Republicans deserve stupid voters, too. We can't leave them all to the Democrats. But Republicans have got to stop with the groupthink.

What, other than mob behavior, explains some conservatives touting Newt Gingrich as the "true conservative," while denouncing Romney as the "moderate," "Establishment" candidate? The alleged "moderate" Mitt Romney didn't support amnesty, didn't take $1.7 million from Freddie Mac, didn't cut a global warming commercial with Nancy Pelosi, and didn't denounce Paul Ryan's Medicare reform as "right-wing social engineering." Gingrich did.

What could be worse on a Republican résumé than taking money from Freddie Mac, the government-backed entity that was a key player in taking down the economy? *Oh yeah, that's a point, but Newt was so great when he insulted the media.* Any Republican who took money from Freddie Mac ought to drop out of public life immediately and explain that he's an alcoholic and was abused as a child.

Don't think bringing up "Romneycare" will help you: Newt also supported Romneycare. *Ah, but "Romneycare" sounds like "Obamacare"!*

This is how liberals think, not conservatives: *Hitler's favorite ice cream was strawberry, so is Mitch McConnell's. Hmmmm…*

Voting records tell us nothing in isolation. We need to know where the candidate had to get himself elected. Who cares if a candidate from Arizona is pro-life? If Obama were running in Arizona *he'd* be pro-life. Why, it's even possible to be a pro-life senator from Arizona and be so liberal, you'd push an insane policy like amnesty for illegals. Some Republican candidates are from places very different from Arizona or Pennsylvania—a state so opposed to abortion that even the Democrats pretend to be pro-life. (See Senator Bob Casey.) Being pro-life and anti-amnesty in Massachusetts tells us a lot. That's like going to an AA meeting during Mardi Gras.

The point is, before declaring you the Robert E. Lee of Republican candidates, we need to know if you fought the Battle of Antietam or just won an arm-wrestling contest with Barney Frank.

In 2012, only one Republican candidate arguably *wasn't* pro-life— the one Sarah Palin called the true conservative, despite Gingrich's having lobbied for embryonic stem cell research. Romney vetoed an embryonic stem cell research bill in a state that—unlike Arizona, Pennsylvania, or a small conservative congressional district in Georgia— repeatedly elected Teddy Kennedy.

Consider two recent Republican candidates for president. One was pro-life, pro-gun, pro-marriage. Another was pro-choice, anti-gun, and marched in gay rights parades. And yet Rudy Giuliani was more conservative, and did far more for his country, than Fred Thompson did. On no issue was Giuliani to the Left of his electorate. Thompson was frequently to the Left of Tennessee voters, such as when he voted against tort reform and against convicting President Clinton for perjury. How would his voting record look if he had had to get elected in New York?

Unfortunately, all this is irrelevant to the passionate few because, for them, it's not about getting the best candidate elected. It's about their self-image as diehard conservatives.

The devoted supporters of these stunt candidates are generally people who got interested in politics five minutes ago. A year later, they won't be paying attention. *Oh yeah, that was a bad idea. Anyway, I'm out of here.* The more you try to talk them out of hitching their wagon to a charlatan, the more they're convinced of his greatness. *Don't be bringing me your books and your articles, he killed in that debate. You're just part of the Establishment.*

The party of trial lawyers, abortion ladies, and public sector unions does not allow its passionate base to screw up elections for them.

Finally, remember that Democrats have an advantage that you do not, conservatives: they have the entire mainstream media covering for them. Do not imagine you can say something stupid and have the media ignore it. This is how bad it is—if you're a Republican, you can't even get your mistress pregnant while your wife is dying of cancer and you're running for president and expect the media to ignore it. Do not tell us about double standards. It's never a good excuse to cite something that has been a fact since the Ice Age. The sun's been around as long as media bias, and we don't want to hear the sun was in your eyes either. If you can't operate in a world that holds you to a ridiculously higher standard than a Democrat, then the Republican Party may not be right for you.

Fred Sawyer and Huckabee Finn
October 10, 2007

Conservatives unhappy with our Republican presidential candidates seem to be drifting aimlessly toward Fred Thompson and Mike Huckabee in the misguided belief that these candidates are more conservative than Rudy Giuliani and Mitt Romney. This is like breaking up with Bobby Brown so you can date Phil Spector.

On illegal immigration, Huckabee makes George Bush sound like Tom Tancredo. He has compared illegal aliens to slaves brought here in chains from Africa, saying, "I think frankly the Lord is giving us a second chance to do better than we did before."

Toward that end, when an Arkansas legislator introduced a bill that would prevent illegal aliens from voting and collecting state benefits, Huckabee denounced the bill, saying it would rile up "those who are racist and bigots."

He also made the insane point that companies like Toyota would not invest in Arkansas if the state didn't allow non-citizens to vote because it would "send the message that, essentially, 'If you don't look like us, talk like us and speak like us, we don't want you.'"

Like all the (other) Democratic candidates for president, Huckabee supports a federal law to ban smoking—unless you're an illegal alien smoking at a Toyota plant! (I just realized why Mike Huckabee can't run for president as a Democrat. They've already got Mike Gravel.)

Huckabee also joined with impeached president Bill Clinton in a campaign against childhood obesity. What, O. J. wasn't available?

Bill and Mike's excellent adventure lasted about one week in May 2005—or just long enough to burnish the image of the president who committed perjury and obstruction of justice in a civil rights suit against him, molested the help, and was credibly accused of rape by Juanita Broaddrick.

Huckabee teamed up with *that* guy to talk to children about healthy eating habits. Ironically, the obesity campaign kicked off almost exactly nine years from the very Palm Sunday on which President Clinton used a cigar as a sexual aid on Monica Lewinsky in the Oval Office.

What is with Republicans? Clinton isn't your average ex-president, like Jerry Ford. He isn't even Jimmy Carter or Walter Mondale.

Decent people shun Clinton—but elected Republicans keep trying to rehabilitate him! President Bush sent his own father on a feel-good "tsunami-relief campaign" with this guy, and Huckabee visits schoolchildren with him.

In 1999, Senator Fred Thompson joined legal giants like Senators Jim Jeffords, Olympia Snowe, and Susan Collins to vote against removing Bill Clinton from office for perjury.

Thompson, whom President Nixon once called "dumb as hell," claimed to have carefully studied the Constitution and determined that perjury by the president of the United States did not constitute a "high crime and misdemeanor." He must have been looking at one of those living, breathing Constitutions we've heard so much about.

When the framers chose the phrase "high crimes and misdemeanors" for the Constitution, they were using a term taken from British parliamentary impeachments. There's a six-hundred-year history about what this phrase means—and Clinton met it about a dozen times before he gave a single statement under oath or suborned a single witness's testimony.

It has been used in this country and in Britain to remove one government official for making "uncivil addresses to a women," another for "notorious excesses and debaucheries," and another for "frequenting bawdy houses and consorting with harlots." Or, as Bill Clinton used to call it, "a three-day weekend."

The House didn't even impeach Clinton for his legion of "notorious excesses and debaucheries." He was impeached for excesses that also happen to be felonies. In a nation of laws, there are no more serious offenses than perjury and obstruction of justice.

The entire Supreme Court—including the justices Clinton appointed—boycotted Clinton's State of the Union address after his impeachment trial. That's what they thought of crimes that attack the legal system.

Representative James Rogan lost his congressional seat because he stuck by his principles as a manager of Clinton's impeachment. Lifelong

Democrat David Schippers abandoned his party's lockstep defense of the horny hick to pursue Clinton's impeachment as the House Judiciary Committee's chief counsel. Representative Henry Hyde saw an affair he had in 1965 become front-page news because he wouldn't waver from doing his job under the Constitution.

But, as the *New York Times* recently said, Thompson "agonized over what he saw as two 'bad choices.'"

What bad choices? Punishing a multiple felon or not punishing him? This wasn't exactly a job for King Solomon, pal.

The *Times* reported that calls from Thompson's Tennessee constituents showed that they "overwhelmingly favored removing President Bill Clinton from office." So Thompson could either: (1) follow the Constitution *and* make his constituents happy, or (2) disregard the Constitution and make his Hollywood friends happy.

Only a handful of Republicans voted against all law and reason to keep Clinton in office. Only one of them was from the great state of Tennessee.

This isn't the time to be toying with any Republican who had a Clinton in his sights and ended up shooting himself in the foot. If you're bored with our top candidates, go see a slasher movie. Don't take it out on a presidential election.

Liberals Sing "Huckelujah"
December 26, 2007

A ll I want for Christmas is for Christians to listen to what Mike Huckabee says, rather than what the media say about him. The mainstream media keep flogging Huckabee for being a Christian, apparently unaware that this "God" fellow is testing through the roof in focus groups.

Huckabee is a "compassionate conservative" only in the sense that calling him a conservative is being compassionate.

He responded to my column last week—pointing out that he is on record supporting the Supreme Court's sodomy-is-a-constitutional-right decision—by saying that he was relying on the word of a caller to his radio show and didn't know the details of the case. (Ironically, that's how most people feel about sodomy: they support it until they hear the details.)

First, I'd pay a lot of money to hear how a court opinion finding that sodomy is a constitutional right could be made to sound reasonable. But the caller had the right response when Huckabee asked him, "What's your favorite radio station?" So he seemed like a reliable source.

Second, Huckabee's statement that he agreed with the court's sodomy ruling was made one week after the decision. According to Nexis, in that one week, the sodomy decision had been on the cover of every newspaper in the country, including the *New York Times*. It was the talk of all the Sunday news programs. It had been denounced by every conservative and Christian group in America—as well as other random groups of sane individuals having no conservative inclinations whatsoever.

The highest court in the land had found sodomy was a constitutional right! That sort of news tends to get around. (I was going to say the sodomy ruling got publicity up the wazoo, but this is, after all, Christmas week.)

So the stretch-marked cornpone is either lying, is a complete ignoramus, or has a closed head injury.

Huckabee opposes school choice, earning him the coveted endorsement of the National Education Association of New Hampshire. This is like being a sheriff endorsed by the local whorehouse.

He is, however, in favor of school choice for kids in Mexico: They have the choice of going to school there or here. Huckabee promoted giving in-state tuition in Arkansas to illegal immigrants from Mexico—but not to U.S. citizens from Mississippi. "I don't believe you punish the children," he said, "for the crime and sins of the parents."

Since when is not offering someone lavish taxpayer-funded benefits a form of punishment? That's almost as crazy as a governor pardoning a known sex offender so he can go out and rape and kill. (As Huckabee also did.)

Huckabee claims he's against punishing children for the crimes of their fathers in the case of illegal immigrants. But in the case of slavery, he believes the children of the children's children should be routinely punished for the crimes of their fathers. Huckabee has said illegal immigration gives Americans a chance to make up for slavery. (I thought letting O. J. walk on a double murder made up for slavery.)

Just two years ago, Huckabee cheerfully announced to a meeting of the Hispanic advocacy group League of United Latin American Citizens that "Pretty soon, Southern white guys like me may be in the minority." Who's writing this guy's speeches—Al Sharpton?

He said the transition from Arkansas' Southern traditions would "require extraordinary efforts on both sides of the border." But, curiously, most of the efforts Huckabee described would come entirely from this side. Arkansas, he pledged, would celebrate diversity "in culture, in language and in population." He said America would have to "accommodate" those who come here.

All that he expected from those south of the border was that they have a desire to provide better opportunities for their families. Basically, we have to keep accommodating everyone but U.S. citizens.

For those of you keeping score at home, this puts Huckabee just a little to the Left of Dennis Kucinich on illegal immigration and border control. (The only difference is that Kucinich supports amnesty for aliens from south of the border *and* north of Saturn.)

In a widely quoted remark, Huckabee denounced a Republican bill that would merely require proof of citizenship to vote and receive government benefits as "un-Christian, un-American, irresponsible and anti-life," according to the Arkansas News Bureau. Now, where have I heard this sort of thing before? Hmmm…wait, now I remember: it was during the Democratic debates!

In his current attempt to pretend to be against illegal immigration, Huckabee makes a meaningless joke about how the federal government should track illegals the way Federal Express tracks packages. (Can a Mexican fit in one of those little envelopes?)

In other words, Huckabee is going to address the problem of illegal immigration by making jokes. It's called leadership, folks.

Liberals love Huckabee because he confirms their image of conservatives as dorks. The most uptight white guy in America brags on TV that—unlike other conservatives—he "likes music." What's he doing—running for president or filling out his Facebook profile? *Arkansas former fatty loves to make jokes and play the bass guitar.*

Remember what happened to the last former fatboy from Arkansas trying to be "cool." I'll take "Stained Dresses" for $400, Alex.

Who on earth says conservatives don't like music—other than liberals and Mike Huckabee? This desperate need to be liked by liberals can lead only to calamity.

Huckabee wants to get kids involved in music at an early age because he believes it leads to a more balanced and developed brain. You know, as we saw with the Jackson family. Someone should tell him the Osmonds are voting for Romney.

He supports a nationwide smoking ban anyplace where people work, constitutional protection for sodomy, big government, higher taxes, and government benefits for illegal aliens. According to my calculations, that puts him about three earmarks away from being Nancy Pelosi.

Liberals take a perverse pleasure in touting Huckabee because they know he will give them everything they want—big government and a Christian they can roll.

The Elephant in the Room
January 16, 2008

U nluckily for McCain, snowstorms in Michigan suppressed the turnout among Democratic "Independents" who planned to screw up the Republican primary by voting for our worst candidate. Democrats are notoriously unreliable voters in bad weather. Instead of putting on galoshes and going to the polls, they sit on their porches waiting for FEMA to rescue them.

In contrast to Michigan's foul weather, New Hampshire was balmy on primary day, allowing McCain's base—Democrats—to come out and vote for him.

Assuming any actual Republicans are voting for McCain—or for liberals' new favorite GOP candidate, Mike Huckabee—this column is for you.

I've been casually taking swipes at Mitt Romney for the past year based on the assumption that, in the end, Republicans would choose him as our nominee. My thinking was that Romney would be our nominee because he is manifestly the best candidate.

I had no idea that Republican voters in Iowa and New Hampshire planned to do absolutely zero research on the candidates and vote on the basis of random impulses.

Dear Republicans—please do one-tenth as much research before casting a vote in a presidential election as you do before buying a new car.

One clue that Romney is our strongest candidate is the fact that Democrats keep viciously attacking him while expressing their deep respect for Mike Huckabee and John McCain. This point was extensively covered in Chapter 1 of *How to Talk to a Liberal (If You Must)*. In brief: never take advice from your political enemies.

Turn on any cable news show right now, and you will see Democratic pundits attacking Romney, calling him a "flip-flopper," while heaping praise on McCain and Huckleberry. (It's almost as if they were reading some sort of "talking points.")

Doesn't that raise the tiniest suspicions in any of you? Are you too busy boning up on Consumer Reports' microwave oven reviews to spend one day thinking about who should be the next leader of the free world? Are you familiar with our "no exchange/no return" policy on presidential candidates? Voting for McCain because he was a POW a quarter-century ago or Huckabee because he was a Baptist preacher is like buying a new car because you like the color.

The candidate Republicans should be clamoring for is the one liberals are feverishly denouncing. That is Mitt Romney by a landslide.

New York Times columnist Frank Rich says Romney "is trying to sell himself as a leader," but he "is actually a follower and a panderer, as confirmed by his flip-flops on nearly every issue."

But Rich is in a swoon over Huckabee. He hasn't been this excited since they announced *Hairspray* was coming to Broadway.

Rich continued to praise "populist" charmer Huckabee even after it came to light that Huckabee had called homosexuality an "abomination." Normally, any aspersions on sodomy and/or favorable portrayals of Christianity would lead to at least a dozen hysterical columns by Frank Rich.

Rich treated Mel Gibson's movie *The Passion of the Christ* as if it were a Leni Riefenstahl Nazi propaganda film. (On a whim, I checked to see if Rich had actually compared Gibson to Riefenstahl in one of his many *Passion* reviews. Yes, of course he had.)

Curiously, however, Huckabee's Christianity doesn't bother Rich. In column after column, Rich hails Huckabee as the only legitimate leader of the Republican Party. This is like a girl in high school who hates you telling you your hair looks great.

Liberals claim to be enraged at Romney for being a "flip-flopper." I've looked and looked, and the only issue I can find that Romney has "flipped" on is abortion. When running for office in Massachusetts—or, for short, "the Soviet Union"—Romney said that Massachusetts was a pro-choice state and that he would not seek to change laws on abortion. (Would that Giuliani would say the reverse while running for the nomination of the pro-life Republican Party!)

Romney's first race was against Senator Teddy Kennedy—whom he came closer to beating than any Republican ever had. If Romney needed to quote *The Communist Manifesto* to take out that corpulent drunk, all men of good will would owe him a lifetime of gratitude.

Even when Romney was claiming to support *Roe v. Wade*, he won the endorsement of Massachusetts Citizens for Life—a group I trust more than the editorial board of the *New York Times*. Romney's Democratic opponents won the endorsements of the very same pro-choice groups now attacking him as a "flip-flopper." They didn't believe he was pro-choice when he was running, but now they do.

After his term as governor, NARAL Pro-Choice America assailed Romney, saying, "[A]s governor he initially expressed pro-choice beliefs but had a generally anti-choice record. His position on choice has changed. His position is now anti-choice."

Pro-abortion groups like the Republican Majority for Choice—the evil doppelganger to my own group, Democratic Majority for Life—are now running videos attacking Romney for "flip-flopping" on abortion.

Of all the Republican candidates for president, Romney and Rudy Giuliani are the only ones who had to be elected by pro-choice electorates. Romney governed as a pro-lifer, was viciously attacked by pro-abortion groups, and now calls himself pro-life.

By contrast, Giuliani cleverly avoids the heinous "flip-flopper" label by continuing to embrace baby-killing. (Rudy flip-flops only on trivial matters like his own marital vows.)

And, of course, Romney is a Mormon. Even a loser Mormon like Senator Harry Reid claims to be pro-life. Having a candidate with a wacky religion isn't all bad. (Whatever problems Romney's Mormonism gives some conservative voters, please remember this: Bill Clinton came in third in heavily Mormon Utah in 1992. *Third.*)

At worst, Romney will turn out to be a moderate Republican—a high-IQ, articulate, moral, wildly successful, moderate Republican. Of the top five Republican candidates for president, Romney is the only one who hasn't dumped his first wife (as well as the second, in the case of Giuliani)—except Huckabee. And unlike Huckabee, Romney doesn't have a son who hanged a dog at summer camp. So there won't be any intern issues, and there won't be any Billy Carter issues.

It's also possible that Romney will turn out to be a conservative Republican—probably a lot more conservative than he was as governor of the Soviet Union.

"Straight Talk" Express Takes Scenic Route to Truth
January 23, 2008

John McCain is Bob Dole minus the charm, conservatism, and youth. Like McCain, pollsters assured us that Dole was the most "electable" Republican. Unlike McCain, Dole didn't lie all the time while claiming to engage in "Straight Talk."

Of course, I might lie constantly, too, if I were seeking the Republican presidential nomination after enthusiastically promoting amnesty for illegal aliens, retroactive Social Security benefits for illegal aliens, criminal trials for terrorists, stem-cell research on human embryos, crackpot global warming legislation, and free speech–crushing campaign-finance laws.

I might lie, too, if I had opposed the Bush tax cuts, a marriage amendment to the Constitution, waterboarding terrorists, and drilling in Alaska.

And I might lie if I had called the ads of the Swift Boat Veterans for Truth "dishonest and dishonorable."

McCain angrily denounces the suggestion that his "comprehensive immigration reform" constituted "amnesty"—on the grounds that it imposed a small fine on illegal aliens. Even the guy who graduated fifth from the bottom of his class at the U.S. Naval Academy ought to remember that he was the one calling this plan amnesty a few years ago.

In 2003, McCain told the *Tucson Citizen* that "amnesty has to be an important part" of any immigration reform. (He also rolled out the old chestnut about America's desperate need for illegals, who do "jobs that American workers simply won't do"—always a big vote-getter with American workers.)

McCain's amnesty bill would have immediately granted millions of newly legalized immigrants Social Security benefits. As recently as in 2006, he even supported allowing work performed as an illegal to count toward Social Security benefits—a vote now adamantly denied by Mr. Straight Talk.

McCain keeps boasting that he was "the only one" of the Republican presidential candidates who supported the surge in Iraq.

What is he talking about? All Republicans supported the surge—including Mitt Romney and Rudy Giuliani. Indeed, the only ones who didn't support it were McCain's usual allies, people like Senator Chuck Hagel. The surge is the first part of the war on terrorism that caused McCain to break from Hagel in order to support President Bush.

True, McCain voted for the war. So did Hillary Clinton. Like her, he then immediately started attacking every other aspect of the war on terrorism. (The only difference was, he threw in frequent references to his experience as a POW, which currently outnumber John Kerry's references to being a Vietnam vet.)

Thus, McCain joined with the Democrats in demanding O. J. trials for terrorists at Guantanamo, including his insistence that the terrorists have full access to the intelligence files being used to prosecute them.

These days, McCain gives swashbuckling speeches about the terrorists who "will follow us home." But he still opposes dripping water down their noses. (He was a POW, you know.)

Though McCain was far from the only Republican to support the surge, he does have the distinction of being the only Republican who voted against the Bush tax cuts. (Also the little lamented Senator Lincoln Chafee, who then left the Republican Party.) Now McCain claims he opposed the tax cuts because they didn't include enough spending cuts. But that wasn't what he said at the time.

When McCain voted against Bush's 2001 tax cuts he cited the idiotic talking point of the Democrats, calling them tax cuts for the rich! "I cannot in good conscience," McCain said, "support a tax cut in which so many of the benefits go to the most fortunate among us at the expense of middle-class Americans who need tax relief."

The *New York Times* was in a swoon.

McCain started the vicious anti-Bush myth that, before the 2000 South Carolina primary, the Bush campaign made phone calls to voters calling McCain a "liar, cheat, and a fraud" and accusing him of having an illegitimate black child. On the thin reed of a hearsay account from a random woman at a town hall meeting, McCain immediately blamed the calls on Bush. "I'm calling on my good friend George Bush," McCain said, "to stop this now. He comes from a better family. He knows better than this."

Bush denied that his campaign had anything to do with the alleged calls and, in a stunning act, ordered his campaign to release the script of the calls being made in South Carolina.

Bush asked McCain to do the same for his calls implying that Bush was an anti-Catholic bigot, but McCain refused. Instead, McCain responded with a campaign commercial calling Bush a liar on the order of Bill Clinton:

McCAIN: His ad twists the truth like Clinton. We're all pretty tired of that.

ANNOUNCER: Do we really want another politician in the White House America can't trust?

After massive investigations by the *Los Angeles Times* and investigative reporter Byron York, among others, it turned out that no such calls had been made by the Bush campaign—or by anyone else. With hundreds of thousands of "robo-calls" being left on answering machines across the state, that's pretty solid evidence that the "illegitimate-child" calls, as well as the "liar, cheat, fraud" calls, were never made.

And yet, to this day, the media weep over Bush's underhanded tactics against McCain in the 2000 South Carolina primary.

In fact, the most vicious attack before the 2000 South Carolina primary came from McCain.

Seeking even *more* favorable press from the *New York Times*, McCain launched an unprovoked attack against the Reverend Jerry Falwell and Pat Robertson, calling them "agents of intolerance." Unlike the phantom "black love child" calls, there's documentary evidence of this smear campaign.

To ensure he would get full media coverage for that little gem, McCain alerted the networks in advance that he planned to attack their favorite whipping boys. Newspaper editors across the country stood in awe of McCain's raw bravery. The *New York Times* praised him in an editorial that said the Republican Party "has for too long been tied to the cramped ideology of the Falwells and the Robertsons."

Though McCain generally votes pro-life—as his Arizona constituency demands—he embraces the loony lingo of the pro-abortion set, repeatedly assuring his pals in the media that he opposes the repeal of *Roe v. Wade* because it would force women to undergo "illegal and dangerous operations."

The more one examines the facts, the clearer it becomes that Dole was a million times better than McCain. Why not run him again?

Newt: Speak Bombastically and Carry a Tiny Stick
December 14, 2011

Fellow right-wingers: Is our objective to taunt Obama by accusing him of "Kenyan, anti-colonial behavior," of being "authentically dishonest" and a "wonderful con"—and then lose the election—or is it to defeat Obama, repeal Obamacare, secure the borders, enforce e-verify, reform entitlement programs, reduce the size of government, and save the country?

If all you want is to lob rhetorical bombs at Obama and then lose, Newt Gingrich—like recent favorite Donald Trump—is your candidate. But if you want to save the country, Newt's not your guy.

Gingrich makes plenty of bombastic statements, but these never seem to translate into actual policy changes.

After becoming the first Republican speaker of the House in nearly half a century, for example, Newt promptly proposed orphanages and janitorial jobs for children on welfare. It was true that welfare had destroyed generations of families shorn of the work ethic and led to soaring illegitimacy rates, child abuse, and neglect. Maybe orphanages and child labor would have been better.

But we didn't get any orphanages. We didn't get jobs for children in families where no one works. What we got was the cartoonish image of Republicans as hard-hearted brutes who hated poor kids.

Ronald Reagan was also accused of waging a war on the poor. But that was on account of his implementing historic tax cuts that produced not only record revenues for the government, but decades of prosperity for the entire nation.

With Newt you get all the heat, but you don't get the legislative victories.

To the contrary, his pointless bloviating about orphanages and child janitors harmed the chances for welfare reform, despite the fact that the American people, the Republican Congress, and the Democratic president (publicly, at least) supported it.

Indeed, when it came time to make vital changes to welfare policy, such as work requirements and anti-illegitimacy provisions, Gingrich tried to scuttle them. He denounced such provisions—the very heart of welfare reform—as, yes, "social engineering of the right" (e.g., Republican Governors Conference, Williamsburg, Virginia, November 22, 1994).

The guy who wanted orphanages for children on welfare suddenly called work requirements for *adults* receiving welfare right-wing "social engineering."

Gingrich went on to lose almost every negotiation with Bill Clinton—and that was with solid Republican majorities in both the House and Senate. His repeated capitulation to Clinton led former Vice President Dan Quayle to remark that the Republican "Contract with America" had become the "Contract with Clinton." (Not to be confused with Newt's book, *A Contract with the Earth*.)

Perfectly good policies are constantly being undermined by Newt's crazy statements—such as his explanation that women couldn't be in combat because they get infections, whereas men "are basically little piglets" who are "biologically driven to go out and hunt giraffes."

Hunt giraffes?

With Gingrich we get the worst of all worlds. He talks abrasively—offending moderates and galvanizing liberals—but then carries a teeny, tiny stick. We want someone who will talk softly and unthreateningly while implementing vital policy changes. Even when Gingrich doesn't completely back off conservative positions, his nutty rhetoric undermines the ability of Republicans to get anything done.

By the time of the 1996 Republican National Convention, Gingrich was so widely reviled that the Democrats' main campaign strategy against all Republican candidates for office was to link them with Gingrich. The speaker was forced into a minor speaking role at the convention, which he used to promote...beach volleyball.

That's right, Republicans were trying to defeat Clinton and Newt was talking about beach volleyball, which is apparently the essence of freedom—as well as evidence of Newt's cuddly side! (During the House ethics investigation of Gingrich, he produced notes in which he reminds himself to "allow expression of warm/smiling/softer side.")

After Gingrich had been Speaker for a brief two years, the Republican House voted 395–28 to reprimand him and fine him $300,000 for ethics violations. (Senator Bob Dole loaned Gingrich the money in what was called the first instance of an airbag being saved by a person.)

It's true that Newt has had some good ideas—but also boatloads of bad ones, such as his support for experimentation on human embryos, cap and trade, policies to combat imaginary manmade global warming, an individual health insurance mandate, Dede Scozzafava (Romney supported the Tea Party candidate), amnesty for illegal aliens, Al Gore's bill to establish an "Office of Critical Trends Analysis" to prepare government reports on "alternative futures" (co-sponsored by Gingrich), and thinking he could get away with taking $1.6 million from Freddie Mac without anyone noticing.

During the ethics investigation, the committee also found among Newt's personal papers a sketch of himself as a stick figure at the center of the universe.

On one page, Newt called himself: "definer of civilization, teacher of the rules of civilization, arouser of those who fan civilization, organizer of the pro-civilization activists, leader (possibly) of the civilizing forces."

This is not a small-government conservative talking. It is not a conservative at all.

Romney Doing the Job Republican Establishment Just Won't Do
April 25, 2012

The actual Republican Establishment—political consultants, the *Wall Street Journal*, corporate America, former Bush advisors, and television pundits—are exhorting Mitt Romney to flip-flop on his very non-Establishment position on illegal immigration. Both as governor of Massachusetts and as a presidential candidate, Romney has supported a fence on the border, E-Verify to ensure that employees are legal, and allowing state police to arrest illegal aliens. He is the rare Republican who recognizes that in-state tuition, driver's licenses, and amnesty are magnets for more illegal immigration.

These positions are totally at odds with Establishment Republicans. The Establishment panders to the business lobby by supporting the cheap labor provided by illegal immigration—then accuse Americans opposed to slave labor in America of racism. Unless voters wise up, America will become California and no Republican will ever be elected president again. Big business doesn't care, and Establishment Republicans are too stupid to notice.

If you're not sure how you feel about illegal immigration, ask yourself this: "Do I have a nanny, a maid, a pool boy, a chauffeur, a cook, or a business requiring lots of cheap labor that the rest of America will have to subsidize with social services to make up for the wages I'm paying?" Press "1" to answer in English. If the answer is "no," illegal immigration is a bad deal for you. Cheap labor is cheap only for the employer.

Today, 70 percent of illegal immigrant households collect government benefits—as do 57 percent of all immigrant households—compared to 39 percent of native households. Immigrant households with the highest rate of government assistance are from the Dominican Republic (82 percent), Mexico, and Guatemala (tied at 75 percent). This is based on the latest available data from 2009. The immigrant households least likely to be on any welfare program are from the United Kingdom (7 percent). But British immigrants aren't picking the tomatoes Karl Rove doesn't want his son to pick. (That's how he justified Bush's amnesty plan.)

You can either pay a little more for tomatoes picked by Americans or you can pay a lot more in welfare to the illegal immigrants who pick them, as well as to generations of their descendants. Yes, many illegal immigrants work hard, but it's not our responsibility if their employers don't pay them a living wage. This is known as an "externality," which we hear a lot about in the case of greedy businesses polluting the land, but not when it's greedy businesses making the rest of us subsidize their underpaid employees.

Romney is one of the few Republicans to recognize that there is no need to "round up" illegal aliens (in the lingo of amnesty supporters) to get them to go home. Illegal aliens will leave the same way they arrived. They decided to walk across the border to get jobs—and welfare, apparently—and they'll walk back across the border as soon as the jobs and welfare dry up. (Obama has a similar plan, but instead of using E-Verify to stop illegal aliens from taking American jobs, he did it by destroying the entire job market. *Hmmmm, drug-ravaged Juarez or Obama's America ... I'll take Juarez!*)

Wrecking the American economy is not a good long-term solution to the illegal immigration problem. Romney could get elected, and then we'll need a fence in a hurry. It didn't take a government administrator "rounding up" foreigners and putting them on buses to get 20 million illegal aliens here, and it won't take a government program "rounding them up" to get them home.

While Romney's views on immigration are wildly popular with Americans, they are extremely unpopular with the Republican Establishment—Bush, Rove, McCain, Huckabee, Perry, Gingrich, Giuliani, Krauthammer, Kristol, Gillespie, etc., etc. It's the Establishment calling Romney "Establishment." So now the elites are demanding that Romney "moderate" his position on immigration. To justify their underpaying the maid, they claim support for illegal immigration is crucial to victory!

The truth is, a tough stance on illegal immigration can only help Romney, not only with the vast majority of Americans, but with any Latino voters who would ever possibly consider voting Republican in the first place. As Romney said in one of the early debates, Republicans appeal to Latinos "by telling them what they know in their heart, which is they or their ancestors did not come here for a handout. If they came here for a handout, they'd be voting for Democrats. They came here for opportunity and freedom. And that's what we represent."

Romney crushed pro-amnesty Newt Gingrich in the Florida primary, winning a huge majority of that state's substantial Hispanic population. (And Gingrich promised Hispanics their own moon base!) Before the primary, Gingrich played up his support for amnesty, while accusing Romney of wanting to "round up" illegal alien grandmothers. The one thing every Florida primary voter knew was that Romney said he'd veto the Dream Act, giving citizenship to illegal alien children. And then Romney won the primary with an even larger percentage of the Hispanic vote than Florida at large. Romney beat Gingrich statewide, 46 percent to 32 percent. But among Latino voters, Romney routed Gingrich, 54 percent to 29 percent.

It's not just Florida. In 2006, Arizona Hispanics supported four anti-illegal immigration propositions by 40 to 50 percent—which is a lot more than voted for pro-amnesty Republican presidential candidates John McCain or George W. Bush. Among the propositions supported by Hispanics in larger numbers than they typically vote Republican was one making English the official language of Arizona (49 percent). As governor of Massachusetts, Romney pushed English-immersion programs. That's my kind of Hispandering!

These are our Latinos—the ones, as Romney said, who came here for opportunity and freedom. Any race-mongering, welfare-collecting, ethnic-identity rabble-rousers are voting for the Democrat.

CHAPTER FOUR

Democrats:
They Can't Be Trained—
They Can Only Be Beaten

had to cut the column on my favorite Democrat, Alvin Greene, so these are just the losers. A party that's willing to overlook the horrors of Stalin can certainly overlook Al Franken.

When Obama won the presidency in 2008, it was the first time in thirty-two years that a Democratic president got as much as half the country to vote for him, but liberals presume to lecture Republicans on how it's done. Listen to me, not them. I've never been elected to anything, so I bring a fresh perspective.

Without Obama on the ticket, it won't be magic again. The only people fainting at Hillary's speeches will be chubby gals from NOW. After all the embarrassing revelations about previous Democratic presidential candidates—from Michael Dukakis releasing first degree murderers on weekend furloughs to John Kerry's inspiring the undying hatred of his comrades in Vietnam, Obama's main selling point for the Democrats was: *Guess what? He has no record!*

Not only that, but the hidden goldmine of votes in the 2012 election came from elderly black women. So, for one thing, that Republican suppression of black voters I kept hearing about on MSNBC didn't seem to work. But for a second thing, I don't know that the black ladies will be rushing out to vote for Hillary.

The media act as if, of course, we all know that America owes Hillary the presidency. They think the rest of us should feel as guilty as liberals do for dumping her for a half-black trophy wife in 2008. It was a power beyond their control—they were swept up in Obamamania! *I don't know why I did it, honey. It just kind of happened.* They betrayed Hillary and took away her rightful place as the Democratic nominee.

I'm not sure the rest of the country thinks it owes Hillary just because she put up with Bill. We did, too. And unlike Obama in 2008, she has a record, so Democrats are back to their old problems.

Obama Woos Gun-Toting God Nuts
April 16, 2008

The Democrats' "Fake-Out America" advisor, Berkeley linguistics professor George Lakoff, must be beside himself. Lakoff has spent years training Democrats to "frame" their language so they would stop scaring Americans. But just last week, B. Hussein Obama was caught on tape speaking candidly to other liberals in San Francisco.

One minute Obama was bowling in Pennsylvania with ordinary people wearing "Beer Hunter" t-shirts, and the next thing you know, he was issuing a report on the psychological traits of these same Americans.

Obama informed the San Francisco plutocrats that working-class Americans are so bitter...they actually believe in God! And not just the twelve-step, higher power, "as you conceive him or her to be" kind of God. The regular, old-fashioned, almighty sort of God!

As Obama put it, "[T]hey get bitter, they cling to guns or religion or antipathy to people who aren't like them or anti-immigrant sentiment or anti-trade sentiment as a way to explain their frustrations." The rich liberals must have nearly fainted at the revelation that the denizens of small towns in Pennsylvania have absolutely *no* concern for the rich's ability to acquire servants from Mexico at a reasonable price.

He gave these remarks at one of the four fundraisers on April 6 at the homes of San Francisco's high and mighty, such as Alex Mehran, an Iranian who went into daddy's business and married an IBM heiress, and Gordon Getty, heir to the Getty Oil fortune.

It is not known whether any of Getty's three illegitimate children attended the Obama fundraiser   which turned out to be more of a McCain fundraiser—but photos from the event indicate that there were a fair number of armed (and presumably bitter) policemen providing security for the billionaires' soirée. In 1967, Gordon sued his own father to get his hands on money from the family trust—and lost. So Gordon Getty knows from bitter. It's a wonder he hasn't turned to guns—or at least to immigrant-bashing. There are enough of them working on his home.

These are the sort of well-adjusted individuals to whom Obama is offering psychological profiles of average Americans, such as their bizarre theories about how jobs being sent to foreign countries and illegal-alien labor at home might have something to do with their own economic difficulties.

It's going to take a lot of "framing" for Democrats to recast Obama's explanation to café society that gun ownership and a belief in God are the byproducts of a mental disorder brought on by economic hardship.

A crucial element of the Democrats' playbook is that they must fool the public by simulating agreement with normal people. The winner of the Democratic primary is always the candidate who does the best impersonation of an American. But then, after all their hard work at making believe they're into NASCAR and God, some Democrat invariably slips and lets us know it's all a big fake-out. They're like a gay guy trying to act straight who accidentally refers to Brad Pitt as "yummy!"

The Democrats' last phony American was John Kerry, who famously said that if "you study hard and you do your homework, and you make an effort to be smart, you can do well. If you don't, you get stuck in Iraq." Kerry claimed this was not an accurate reflection of his feelings about the troops, despite a four-decade record of contempt for them, including accusing American troops of being baby-killers during the Vietnam War.

Rather, he said, it was a "botched joke." (In Kerry's defense, he was the opening act for Randi Rhodes's stand-up comedy show at the time.) In case there was any confusion, other Democrats immediately clarified their position by going on television and saying—as Representative Charlie Rangel did—that our troops are people who don't have the option of having "a decent career."

These Democrats can't even pull off attending a NASCAR race without embarrassing themselves. In August 2004, Kerry exclaimed, "Who among us does not love NASCAR?" Then, a few years later, in October 2007, Democratic congressional staffers to Representative Bennie Thompson, D-MS, sent out a memo urging aides going to NASCAR races to get inoculated before attending. (This entire paragraph is completely true.)

Obama had been so careful until now, "framing" his message as "change"—rather than tax hikes, partial-birth abortion, driver's licenses for illegal aliens, socialized medicine, and abandoning mandatory minimum prison sentences for federal crimes. (Or any prison sentences, really.) One can only hope that Obama got his shots before bowling in Altoona, Pennsylvania.

Only His Hairdresser Knows for Sure
August 6, 2008

The mainstream media's reaction to reports on John Edwards's "love child" is reminiscent of the Soviet press. Edwards's name has simply been completely excised from the news. *Say, why isn't anyone talking about John Edwards for vice president anymore? No, seriously— hey! Why are we cutting to a commercial break?*

I suspect that if I tried to look up coverage of the Democratic primaries in Nexis news archives, Edwards's name will have disappeared from the database. By next week, there will be no evidence that Edwards was John Kerry's running mate in 2004.

Do you know what this means? At this precise moment in time, I could call Edwards any name, and the media would be unable to report it.

A *Washington Post* reporter defended the total blackout on the *National Enquirer*'s love child story, telling the *Times* of London, "Edwards is no longer an elected official and he is not running for office now. Don't expect wall-to-wall coverage." This was the perfect guy to say that to because, if there's one thing they're careful about in London, it's tabloid excess.

Isn't there some level of coverage between "wall-to-wall" and "double-secret probation, total news blackout" when it comes to a sex scandal involving a Democrat?

Hey, what sort of "elected official" was Ted Haggard again? He was the Christian minister no one outside of his own parish had ever heard of until he was caught in a gay sex scandal last year. Then he suddenly became the pope of the Protestants. And yet, despite the fact that Haggard was not an "elected official," the *Post* gave that story wall-to-wall coverage. And what sort of "elected officials" were Mel Gibson, Rush Limbaugh, and Bill Bennett?

The MSM justify banner coverage of the smallest malfeasance by any Christian or conservative with the lame excuse of "hypocrisy." But if all it takes to get the Edwards story into the establishment press is a little hypocrisy, boy, have I got a story for you!

Based on information currently saturating the internet: (1) the entire schmaltzy Edwards campaign consisted of this self-professed moralist telling us how much he loved the poor and was devoted to his cancer-stricken wife; (2) the following was Edwards's response to CBS News anchor Katie Couric's question about whether voters should care if a presidential candidate is faithful to his spouse: "Of course. I mean, for a lot of Americans—including the family that I grew up with, I mean, it's fundamental to how you judge people and human character—whether you keep your word, whether you keep what is your ultimate word, which is that you love your spouse, and you'll stay with them.... I think the most important qualities in a president in today's world are trustworthiness—sincerity, honesty, strength of leadership. And—and certainly that goes to a part of that."

There you have it, boys. Go to town, MSM!

Moreover, the *National Enquirer* reports that Edwards is paying Rielle Hunter—the former "Lisa Druck"—$15,000 a month in "hush money." Shouldn't the IRS be investigating whether Edwards is deducting those payments as a "campaign expense"?

Maybe the *Washington Post* didn't hear about the *Enquirer* catching Edwards in a hotel with his mistress and love child since it happened way out in the sleepy little burg of Los Angeles near the corner of Wilshire and Santa Monica Boulevards. You know, the middle of nowhere. But surely the public can count on the *Los Angeles Times* to report on a tabloid scandal occurring under its very nose.

Kausfiles produced this email from an *LA Times* editor to its bloggers soon after the *Enquirer*'s stakeout of Edwards and his alleged mistress at the Beverly Hilton:

> From: "Pierce, Tony"
> Date: July 24, 2008 10:54:41 AM PDT
> Subject: john edwards
>
> Hey bloggers,
>
> There has been a little buzz surrounding John Edwards and his alleged affair. Because the only source has been the National Enquirer we have decided not to cover the rumors or salacious speculations. So I am asking you all not to blog about this topic until further notified.
>
> If you have any questions or are ever in need of story ideas that would best fit your blog, please don't hesitate to ask.
>
> Keep rockin',
>
> Tony

Hey, I have a story idea I think the *LA Times* might like: How about something on the glorious workers' revolution that will restore the means of production to the people and create a workers' paradise right here on Earth, free of the shackles of capitalism? *Keep rockin'*.

I assume it would be jejune to point out that the MSM would be taking the wall-to-wall approach to this story, rather than the total blackout approach, if it were a story about Mitt Romney's love child or, indeed,

Larry Craig's love child. They'd bring Ted Koppel out of retirement to cover that. Katie Couric, Brian Williams, and Charles Gibson would be anchoring the evening news from Romney's front yard. They might even get Dan Rather to produce some forged documents for the occasion.

But with a Democrat sex scandal, the *LA Times* is in a nail-biting competition with the *Washington Post*, the *New York Times*, ABC, NBC, and CBS for the Pulitzer awarded for "Best Suppressed Story."

Biden Secret Service Code Name: "Assassination Insurance"
October 1, 2008

While Governor Sarah Palin is being grilled on her position on mark-to-market accounting rules, the press can't bother to ask Joe Biden if he could give us a ballpark estimate on when Franklin D. Roosevelt was president—or maybe take a stab at the decade when televisions became widely available to the public.

Being interviewed by Katie Couric on the *CBS Evening News*, Biden said: "When the stock market crashed, Franklin D. Roosevelt got on the television and didn't just talk about the, you know, the princes of greed. He said, 'Look, here's what happened.'" For those of you who aren't hard-core history buffs, Biden not only named the wrong president during the 1929 stock market crash, he also named a man who was president before Americans had TVs.

Other than that, the statement holds up pretty well. At least Biden managed to avoid mentioning any "clean" Negroes he had met.

Couric was nearly moved to tears by the brilliance of Biden's brain-damaged remark. She was especially intrigued by Biden's claim that FDR had said the new iPhone was the bomb! Here is Couric's full response to Biden's bizarre outburst about FDR (a) being president and (b) going on TV in 1929: "Relating to the fears of the average American is one of Biden's strong suits."

But when our beauteous Sarah said that John McCain was a better leader on the economy than Barack Obama, Couric relentlessly badgered her for evidence. "Why do you say that?" Couric demanded. "Why are they waiting for John McCain and not Barack Obama? ... Can you give us any more examples of his leading the charge for more oversight?"

The beauteous Sarah had cited McCain's prescient warnings about Fannie Mae and Freddie Mac. But Couric, the crackerjack journalist who didn't know FDR wasn't president in 1929, continued to demand *more* examples from Palin. We are currently in the middle of a massive financial crisis brought on by Fannie Mae. McCain was right on Fannie Mae; Obama was wrong. That's not enough?

Not for the affable Eva Braun of evening TV! "I'm just going to ask you one more time," Couric snipped, "not to belabor the point. Specific examples in his twenty-six years of pushing for more regulation?" This would be like responding to someone who predicted the 9/11 attacks by saying, *OK, you got one thing right. Not to belabor the point, but what else?*

Obama was not merely wrong on Fannie Mae: he is owned by Fannie Mae. Somehow Obama managed to become the second biggest all-time recipient of Fannie Mae political donations after only three years in the Senate. The biggest beneficiary, Democratic senator Chris Dodd, had a thirty-year head start on receiving loot from Fannie Mae—the government-backed institution that caused our current crisis.

How does the Democratic ticket stack up on other major issues facing the nation, say, gas prices?

Shockingly, Senator Joe Biden was one of only five senators to vote against the first Alaskan pipeline bill in 1973. This is like having been a

Nazi sympathizer during World War II. If Sarah Palin does nothing else, she has got to tie that idiotic vote around Biden's neck.

The Senate passed the 1973 Alaskan pipeline bill by an overwhelming 80–5 vote. Only five senators voted against it on final passage. Senator Biden is the only one who is still in the Senate—the other four having been confined to mental institutions long ago.

The stakes were clear: this was in the midst of the first Arab oil embargo. Even liberal Democrats, such as Senators Robert Byrd, Mike Mansfield, Frank Church, and Hubert Humphrey, voted for the pipeline.

But Biden cast one of only five votes against the pipeline that has produced more than fifteen billion barrels of oil, supplied nearly 20 percent of this nation's oil, created tens of thousands of jobs, added hundreds of billions of dollars to the U.S. economy, and reduced money transfers to this nation's enemies by about the same amount.

The only argument against the pipeline was that it would harm the caribou, which was both trivial and wrong. The caribou population near the pipeline increased from five thousand in the 1970s to thirty-two thousand by 2002.

It would have been bad enough to vote against the pipeline bill if it had hurt the caribou. A sane person would still say, *Our enemies have us in a vise grip. Sorry, caribou, you've got to take one for the team.* But when the pipeline goes through and the caribou population sextuples in the next twenty years, you really look like a moron.

We couldn't possibly expect Couric to ask Biden about a vote that is the equivalent of voting against the invention of the wheel. But couldn't she have come up with just one follow-up question for Biden on FDR's magnificent handling of the 1929 stock market crash?

Or here's a question the public is dying to know: If Obama wanted a delusional vice president, why not Lyndon LaRouche? At least LaRouche didn't vote against the Alaskan pipeline.

One Plus One Equals Twenty Extra Votes for Franken
December 17, 2008

I t's bad enough that the Republican Party can't prevent Democrats from voting in its primaries and saddling us with the *New York Times*' favorite Republican as our presidential nominee. If the Republican Party can't protect an election won by the incumbent U.S. senator in Minnesota, there is no point in donating to the Republican Party.

The day after the November election, Republican Senator Norm Coleman had won his reelection to the U.S. Senate, beating challenger Al Franken by 725 votes. Then one heavily Democratic town magically discovered one hundred missing ballots. In another marvel, they were all for Al Franken! It was like a completely evil version of a Christmas miracle.

As strange as it was that all one hundred post-election, "discovered" ballots would be for one candidate, it was even stranger that the official time stamp on the miracle ballots showed that the votes had been cast on November 2—two days before the election. Democratic election officials in the magical-ballot county simply announced that the date stamp on their voting machine must have been broken. Don't worry about it—they were sure those one hundred votes for Franken were legit.

Next, another four-hundred-odd statistically improbable "corrections" were made in other Democratic strongholds until—by the end of election week—Coleman's lead had been whittled down to a mere 215 votes.

Since then, highly irregular counting methods have added to Franken's total bit by bit, to the point that Coleman is now ahead by only 188 votes.

As long as Coleman maintains any lead at all, Republicans don't seem to care that his advantage is being shrunk by laughable ballot "discoveries" and different vote-count standards being applied from one precinct to the next—depending on which method of counting ballots is most advantageous to Franken.

Consider a few other chilling examples of Democrats thieving their way to victory over the years. In 1974, Republican Louis Wyman won his race for U.S. Senate in New Hampshire, beating Democrat John Durkin by 355 votes. Durkin demanded a recount—which went back and forth by a handful of votes until the state's Ballot Law Commission concluded that Wyman had indeed won by (at least) two votes. Wyman was certified the winner by the New Hampshire secretary of state and was on his way to Washington when...the overwhelmingly Democratic U.S. Senate refused to seat Wyman.

Despite New Hampshire's certification of Wyman as the winner of the election, this was the post-Watergate Senate, when Democrats could get away with *anything*—including a madcap prank known as "President Jimmy Carter." The U.S. Senate spent months examining disputed ballots from the New Hampshire election. Unable to come up with a method to declare the Democrat the winner that didn't involve a guillotine, the U.S. Senate forced New Hampshire to hold another election.

It was a breathtaking abuse of power. New Hampshire had certified a winner of its Senate election, but it was a Republican, so the Democratic Senate simply ordered a new election. Demoralized Republicans stayed away from the race and, this time, the Democrat won the re-vote.

Even more egregious was a 1984 congressional race in Indiana. On election night, the incumbent Democrat Frank McCloskey appeared to have won a razor-thin victory of seventy-two votes. But after a correction was made in one county, it turned out his Republican opponent, Richard McIntyre, had won by thirty-four votes.

Republican McIntyre was certified the winner—which is when the trouble usually starts. Again, a majority Democrat House refused to seat the certified winner in a close election. (I'm sure it was just a coincidence that the winner was a Republican.)

Consequently, Indiana performed yet another recount of the entire district, which *again* showed that Republican McIntyre was the winner—this time by 418 votes. As the *Washington Post* reported at the time: there were "no allegations of fraud" in the recount and 90 percent of ballot disqualifications had been agreed to "by election commissions dominated by Democrats." So, naturally, the House refused to seat the Republican even though he had received the most votes in the election, which in most jurisdictions would make him "the winner."

This time, instead of ordering the district to hold another election, the Democratic House saved everyone a lot of trouble by simply declaring Democrat Frank McCloskey the winner. By exactly four votes, according to the House's count.

Rounding out our stories of Democratic vote-theft is the infamous 2004 gubernatorial election in Washington State. Eerily similar to the ongoing "recount" in Minnesota, the Republican won the race on election night, but ballots favoring the Democrat kept being "discovered" until the Democrat finally eked out a majority. At that point, the recount was immediately halted and the Democrat declared the victor.

You would have to go back to Reconstruction to find an election that was stolen by the Republicans this way, but it's all in a day's work for the Democrats. Win or lose, Democrats will steal any close election.

That's why they were so testy about the 2000 Florida election. It was the one time in the last century Republicans wouldn't let Democrats steal an election they lost by less than a thousand votes.

No matter how many times Democrats steal elections, Republicans keep thinking the next time will be different. *Minnesota is famously clean! It's not like those other states.* It's not different. It's still the Democrats.

Obama Birth Certificate Spotted in Bogus Moon Landing Footage
August 5, 2009

Tardy though they are, we welcome MSNBC to finally joining every major conservative news outlet—including Fox News, the *American Spectator*, *Human Events*, *National Review*, and *Sweetness & Light*—in discrediting the idea that President Obama wasn't born in this country and, therefore, is ineligible to be president.

Now the big question: Was Joe Biden born on this planet?

Inasmuch as the "birther" movement was hatched in the station wagon of MSNBC's favorite left-wing fantasist, Larry Johnson, and pushed by Hillary's supporters, maybe the mainstream media can stop acting as if it's a creation of the Republican National Committee.

Which political party is more likely to house nutty conspiracy theorists? For example, which party contains 99 percent of the people who believe:

- O. J. is innocent;
- Bush shirked his National Guard duty;
- Sarah Palin's infant child, Trig, was actually the child of her daughter;
- Justice Antonin Scalia threw the 2000 election to Bush so that his son could get a legal job with the Labor Department;
- The spectacularly guilty Mumia Abu-Jamal was framed;
- The Diebold Corporation secretly stole thousands of Kerry votes in 2004;
- Duke lacrosse players gang-raped a stripper;
- Bill Clinton did not have sex with "that woman";

- Heterosexuals are just as likely to contract AIDS as gays; and,
- John Edwards didn't have an affair with Rielle Hunter and father her "love child."

Add to this a 2007 Rasmussen poll that showed 35 percent of Democrats believe Bush knew about the 9/11 attacks in advance, while 26 percent aren't sure.

Holy mackerel.

A favorite MSNBC guest, Janeane Garofalo, believes Enron's Ken Lay faked his own death. (It's weird that Keith Olbermann didn't ask her about that when she was on his show a couple of months ago, given his sudden interest in stamping out conspiracy theories.)

Trying to revive his failing TV show, MSNBC's Chris Matthews has been denouncing the birthers on *Hardball* nightly and demanding that every elected Republican who appears on his show do the same.

How many times has Matthews forced Democratic officeholders to denounce Al Sharpton for the Tawana Brawley hoax? Or for that matter, how many times has he forced Sharpton—a frequent guest on his show—to admit the case was a fraud? Sharpton has veto power over all Democratic presidential candidates. Even Al Gore, a former vice president of the United States, was required to kiss Sharpton's ring.

If there ever comes a time when Republican presidential candidates have to get the blessing of the head of the birther movement, I'll say: I'm wrong—Republicans *do* have as many conspiracy nuts as the Democrats.

Not content with merely humoring their nuts, Democratic officeholders actively promote conspiracy theories themselves. In 2003, Democratic presidential candidate and future Democratic National Committee Chairman Howard Dean approvingly cited the left-wing lunacy that Saudi Arabia had warned Bush in advance about the 9/11 attacks. He promised a caller to National Public Radio that, if elected, he would investigate.

In the fall of 2004, Clinton's secretary of state Madeleine Albright said she believed Bush was holding Osama bin Laden and planned to release him just before the election. (She later claimed she was joking—a surprise to all three witnesses who heard her say it.)

Senator Barbara Boxer officially objected—on the Senate floor—to the certification of Ohio's votes in the 2004 election and demanded an investigation into the "Diebold stole Kerry votes" conspiracy theory.

And, of course, a Democratic House and Senate actually used official government proceedings to investigate the original nut-job conspiracy theory, the "October Surprise," the thesis of which was that Reagan struck a secret deal with the Iranians *not* to release the hostages until after the 1980 election.

Now, the only October surprise we have is Obamacare: order an MRI in April and get it by...October. Surprise!

Rosie O'Donnell—who has headlined many a Democratic fund-raiser—is a prominent 9/11 "truther." She believes the World Trade Center was blown up with explosives, not terrorists in airplanes.

Most shockingly, the Democrats have a hand-in-glove relationship with Michael Moore, crackpot documentarian, whose *Fahrenheit 9/11* is chock-a-block with demented conspiracy theories, including:

- The 2000 election was stolen;
- The Bush family clandestinely spirited the bin Laden family out of the U.S. after the 9/11 attacks; and
- Bush went to war in Afghanistan, not to avenge the 9/11 terrorist attack, but to help the Unocal Corporation obtain a natural gas pipeline in Afghanistan.

Terry McAuliffe, then chairman of the Democratic National Committee attended the glittering Washington, D.C., premiere of *Fahrenheit 9/11* and emerged endorsing Moore's wacko Unocal conspiracy theory. "I believe it after seeing that," McAuliffe said.

Show me RNC Chairman Michael Steele saying, "I believe the birthers," and I'll give 10 percent of my book profits to Air America, raising their profits to, let's see ... about 10 percent of my book profits.

Democratic presidential candidate Wesley Clark proudly accepted Moore's endorsement in 2004, and Moore was an honored guest at the 2004 Democratic National Convention, sitting with former President Carter.

What is the likelihood that a birther will be sitting with former President Bush at the 2012 Republican National Convention?

Other Democrats who attended Moore's movie screening included Senators Tom Daschle, Tom Harkin, Max Baucus, Ernest Hollings, Debbie Stabenow, Bill Nelson, and Representatives Charles Rangel and Jim McDermott.

Show me a half dozen Republican senators attending a birther movie premiere, and I'll pretend to believe that Olbermann went to an Ivy League college.

Let's Play "Spot the Democrat!"
August 11, 2010

I n the greatest party-affiliation cover-up since the media tried to portray Gary Condit as a Republican, the media are refusing to mention the party affiliation of the thieving government officials in Bell, California.

There have been hundreds of news stories about Bell city officials' jaw-dropping compensation packages. In this poor city on the outskirts of Los Angeles, where the per capita annual income is $24,800 a year, the city manager, Robert Rizzo, had a salary of $787,637. That's about twice what the president of the United States makes. (To be fair, Rizzo was doing a better job.)

Rizzo was the highest-paid government employee in the entire country, not counting Maxine Waters's husband. With benefits, Rizzo's total annual compensation, according to the *Los Angeles Times*, came to $1.5 million a year. (Alerted to the Bell situation, the White House quickly added "Bell city manager" to the list of jobs saved by its stimulus plan.) Not only that, but Rizzo was entitled to twenty-eight weeks off a year for vacation and sick leave. To put that in perspective, that's almost as much vacation time as public school teachers get!

Reached in Spain, even Michelle Obama was outraged.

Rizzo responded to the anger over his preposterous salary by saying: "If that's a number people choke on, maybe I'm in the wrong business. I could go into private business and make that money." Good luck to him. After leaving Bell, Rizzo will be lucky to land a job at Taco Bell. Before being anointed the King Tut of Bell, Rizzo was the city manager of Hesperia, California, where he was overpaid only to the tune of $78,000 a year.

The police chief of Bell, Randy Adams, was making $457,000— $770,046 including benefits. The assistant city manager, Angela Spaccia, had a $376,288 salary, with a total compensation package of $845,960. Being just an assistant city manager, Angela could barely afford her own yacht.

As soon as the *Los Angeles Times* reported these stratospheric government salaries in little Bell, the millionaire government employees all resigned. Upon their resignations, they qualified for lifetime pensions worth, by some estimates, more than $50 million.

These insane salary packages were granted by the mayor and four city council members—who also set their own salaries. As a result, all but one were making $100,000 a year for their part-time city jobs. After the council members' salaries came to light, the four looters cut their salaries by 90 percent.

According to Nexis, there have been more than three hundred news stories reporting on the Bell scandal. Guess how many mentioned the party affiliation of the corrupt government bureaucrats? One. Yes, just one. Now guess if the government officials were Democrats or Republicans? Yes, that is correct. Congratulations—you've qualified for our bonus round!

The one newspaper to cough up party affiliations, the *Orange County Register*, admitted that the corrupt officials were all Democrats only in response to reader complaints about the peculiar omission. Lots of news stories on the scandal in Bell used the word "Democrat" or "Democratic." But that was only to say that the DEMOCRATIC attorney general of California, Jerry Brown, who is running on the DEMOCRATIC ticket for governor, is investigating the Bell officials' salaries.

Yes, in fact, you might want to vote for that DEMOCRATIC attorney general who is apparently a great crusader against corruption…despite his years of ignoring the public employee salary and pension looting that has driven the state into insolvency.

So we know the media are aware of party affiliations. They just chose not to mention them when it would require identifying shockingly corrupt government officials as Democrats.

Unlike political corruption involving sex or bribery, the outrage in Bell isn't a scandal that hits both parties from time to time. This is how the Democrats govern. Elected Democratic officials bestow ludicrous salaries and benefits packages on government employees, and, in return, public employee unions make sure the Democrats keep getting reelected.

The scandal in Bell isn't a scandal at all for the Democrats. It is the governing strategy of the Democrats.

[UPDATE: Say, whatever happened to Jerry Brown's investigation of Bell city officials? Dropped, I imagine.]

Patty Murray: The Stupidest Person in America
September 29, 2010

No liberal has standing to call any Republican stupid as long as Patty Murray remains in the U.S. Senate.

Soon after being elected to the U.S. Senate in 1992, Murray went on a radio show and said: "When I was growing up, the big fear in my life was the nuclear war. I remember second- and third-grade teachers giving us skills to deal with it, if that big alarm goes off, which was 'Hide under your desk.' Would that do any good? I don't know. But as a child, that gives you a feeling there's something to do beyond panic. Today the biggest fear our kids live with is whether ... the kid beside them has a gun. We have to give them skills so they feel confident to deal with it."

The woman is not sure if ducking under a school desk would help in a nuclear attack. Not only that, but she wants to teach children to do something similarly pointless to help them "deal with" school shootings. Maybe imaginary bulletproof vests!

With amazing understatement, one of Murray's Democratic colleagues in the state senate told the *Seattle Times* in 1992, "She just doesn't strike you as somebody who's been reading the *New York Times* every day for the past five years." I wonder when Katie Couric is going to ask Murray what newspapers she reads.

After Murray was elected to the U.S. Senate, the Democrats tried to keep her locked in her office to prevent her from saying anything that might end up in a newspaper. But in the confusion after the 9/11 attack, the leadership must have lost the keys and Murray escaped to say this about Osama bin Laden: "He's been out in these countries for decades, building schools, building roads, building infrastructure, building day-care facilities, building health-care facilities, and the people are extremely grateful. He's made their lives better."

Yes, Osama was out building "schools" and "day-care facilities"—and probably sponsoring "Bring Your Daughter to Work" days! I defy anyone to produce something stupider ever uttered by a *homo sapien*. Not Barbara Boxer, Joe Biden, or even John Edwards can hold their dimly lit candles to her.

Murray, whose college major was "recreation," got her start in politics fighting to save her own useless government job. The apocryphal story she tells is that she was told by some crusty old male politician—still unnamed decades later: "You're just a mom in tennis shoes—you can't make a difference!" (You know how politicians love gratuitously insulting their constituents.) This stuck in Murray's craw and so, filled with righteous anger, she ran for state office and won as a "mom in tennis shoes."

The real story is that Murray was teaching a "parenting" class at a community college, which no one was taking, so the state decided to cut it. Murray's reaction was, "Wait—I'm a public employee! You have no right to fire me!"

She wasn't a parent upset that her child's school was dropping an art history class. She was a deadbeat public employee who didn't want her job cut. No one was taking her course, but she thought taxpayers should be required to pay her anyway.

Fighting to keep your own cushy job isn't a point of principle; it's evidence of a narcissistic personality disorder.

But you have to do a lot of research to find out that the class being eliminated was Murray's own. The media's deliberate policy of hiding Murray's utterly self-serving motive for saving the class tells me they know this is a problem for her.

Admiring Murray's tenacious political start is like applauding the pluck of a stalker: "That guy sure has moxie and determination!" You're not supposed to be canonized for fighting to keep your own job. Murray is the equivalent of a Wall Street fat cat saying, "I'm going to fight for my $50 million severance package because it's the right thing to do!"

This remarkably unimpressive woman has tried to turn being a flat-footed dork into an advantage by selling herself as a tribune of regular folks. Yes, like most regular folk, she listed no religious affiliation whatsoever in the first few editions of the *Congressional Almanac*. (She probably couldn't remember she was supposed to pretend to be a Catholic.)

Soon after being elected to the Senate in 1992, Murray fought for a federal government jobs program by saying, "The highest-paying job I had before coming to Washington, D.C., paid $23,000 a year.… I know what it's like to tell my kids they can't buy everything they want." Is that what Murray thinks a senator should be doing? Ensuring that parents can tell their children they *can* buy everything they want? Or just ensuring that Patty Murray's children can buy everything they want?

True, Murray is a mom. You could also describe Hitler as a "war veteran and painter," but I think the more salient fact is that he was a German dictator. Similarly, Murray's most important characteristic is that she is a lifelong public-sector union zealot.

Again, Murray's class was on "parenting"—the very definition of a pointless government program. Imagine going back in a time machine and trying to explain to someone from 1950 why the government was paying for classes on "parenting." How about classes on "waking up" or "getting dressed"?

Democrats have completely infantilized the populace in order to create jobs for useless social workers like Murray. And people wonder why states are going bankrupt under crushing debt burdens.

But I guess we have to fund these idiotic programs in order not to be outshone by Osama bin Laden's "Partnership With Working Mothers Initiative" in Peshawar.

Weiner's Penis Headed to Small Claims Court
June 1, 2011

Sometimes I wonder if Representative Anthony Weiner, D-NY, is too nice for his own good.

An evil swine hacks into Weiner's Twitter account and posts an embarrassing photo of spindly legs topped by a small erect penis draped in dingy gray briefs no male over the age of eleven would wear—and Anthony just wants to forget the whole thing! Instead of angrily demanding an investigation like anyone else would, Anthony has gone all St. Francis of Assisi on us.

He doesn't want an investigation! How big-hearted is that? Talk about a forgiving nature! He's almost too magnanimous. I wish I had that kind of forbearance.

Maybe he's ready to live and let live, but speaking as one of Anthony's biggest Twitter followers, I am not. Otherwise, Weiner's hacker is just going to go out and hack and hack again. So while I admire Anthony's selfless refusal to be "distracted" by the penis tweets, I would urge him to reconsider.

Only a full and complete investigation will show that he had absolutely nothing to do with that humiliating photo of the tiny stub of a male organ sent to a twenty-one-year-old coed from his Twitter address last Friday night. Anthony needs to remember that hacking is a serious crime. In fact, there probably will have to be a federal investigation whether or not our hero requests one.

Another example of Anthony's amazing forbearance is how he has not retaliated against CNN for its malicious editing of Weiner's press conference on Tuesday. CNN obviously sabotaged the tape to make it look as if he was refusing to answer the simplest, most direct questions. (I confess I did not see the entire conference live; I was too busy sending private messages to the hundreds of college coeds I follow on Twitter, just like Anthony.) Through sheer trickery, CNN made it appear as if Anthony kept lurching back to the same irrelevant story about a heckler in an audience of forty-five thousand people.

Anyone could see there was something off about the video because no matter what reporters asked him, CNN kept looping back to that clip of Anthony telling his long, pointless parable about a heckler in an audience and then demanding that he be allowed to finish, when he obviously had already finished. This falsely suggested that he was stonewalling reporters. Perhaps the CNN tape was hacked, too!

It's time for Anthony to stand up for himself, if you'll pardon the expres—*Hey, wait a minute! Now my column is being hacked!!!*—and demand an investigation of both the hacker and CNN. You don't need to apologize for anything, congressman. Your only problem is, you're just too damn nice.

But knowing Anthony, he'll probably forgive CNN. There's a reason why, year in and year out, Anthony Weiner has been voted Congress's most forgiving person. I try to be a good Christian, but it took Anthony Weiner to show me what true mercy is. I salute you, congressman!

The preceding several paragraphs are what we call "irony," i.e., saying one thing while meaning the opposite. What I meant to say is: OF

COURSE ANTHONY WEINER DOESN'T WANT AN INVESTIGA-
TION! IT WOULD ONLY PROVE THAT HE HIMSELF POSTED THE
PHOTO OF HIS SMALL ERECT PENIS!

The reason the congressman is so eager to "forgive" the hacker is that
there is no hacker. He cannot have an investigation for the simple reason
that it will show that he sent the penis photo himself.

In a panic when he saw he had hit the wrong button and sent a private tweet of his pecker to his entire Twitter following, Weiner blurted
out the hacker defense, quickly typing: "FB hacked. Is my blender gonna
attack me next?" Unfortunately, there was no lawyer in the room to tell
him: "Don't say that! They'll have to investigate!"

On Sunday, his staff followed up with a press release, saying, "Anthony's accounts were obviously hacked." So now he really can't claim he
didn't say it.

Nonetheless, after hiring a lawyer, Weiner quickly backpedaled from
the "hacker" claim and began insisting, in another press release, "This
was a prank. We are loath to treat it as more." If it was a prank, then why
did he hire a lawyer?

Weiner isn't a celebrity: he's a CONGRESSMAN. Whoever can hack
into his Twitter account may be able to hack into other congressmen's
accounts—or into briefing files from, say, the Department of Defense.
(Indeed, unless the alleged hacker is arrested, who knows how many
Anthony Weiner penis shots could start circulating on Twitter?)

But when one of Weiner's colleagues, Representative Cliff Stearns,
R-FL, requested a congressional investigation into cybersecurity based
on Weiner's self-proclaimed computer attack on his Twitter account,
Weiner denounced and insulted Stearns. He's stuck angrily announcing
that he wants to move on, there's important work to be done, and calling
a CNN reporter a "jackass" merely for asking him if he sent the penis
photo.

For a guy who's suddenly taking the position that this was all just a harmless prank, Weiner seemed pretty bent out of shape at that CNN press conference. If that condition persists for more than four hours, congressman, consult your doctor.

CHAPTER FIVE

Liberal Behavior: Porn Surfers, Liars, and Welfare Suppliers

E ven communist dupe Henry Wallace knew American liberals were nuts. Speaking at a conference sponsored by two Red fronts, the National Citizens Political Action Committee and the Independent Citizens Committee of the Arts, Sciences, and Professions—for which he was fired as President Truman's commerce secretary—Wallace said that the great majority of Americans were offended by Russia's suppression of basic liberties in Eastern Europe. The hissing from the audience was so loud at this, that Wallace stepped back from the microphone, commenting, "I'm talking about people outside New York City when I say that. Every Gallup Poll will show it!" (David A. Shannon, *The Decline of American Communism: A History of the Communist Party of the United States Since 1945*, page 119.)

These are the types of people who populate the mainstream media and Democratic administrations.

Communism doesn't work unless everyone has it. The impossibility of "socialism in one state" drives the Left to demand no-exceptions national laws. Otherwise, free market states will always undermine totalitarian regimes. Look at the booming population growth in low-tax, low-regulation states in the U.S., while the big government states like New York, Michigan, Illinois, and California wither away. Having already driven out nearly every other industry, in 2013, the dying blue states began pushing gun manufacturers out of their states—and thousands of good-paying jobs with them.

The same way some countries operate as tax havens, the U.S. used to be a medical haven. That's why nationalizing healthcare has been on liberals' "To Do" list since the 1940s. Now, no one can escape.

By the way, how has nationalizing education worked out? Is public education just as good as private? Does it keep the cost of private school down? If you would die unless you got some medicine from coast to coast overnight, would you request Express Mail from the U.S. Postal Service for $15 or Federal Express for $40?

Still, I can't wait to see the rest of Obama's America. An America where I can use lightning-fast, high-speed internet to file electronically for my unemployment benefits.

Reno 911
August 29, 2007

This week, congressional Democrats vowed to investigate Attorney General Alberto Gonzales's firing of himself.* Gonzales has said he was not involved in the discussions about his firing and that it was "performance-based," but he couldn't recall the specifics.

---

* Gonzales announced his resignation on August 27, 2007, in the midst of liberal fury over Bush firing some of his own U.S. attorneys.

Right-wingers like me never trusted Gonzales. But watching Hillary Rodham Clinton literally applaud the announcement of Gonzales's resignation on Monday was more than any human being should have to bear. Liberals' hysteria about Gonzales was surpassed only by their hysteria about his predecessor, John Ashcroft. (Also their hysteria about Bush, Rove, Rumsfeld, Cheney, Libby, Rice, Barney the dog, and so on. They're very excitable, these Democrats.)

Liberals want to return the office to the glory years of Attorney General Janet Reno!

There is reason to believe Reno is precisely the sort of attorney general that Hillary would nominate, since Reno was widely assumed to be Hillary's pick at the time. As ABC News's Chris Bury reported the day Reno was confirmed: "The search for an attorney general exemplifies Hillary Clinton's circle of influence and its clout.... The attorney general-designate, Janet Reno, came to the president's attention through Hillary Clinton's brother, Hugh Rodham."

Let's compare attorneys general:

- Civilians killed by Ashcroft: 0
- Civilians killed by Gonzales: 0
- Civilians killed by Reno: 80

Reno's military attack on a religious sect in Waco, Texas, led to the greatest number of citizens ever killed by the government in the history of the United States. More Americans were killed at Waco than were killed at any of the various markers on the Left's via dolorosa—more than Kent State (four dead), more than the Haymarket Square rebellion (four dead), more than Three Mile Island (zero dead).

- Innocent people put in prison by Ashcroft: 0
- Innocent people put in prison by Gonzales: 0

- Innocent people put in prison by Reno: at least 1 that I know of

As Dade County (Florida) state attorney, Janet Reno made a name for herself as one of the leading witch-hunters in the notorious "child molestation" cases from the '80s, when convictions of innocent Americans were won on the basis of heavily coached testimony from small children.

Charged by Reno's office in 1984 with child molestation, Grant Snowden was convicted on the manufactured testimony of one such child, who was four years old when the abuse allegedly occurred.

Snowden, the most decorated police officer in the history of the South Miami Police Department, was sentenced to five life terms—and was imprisoned with people he had put there. Snowden served eleven years before his conviction was finally overturned by a federal court in an opinion that ridiculed the evidence against him and called his trial "fundamentally unfair."

In a massive criminal justice system, mistakes will be made from time to time. But Janet Reno put people like Snowden in prison not for crimes that they didn't commit—but for crimes that never happened. Such was the soccer mom–induced hysteria of the '80s, when average Americans were prosecuted for fantastical crimes concocted in therapists' offices.

- Number of obvious civil rights violations ignored by Ashcroft: 0
- Number of obvious civil rights violations ignored by Gonzales: 0
- Number of obvious civil rights violations ignored by Reno: at least 1

On Aug. 19, 1991, rabbinical student Yankel Rosenbaum was stabbed to death in Crown Heights by a black racist mob shouting "Kill the Jew!" as retaliation for another Hasidic man killing a black child in a car accident hours earlier.

In a far clearer case of jury nullification than the first Rodney King verdict, a jury composed of nine blacks and three Puerto Ricans acquitted Lemrick Nelson Jr. of the murder—despite the fact that the police found the bloody murder weapon in his pocket and the victim's blood on his clothes. Oh, also, Rosenbaum, as he lay dying, had identified Nelson as his assailant.

The Hasidic community immediately appealed to the attorney general for a federal civil rights prosecution of Nelson. Reno responded with utter mystification at the idea that anyone's civil rights had been violated.

Civil rights? Where do you get that?

Because they were chanting "Kill the Jew," Rosenbaum is a Jew, and they killed him.

Huh. That's a weird interpretation of "civil rights." It sounds a little harebrained to me, but I guess I could have someone look into it.

It took two years from Nelson's acquittal to get Reno to bring a civil rights case against him.

- Number of innocent civilians accused of committing heinous crimes by Ashcroft: 0
- Number of innocent civilians accused of committing heinous crimes by Gonzales: 0
- Number of innocent civilians accused of committing heinous crimes by Reno: at least 1

Janet Reno presided over the leak of Richard Jewell's name to the media, implicating him in the Atlanta Olympic Park bombing in

1996, for which she later apologized. I believe Reno also falsely accused the Miami relatives of Elian Gonzalez of violating the law, which I am not including in her record of false accusations, but that reminds me…

- Number of six-year-old boys deported to totalitarian dictatorships by Ashcroft: 0
- Number of six-year-old boys deported to totalitarian dictatorships by Gonzales: 0
- Number of six-year-old boys deported to totalitarian dictatorships by Reno: 1

So it's strange that the media only became interested in the short-comings of attorneys general after Bush became president. Whatever flaws Alberto Gonzales has (John Ashcroft has none), we don't have to go back to the Harding administration to find a worse attorney general.

From the phony child abuse cases of the '80s to the military assault on Americans at Waco, Janet Reno presided over the most egregious attacks on Americans' basic liberties since the Salem witch trials. These outrageous deprivations of life and liberty were not the work of fanatical right-wing prosecutors, but liberals like Janet Reno.

Reno is the sort of wild-eyed zealot trampling on real civil rights that Hillary views as an ideal attorney general, unlike that brute Alberto Gonzales. At least Reno didn't fire any U.S. attorneys!

Oh wait!

- Number of U.S. attorneys fired by Ashcroft: 0
- Number of U.S. attorneys fired by Gonzales: 8
- Number of U.S. attorneys fired by Reno: 93

Obama's Recipe for Change Not My Cup of Tea
April 15, 2009

I had no idea how important the nationwide anti-tax tea parties were until hearing liberals denounce them with such ferocity. The *New York Times'* Paul Krugman wrote a column attacking the tea parties, apologizing for making fun of "crazy people." (It's OK, Paul, you're allowed to make fun of crazy people for the same reason Jews can make fun of Jews.)

On MSNBC, hosts Keith Olbermann and Rachel Maddow have been tittering over the similarity of the name "tea parties" to an obscure homosexual sexual practice known as "tea bagging." Night after night, they sneer at Republicans for being so stupid as to call their rallies "tea bagging," a practice they show a surprising degree of familiarity with.

Except no one is calling the tea parties "tea bagging." Only Olbermann and Maddow call them that. Republicans call them "tea parties." But if the Republicans *were* calling them "tea-bagging parties," the MSNBC hosts would have a fantastically hilarious segment for viewers in San Francisco and the West Village and not anyplace else in the rest of the country. On the other hand, they're not called "tea-bagging parties."

You know what else would be hilarious? It would be hilarious if Hillary Clinton's name were "Ima Douche." Unfortunately, it's not. It was just a dream. Most people would wake up, realize it was just a dream, and scrap the joke. Not MSNBC hosts.

One point of the tea parties is to note that Democrats always tell voters they have absolutely no intention of raising taxes. (Most people who actually pay taxes consider raising them a bad idea.) Then they get elected and immediately raise taxes. Obama's biggest shortcoming is that he believes all the things believed by Democrats, which have devastating consequences when put into effect. Among these is the Democrats' admiration for raising taxes on the productive.

For the last fifty years, Democrats have tried to stimulate the economy by giving "tax cuts" to people who don't pay taxes. Obviously, these are simple welfare payments, but campaigning on a promise to grow welfare, evidently, isn't a big vote-getter. Even Bush had a "stimulus" bill that sent government checks to lots of people last year. Guess what happened? It didn't stimulate the economy.

Obama's stimulus bill is the mother of all pork bills for friends of Congressional Democrats and friends of O. ("O" stands for Obama, not Oprah, but there's probably a lot of overlap.) And all that government spending on the Democrats' constituents will be paid for by raising taxes on the productive. Raise taxes and the productive job holders will work less, adopt tax shelters, barter instead of sell, turn to an underground economy—and the government will get less money.

The perfect bar bet with a liberal would be to wager that massive government deficits in the '80s were not caused by Reagan's tax cuts. Casually mention that you thought Reagan's tax cuts brought the government *more* revenue—they did—and you could get odds in Hollywood and Manhattan. (This became a less attractive wager in New York this week after Governor David Paterson announced his new plan to tax bar bets.)

The lie at the heart of liberals' mantra on taxes—"tax increases only for the rich"—is the ineluctable fact that unless taxes are raised across the board, the government won't get enough money to fund layers and layers of useless government bureaucrats, none of whom can possibly be laid off. How much would you have to raise taxes before any of Obama's constituents noticed? They don't pay taxes, they engage in "tax-reduction" strategies, they work for the government, or they're too rich to care. (Or they have offshore tax shelters, like George Soros.)

California tried Obama's soak-the-productive plan years ago and was hailed as the perfect exemplar of Democratic governance. In June 2002, the liberal *American Prospect* magazine called California a "laboratory" for Democratic policies, noting that "California is the only one of the nation's 10 largest states that is uniformly under Democratic control." They said this, mind you, as if it were a good thing. California, the article proclaimed, "the next New Deal is in tryouts."

In just a few years, Democrats had turned California into a state—or as it's now known, a "job-free zone"—with a $41 billion deficit, a credit rating that was slashed to junk-bond status and a middle class now located in Arizona.

Democrats governed California the way Democrats always govern. They bought the votes of government workers with taxpayer-funded jobs, salaries, and benefits—and then turned around and accused the productive class of "greed" for wanting not to have their taxes raised through the roof. Having run out of things to tax, now the California legislature is considering a tax on taxes. At this point, the only way out may be a tax on Botox and steroids.

California was, in fact, a laboratory of Democratic policies. The rabbit died. Now Obama is trying it on a national level. That's what the tea parties are about.

What a Sack of Sacrosanct
June 23, 2010

I n the *New York Times'* profile of Supreme Court nominee Elena Kagan, her aunt was quoted as saying, "There was thinking, always thinking" at the family's dinner table. "Nothing was sacrosanct." Really? Nothing was sacrosanct? Because in my experience, on a scale of

1 to infinity, the range of acceptable opinion among New York liberals goes from 1 to 1.001.

How would the following remarks fare at a dinner table on the Upper West Side where "nothing was sacrosanct"?

- *"Hey, maybe that Joe McCarthy was onto something."*
- *"What would prayer in the schools really hurt?"*
- *"How do we know gays are born that way?"*
- *"Is it possible that union demands have gone too far?"*
- *"Does it make sense to have three recycling bins in these microscopic Manhattan apartments?"*
- *"Say, has anyone read Charles Murray's latest book?"*

Those comments, considered "conversation starters" in most of the country, would get you banned from polite society in New York. And unless you want the whole room slowly backing away from you, also avoid: *"May I smoke?," "Merry Christmas!,"* and *"I heard it on Fox News."*

Even members of survivalist Christian cults in Idaho at least know people who hold opposing views. New York liberals don't. As Kagan herself described it, on the Upper West Side of New York where she grew up, "Nobody ever admitted to voting Republican." So, I guess you could say that, in the Kagan household, being a Democrat was "sacrosanct."

Even within the teeny, tiny range of approved liberal opinion, disagreement will get you banned from the premises.

When, as dean of the Harvard Law School, Kagan disagreed with the Bill Clinton policy of "Don't Ask, Don't Tell" for gays in the military, she open-mindedly banned military recruiters from the law school, denouncing Clinton's policy as "discriminatory," "deeply wrong," "unwise and unjust." From this, I conclude that having gays serving openly in the military is "sacrosanct" for liberals like Kagan.

The opposite position is held by lots of people in other parts of the country, but I do not recall any Christian colleges banning military recruiters because the schools believed "Don't Ask, Don't Tell" went too far the other way.

Not only is every weird, shared delusion of the New York liberal deemed sacrosanct, but what ought to be sacrosanct—off the top of my head, human life—isn't. As Stan Evans says, whatever liberals disapprove of, they want banned (smoking, guns, Christianity, ROTC, the Pledge of Allegiance), and whatever they approve of, they make mandatory (abortion-on-demand, gay marriage, pornography, condom distribution in public schools, screenings of *An Inconvenient Truth*).

When liberals say, "nothing is sacrosanct," they mean "nothing *other Americans consider sacrosanct* is sacrosanct." They demonstrate their open-mindedness by ridiculing other people's dogma but will not brook the most trifling criticism of their own dogmas.

Thus, for example, liberals sneer at the bluenoses and philistines of the "religious right" for objecting to taxpayer funding of a crucifix submerged in a jar of urine but would have you banned from public life for putting Matthew Shepard in a jar of urine, with or without taxpayer funding. These famously broad-minded New Yorkers—"thinking, always thinking"—actually booed Mayor Rudy Giuliani when he showed up at the opera after pulling city funding from a museum exhibit that included a painting of the Virgin Mary plastered with close-up pornographic photos of women's vulvas. (The *New York Times* fair-mindedly refused to ever mention the vulvas, instead suggesting that the mayor's objection was to the cow dung used in the composition.)

Has a decision on funding "art" ever gotten a politician in any other part of the country booed in public? And how might the *Times* refer to citizens booing a mayor who had withdrawn taxpayer funding for a painting of Rosa Parks covered in pornography?

If New York liberals insist on bragging about their intellectual courage in believing "nothing is sacrosanct," it would really help if they could stop being the most easily offended, thin-skinned weenies in the entire universe. They also might want to ease up on the college "hate speech" codes, politically correct firings, and bans on military recruiters.

With that in mind, here are some questions it would be fun to ask a New York liberal like Supreme Court nominee Elena Kagan at her hearings next week:

- Roughly one-third of Americans are Evangelical Christians. Do you personally know any Evangelical Christians? Name two.
- In 1972, Richard Nixon was elected president with more than 60 percent of the vote, winning every state except Massachusetts and the District of Columbia. How many people do you know who voted for Nixon?
- Appropriate or inappropriate: Schools passing out condoms to seventh-graders? Schools passing out filtered cigarettes to seventh-graders?
- Who is a greater threat to America, Sarah Palin or Mahmoud Ahmadinejad?

Bonfire of the Insanities
September 8, 2010

In response to General David Petraeus's denunciation of Florida pastor Terry Jones's right to engage in a symbolic protest of the 9/11 attacks by burning copies of the Quran this September 11, President

Obama said: "Let me be clear: As a citizen, and as president, I believe that members of the Dove World Outreach Center have the same right to freedom of speech and religion as anyone else in this country."

Governor Charlie Crist of Florida lauded Obama's remarks, saying America is "a place where you're supposed to be able to practice your religion without the government telling you you can't."

New York City mayor Michael Bloomberg called Obama's words a "clarion defense of the freedom of religion"—and also claimed that he had recently run into a jihadist who actually supported the Quran-burning!

Keith Olbermann read the poem "First they came ..." on air in defense of the Quran-burners, nearly bringing himself to tears at his own profundity.

No wait, my mistake. This is what liberals said about the Ground Zero mosque only five minutes ago when they were posing as First Amendment absolutists. Suddenly, they've developed amnesia when it comes to the free-speech right to burn a Quran.

Weirdly, conservatives who opposed building the mosque at Ground Zero are also against the Quran-burning. (Except in my case. It turns out I'm for it, but mostly because burning Qurans will contribute to global warming.)

Liberals couldn't care less about the First Amendment. To the contrary, censoring speech and religion is the Left's specialty! (Unless the religion is Islam.) They promote speech codes, hate crimes, free speech zones (known as "America" off college campuses), and go around the country yanking every reference to God from the public square via endless lawsuits by the ACLU.

Whenever you see a liberal choking up over our precious constitutional rights, you can be sure we're talking about the rights of Muslims at Ground Zero, "God Hates Fags" funeral protesters, strippers, the *New*

York Times publishing classified documents, pornographers, child molesters, murderers, traitors, saboteurs, terrorists, flag-burners (but not Quran-burners!), or women living on National Endowment for the Arts grants by stuffing yams into their orifices on stage.

Speaking of lying dwarves, last week on *The Daily Show* Bloomberg claimed he was having a hamburger with his "girlfriend" when a man came up to him and said of the Ground Zero mosque: "I just got back from two tours fighting overseas for America. This is what we were all fighting for. You go and keep at it." We're fighting for the right of Muslims to build mosques at Ground Zero? I thought we were trying to keep Muslims AWAY from our skyscrapers. (What an embarrassing mistake.) PLEASE PULL THE TROOPS OUT IMMEDIATELY.

But back to the main issue: Was Bloomberg having a $150 Burger Double Truffle at DB Bistro Moderne or a more sensible $30 burger at the 21 Club when he bumped into the imaginary veteran? With the pint-sized mayor shrieking at the sight of a saltshaker, I assume he wasn't having a Hardee's No. 4 Combo Meal. Adding an element of realism to his little vignette, Bloomberg said: "I got a hamburger and a pickle and a potato chip or something."

A potato chip? Translation: "I don't know what I was eating, because I'm making this whole story up—I wouldn't be caught dead eating 'a potato chip' or any other picaresque garnish favored by the peasants." At least Bloomberg didn't claim the man who walked up to him took credit for setting the Times Square bomb because he was a Tea Partier upset about Obamacare—as Sherlock Bloomberg had so presciently speculated at the time.

General Petraeus objected to the Quran-burning protest on the grounds that it could be used by radical jihadists to recruit Muslims to attack Americans. This is what liberals say whenever we do anything displeasing to the enemy—invade Iraq, hold terrorists in Guantanamo, interrogate jihadists, or publish Muhammad cartoons. Is there a website somewhere listing everything that encourages terrorist recruiting?

If the general's objective is to hamper jihadist recruiting, may I respectfully suggest unconditional surrender? Because on his theory, you know what would really kill the terrorists' recruiting ability? If we adopted Sharia law!

But wait—weren't we assured by Fire Island's head of national security, Andrew Sullivan, that if America elected a "brown-skinned man whose father was an African, who grew up in Indonesia and Hawaii, who attended a majority-Muslim school as a boy," the terrorists would look like a bunch of lunkheads and be unable to recruit?

It didn't work out that way. There have been more terrorist attacks on U.S. soil by these allegedly calmed Muslims in Obama's first eighteen months in office than in the six years under Bush from the moment he invaded Iraq. Also, as I recall, there was no Guantanamo, no Afghanistan War, and no Iraq War on September 10, 2001. And yet, somehow, Osama bin Laden had no trouble recruiting back then. Can we retire the "it will help them recruit" argument yet?

The reason not to burn Qurans is that it's unkind—not to jihadists, but to Muslims who mean us no harm. The same goes for building a mosque at Ground Zero—in both cases, it's not a question of anyone's "rights," it's just a nasty thing to do.

Look for the Union Fable
February 23, 2011

In February 2011, thousands of government workers in Wisconsin began a months-long protest outside the state capitol,

shutting down public schools and other government services.
Democratic lawmakers fled the state to block the quorum
needed to pass the governor's bill, which would have ended
collective bargaining over work conditions.

The good news out of Wisconsin is that public school students' test scores skyrocketed last week, mystifying educators. The bad news is many student-teacher love affairs were hard-hit without access to janitors' closets and locker rooms.

Democrats are acting as if Wisconsin governor Scott Walker's demand that public sector employees give up collective bargaining would have George Washington rolling in his grave (a clear violation of Gravediggers' Local 803 regulations concerning the rolling of the dead).

In fact, government employees should never, ever be allowed to organize. The need for a union comes down to this question: Do you have a boss who wants you to work harder for less money? In the private sector, the answer is yes. In the public sector, the answer is a big, fat NO. Government unions have nothing in common with private sector unions because they don't have hostile management on the other side of the bargaining table. The "bosses" of government employees aren't antagonists, they're co-conspirators.

Far from being careful stewards of the taxpayers' money, politicians are on the same side of the table as government employees—against the taxpayers, who aren't allowed in on the negotiation. This is why the head of New York's largest public union in the mid-'70s, Victor Gotbaum, gloated, "We have the ability to elect our own boss." Democratic politicians don't think of themselves as "management." They don't respond to union demands for more money by saying, "Are you kidding me?" They say, "Great—get me a raise too!"

Democrats buy the votes of government workers with generous pay packages and benefits—paid for by the taxpayer—and then expect a kickback from the unions in the form of hefty campaign donations, rent-a-mobs, and questionable union political activity when they run for reelection.

In 2006, ten thousand public employees staged a rally outside the New Jersey State House to protest the mere discussion of a cut to their gold-plated salaries and benefits. Then governor Jon Corzine leapt onto the stage shouting, "We will fight for a fair contract!" (It takes a special kind of courage to promise ten thousand union agitators that you'll fight to get them more money.)

Only later, someone noticed: Wait—isn't he management?

Service Employees International Union officials openly threaten California legislators. At a 2009 legislative hearing, an SEIU member sneered into a microphone: "We helped to getchu into office, and we gotta good memory. Come November, if you don't back our program, we'll getchu out of office."

It used to be widely understood that collective bargaining has no place in government employment. In 1937, liberals' most beloved president, FDR, warned that collective bargaining "cannot be transplanted into the public service." George Meany, head of the AFL-CIO for a quarter century, said unions were not appropriate for civil servants. As recently as 1978, the vast majority of states prohibited unionization of government employees.

Public sector unions take advantage of the perception that all union members are tough manual laborers being abused by greedy capitalist overseers. Anytime there is the slightest suggestion that perhaps in the middle of a deep recession, public school teachers should pay 1.5 percent of their salaries toward their fabulous healthcare plans, suddenly we get television ads of muscular men, covered in soot, doing dangerous jobs on docks and in foundries.

The unions must be desperately hoping that no one will notice... *Wait a minute! WE'RE TALKING ABOUT TEACHERS!* This isn't the Discovery Channel's *Dirty Jobs*—it's Mrs. Cooper's seventh grade "values clarification" class. With heavy union dues, labor has plenty of money to pay for propaganda and to threaten and bribe politicians.

Government workers think the job of everyone else in society is to protect their high salaries, crazy work rules, and obscene pensions. They self-righteously lecture us about public service, the children, a "living wage"—all in the service of squeezing more money from the taxpayer to fund their breathtakingly selfish job arrangements.

There's never a recession if you work for the government. The counties with the highest per capita income aren't near New York City or Los Angeles—they're in the Washington, D.C., area—a one-company town where the company is the government. The three counties with the highest incomes in the entire country are all suburbs of Washington. Eleven of the twenty-five counties with the highest incomes are near Washington.

For decades now, the Democrats have had a good gig buying the votes of government workers—and then sticking the productive class with the bill. But now we're out of money, no matter how long Wisconsin Democrats hide out in Illinois.

This Is What a Mob Looks Like
October 5, 2011

I am not the first to note the vast differences between the Wall Street protesters and the Tea Partiers. To name three: the Tea Partiers have jobs, showers, and a point.

No one knows what the Wall Street protesters want—as is typical with mobs. They say they want Obama reelected but claim to hate "Wall Street." You know, the same Wall Street that gave its largest campaign donations in history to Obama, who, in turn, bailed out the banks and made Goldman Sachs the fourth branch of government. This would be like opposing fattening processed foods but cheering Michael Moore—which the protesters also did this week.

But to me, the most striking difference between the Tea Partiers and the "Occupy Wall Street" crowd—besides the smell of patchouli—is how liberal protesters must claim their every gathering is historic and heroic. They chant: "The world is watching!" "This is how democracy looks!" "We are the ones we've been waiting for!" At the risk of acknowledging that I am, in fact, "watching," this is most definitely not how democracy looks.

Sally Kohn, a self-identified "community organizer," praised the Wall Street loiterers on CNN's website, comparing the protest to the Boston Tea Party, which she claimed, "helped spark the American Revolution," adding, "and yes, that protest ultimately turned very violent."

First of all, the Boston Tea Party was nothing like tattooed, body-pierced, sunken-chested nineteen-year-olds getting in fights with the police for fun. Paul Revere's nighttime raid was intended exclusively to protest a new British tea tax. (The Wall Street protesters would be more likely to fight *for* a new tax.)

Second, so far from violent was it, that Revere made sure to replace a broken lock on one of the ships and severely punished a participant who stole some tea for his private use. Samuel Adams defended the raid by saying that all other methods of recourse—say, voting—were unavailable.

Our revolution—the only revolution that led to greater freedom since at least 1688—was not the act of a mob. As specific and limited as it was, however, even the Boston Tea Party was too mob-like to spark anything other than retaliatory British measures. Indeed, it set back the cause of American independence by dispiriting both American and British supporters, such as Edmund Burke.

George Washington disapproved of the destruction of the tea. Benjamin Franklin demanded that the East India Company be reimbursed for it. Considered an embarrassment by many of our Founding Fathers, the Boston Tea Party was not celebrated for another fifty years.

It would be three long years after the Boston Tea Party when our Founding Fathers engaged in their truly revolutionary act: the signing of the Declaration of Independence. In that document, our Christian forebears set forth in blindingly clear terms their complaints with British rule, their earlier attempts at resolution, and an appeal to the Supreme Judge of the world for independence from the crown.

The rebel armies defending that declaration were not a disorganized mob, chanting slogans for the press and defacing public property. Even the Minutemen, whose first scuffle with the British began the war, were a real army with ranks, subordination, coordination, drills, and supplies. There is not a single mention in the historical record of Minutemen playing hackysack or sitting in drum circles.

A British lieutenant general who fought the Minutemen observed, "Whoever looks upon them as an irregular mob will find himself very much mistaken."

By contrast, the directionless losers protesting "Wall Street"—Obama's largest donor group—pose for the cameras while uttering random liberal clichés lacking any reason or coherence. But since everything liberals do must be heroic, the "Occupy Wall Street" crowd insists on comparing themselves to this nation's heroes. One told Fox News's Bill Schulz, "I was born to be here, right now, the Founding Fathers have been passing down the torch to this generation to make our country great again."

The Canadian environmental group behind Occupy Wall Street, Adbusters, has compared the Wall Street "revolutionaries" to America's Founding Fathers. (Incidentally, those who opposed the American Revolution fled after the war to...Canada.)

The—again—*Canadians* exulted, "You sense they're drafting a new Declaration of Independence." I suppose you only "sense" it because they're doing nothing of the sort. They say they want Mao as the president—as one told Schulz—and the abolition of "capitalism."

The modern Tea Partiers never went around narcissistically comparing themselves to General George Washington. And yet they are the ones who have engaged in the kind of political activity Washington fought for. The Tea Party name is meant in fun, inspired by an amusing rant from CNBC's Rick Santelli in February 2009, when he called for another Tea Party in response to Obama's plan to bail out irresponsible mortgagers.

The Tea Partiers didn't arrogantly claim to be drafting a new Declaration of Independence. They're perfectly happy with the original. Tea Partiers didn't block traffic, sleep on sidewalks, wear ski masks, fight with the police, or urinate in public. They read the Constitution, made serious policy arguments, and petitioned the government against Obama's unconstitutional big government policies, especially the stimulus bill and Obamacare. Then they picked up their own trash and quietly went home. Apparently, a lot of them had to be at work in the morning.

In the two years following the movement's inception, the Tea Party played a major role in turning Teddy Kennedy's seat over to a Republican, making the sainted Chris Christie governor of New Jersey, and winning a gargantuan, historic Republican landslide in the 2010 elections. They are probably going to succeed in throwing out a president in next year's election.

That's what democracy looks like.

Who Wouldn't Enjoy Firing These People?
January 11, 2012

Earlier this week, Mitt Romney got into trouble for saying, "I like being able to fire people who provide services to me." To comprehend why the political class reacted as if Romney had just praised Hitler, you must understand that his critics live in a world in which no one can ever be fired—a world known as "the government."

Romney's statement about being able to fire people was an arrow directed straight to the heart of Obamacare. (By the way, arrows to the heart are not covered by Obamacare.)

Talking about insurance providers, he said, "I want individuals to have their own insurance. That means … if you don't like what they do, you can fire them. I like being able to fire people who provide services to me. You know, if someone doesn't give me a good service that I need, I want to say I'm going to go get someone else to provide that service to me."

Obamacare, you recall, will be administered by the same people who run the Department of Motor Vehicles. They will operate under the same self-paced, self-evaluated work rules that have made government offices the envy of efficiency specialists everywhere. And no one will be able to fire them—unless they're caught doing something truly vile and criminal, such as stealing from patients in nursing homes.

Oops, I take that back: government employees who rob the elderly also can't be fired.

The *Los Angeles Times* recently reported that, after a spate of burglaries at a veterans' hospital in California, authorities set up video cameras to catch the perpetrators. In short order, nurse's aide Linda Riccitelli was videotaped sneaking into the room of ninety-three-year-old Raymond Germain as he slept, sticking her hand into his dresser drawer, and stealing the bait money that had been left there. Riccitelli was fired and a burglary prosecution initiated. A few years later, the California Personnel Board rescinded her firing and awarded her three years back pay. The board dismissed the videotape of Riccitelli stealing the money as "circumstantial." (The criminal prosecution was also dropped after Germain died.)

But surely we'll be able to fire a government employee who commits a physical assault on a mentally disturbed patient? No, wrong again.

Psychiatric technician Gregory Powell was working at a government center for the mentally retarded when he hit a severely disturbed individual with a shoe so hard that the impression of the shoe's sole was visible on the victim three hours later. A psychologist who witnessed the attack said the patient was cowering on the couch before being struck. Powell was fired, but, again, the California Personnel Board ordered him rehired.

Now, let's turn to New York City. For years, the New York City school budget included $35 million to $65 million a year to place hundreds of teachers in "rubber rooms," for committing such serious offenses that they were barred from classrooms. Teachers accused of raping students sat in the rooms doing no work all day, but still collecting government paychecks. They couldn't be fired. After an uproar about this, Michael Bloomberg abolished the rooms. But the teachers still can't be fired.

Wherever there is government, there is malfeasance and criminality— and employees who can never be fired.

In 2010, thirty-three employees of the Securities and Exchange Commission—half making $100,000 to $200,000 per year—were found to have spent most of their workdays over a five-year period downloading internet pornography. (Thank goodness there were no financial shenanigans going on then!) One, a senior lawyer at SEC headquarters in Washington, D.C., admitted to spending eight hours a day looking at internet pornography, sometimes even "working" through his lunch hour. Another admitted watching up to five hours a day of pornography in his office. Would that Bernie Madoff had posted naked photos of himself online!

Not one of the porn-surfing employees of the SEC was fired.

In 2009, the inspector general of the National Science Foundation was forced to abandon an investigation of grant fraud when he stumbled across dozens of NSF employees, including senior management, surfing pornographic websites on government computers during work hours. One senior official who had spent 331 workdays talking to nude women online was allowed to resign (but was not fired). I just hope they gave him his computer as a parting gift. The others kept their jobs—including an employee who had downloaded hundreds of pornographic videos and pictures and even developed pornographic PowerPoint slide shows. (And you thought PowerPoint presentations were boring.)

They weren't fired. They weren't even embarrassed. One appealed his *ten-day suspension*, complaining that it was too severe. The government refused to release any of their names.

These are the people who are going to be controlling your access to medical services if Obamacare isn't repealed. There will be only one insurance provider, and you won't be able to switch, even if the service is lousy (and it will be). Obamacare employees will spend their days surfing pornography, instead of approving your heart operation. They can steal from you and even physically assault you. And they can never be fired.

Now, wouldn't you like to be able to fire people who provide services to you?

CHAPTER SIX

Slavery, the KKK, and the Trail of Tears—I Give You the Democrat Party

D iscussions of race in America consist primarily of sanctimonious white liberals getting high and mighty about racial issues to display their moral superiority. Curiously, these moral giants always manage to arrange their lives in a way that minimizes their own contact with black people.

The media invariably play up the exceedingly rare instances of white-on-black crime. In a country of 300 million people, everything happens. But it's shocking how few white-on-black crimes there are. Probably the most extreme differential occurs in the case of interracial rape. Between 1997 and 2008, black-on-white rapes numbered in the thousands per year. During the same time period, the number of white-on-black rapes ranged from 0.0 to "Sample based on 10 or fewer," according to the

Department of Justice's criminal victimization surveys. (Black-on-black rapes are the largest category of all.)

There's an unwritten rule that one simply does not mention the many more black-on-white crimes, compared to white-on-black crimes. Nor is anyone allowed to notice the high rates of murder, rape, illegitimacy, or graffiti in black neighborhoods. (That would be playing the old game of "blame the perpetrator"!) Strict enforcement of racial etiquette makes white liberals feel terrific about themselves but does very little to improve the condition of black Americans.

Harry Reid's Negro Problems and Ours
January 13, 2010

The recently released book *Game Change* reports that Senator Harry Reid said America would vote for Barack Obama because he was a "light-skinned" African American "with no Negro dialect, unless he wanted to have one." The book also says Bill Clinton called Senator Ted Kennedy to ask for his endorsement of Hillary over Obama, saying of Obama, "A few years ago, this guy would have been getting us coffee." And we already knew that Obama's own vice president, Joe Biden, called Obama "articulate" and "clean" during the campaign. (So you can see why Biden got the vice presidential nod over Reid.) Democrats regularly say things that would end the career of any conservative who said them. And still, blacks give 90 percent of their votes to the Democrats.

Reid apologized to President Obama, and Obama accepted the apology. We know he meant it because he was using his "white voice." So all is forgiven. Clinton also called Obama to apologize but ended up asking him to bring everybody some coffee. Now the only people waiting for an apology are the American people, who want an apology from Nevada for giving us Harry Reid.

Reid will be the guest of honor at a luncheon in Las Vegas this week hosted by a group called "African-Americans for Harry Reid." That's if you can call two people a "group." If this gets off the ground, "African-Americans for Harry Reid" will be a political juggernaut that cannot be denied! Their motto: "We Will Be Heard—As Soon As I Get This Gentleman's Coffee."

Reid has also picked up an endorsement from the United Light-Skinned Negro College Fund. And Tiger Woods is considering endorsing him. He is the one light-skinned half-black guy right now who's thrilled with Reid's comments. [Woods's explosive adultery scandal was, at that time, still front-page news.]

Reid's defenders don't have much to work with. Their best idea so far is that at least he said "Negro" and not "Nigra."

Liberals are saying that since Reid supported Obama's run for the presidency, it was OK to praise his skin color and non-Negro dialect. (Reid is denying reports that, in 2007, he said to Obama, "You should run. You people are good at that.") In fact, however, Reid didn't endorse Obama until after Hillary dropped out of the race. (He also admired Hillary for her light skin and the fact that she only uses a Negro dialect when she wants to.)

In the alternative, liberals are defending Reid by claiming he said nothing that wasn't true, though he may have used "an unusual set" of words—as light-skinned Reid-defender Harold Ford Jr. put it.

As long as we're mulling the real meaning of Reid's words and not just gasping in awe at the sorts of things Democrats get away with, I think Reid owes America an apology for accusing the entire country of racism, for only accepting a "light-skinned" black. A country, let us note, that just elected a manifestly unqualified black man president. Of course, Reid couldn't have been expecting Republicans to vote for a Democrat, so maybe Reid was accusing only Democratic voters of racism. I don't disagree with that, but I'd like to get it in writing.

I think the Democratic platform should include a statement opposing dark-skinned blacks with a Negro dialect. Check with Harry Reid on the precise wording but something along the lines of "no one darker than Deepak Chopra." The "whereas" clauses can include the Democrats' history of supporting slavery, segregation, racial preferences, George Wallace, and Bull Connor—and also a review of their treatment of dark-skinned Clarence Thomas.

Democrats couldn't win an election without the black vote, but the Democratic Party keeps treating blacks like stage props, wheeling them out for photo ops now and then but almost never putting them in charge of anything important.

President Bush appointed the first black secretary of state and then the first black female secretary of state. Meanwhile, the closest black woman to Bill Clinton was his secretary, Betty Currie. The one sitting black Supreme Court justice, Clarence Thomas, was appointed by a Republican. The head of the Republican National Committee is black—Michael Steele is light-skinned, but liberals treated him like Black Sambo when they threw Oreo cookies at him during his Maryland gubernatorial campaign in 2002.

After the 2000 election, Democrats had a chance to make one of the rare smart Democrats, Donna Brazile, head of the Democratic National Committee. Brazile had just run a perfectly respectable campaign on behalf of that bumbling buffoon Al Gore. She also happens to be black. Again, blacks give 90 percent of their votes to the Democrats. But the Democrats skipped over Brazile and handed the DNC chairmanship to the goofy white guy in lime green pants. (Howard Dean.)

The single most insulting remark made about blacks in my lifetime was Bill Clinton's announcement—after being caught in a humiliating sex scandal—that he was "the first black president."

He did not call himself "the first black president" when liberals were dancing and singing to Fleetwood Mac at his inauguration. He did not call himself "the first black president" when he was being lionized by the media. He did not call himself "the first black president" when he was negotiating that sixty-second "peace deal" between the Palestinians and Israel.

Oh no. It was not until he became a national laughingstock that Clinton announced he was "the first black president." At least he could finally get his own coffee.

Negroes with Guns
April 18, 2012

Liberals have leapt on the shooting death of Trayvon Martin in Florida to push for the repeal of "stand your ground" laws and to demand tighter gun control. (MSNBC's Karen Finney blamed "the same people who stymied gun regulation at every point.") This would be like demanding more funding for the General Services Administration after seeing how its employees blew taxpayer money on a party weekend in Las Vegas.

We don't know the facts yet, but let's assume the conclusion MSNBC is leaping to is accurate: George Zimmerman stalked a small black child and murdered him in cold blood, just because he was black.

If that were true, every black person in America should get a gun and join the National Rifle Association, America's oldest and most august civil rights organization. Apparently this has occurred to no one because our excellent public education system ensures that no American under the age of sixty has the slightest notion of this country's history. Gun-control laws were originally promulgated by Democrats to keep guns out of the hands of blacks. This allowed the Democratic policy of slavery to proceed with fewer bumps and, after the Civil War, allowed the Democratic Ku Klux Klan to menace and murder black Americans with little resistance.

(Contrary to what illiterates believe, the KKK was an outgrowth of the Democratic Party, with overlapping membership rolls. The Klan was to the Democrats what the American Civil Liberties Union is today: not every Democrat is an ACLU-er, but every ACLU-er is a Democrat. Same with the Klan.)

In 1640, the very first gun-control law ever enacted on these shores was passed in Virginia. It provided that blacks—even freemen—could not own guns. Chief Justice Roger Taney's infamous opinion in *Dred Scott v. Sandford* circularly argued that blacks could not be citizens because if they were citizens, they would have the right to own guns: "[I]t would give them the full liberty," he said, "to keep and carry arms wherever they went."

Dealing with logic like that, Republicans eventually had to fight a Civil War to get the Democrats to give up slavery. Alas, they were Democrats, so they couldn't learn. After the war, Democratic legislatures enacted "Black Codes," denying black Americans the rights of citizenship—such as the rather crucial one of bearing arms—while other Democrats (sometimes the same Democrats) founded the Ku Klux Klan.

For more than a hundred years, Republicans have aggressively supported arming blacks, so they could defend themselves against Democrats. The original draft of the Anti-Klan Act of 1871—passed at the urging of Republican president Ulysses S. Grant—made it a federal felony to "deprive any citizen of the United States of any arms or weapons he may have in his house or possession for the defense of his person, family, or property." This section was deleted from the final bill only because it was deemed both beyond Congress's authority and superfluous, inasmuch as the rights of citizenship included the right to bear arms.

Under authority of the Anti-Klan Act, President Grant deployed the U.S. military to destroy the Klan and pretty nearly completed the job. But the Klan had a few resurgences in the early and mid-twentieth century. Curiously, wherever the Klan became a political force, gun control laws would suddenly appear on the books.

This will give you an idea of how gun control laws worked. Following the firebombing of his house in 1956, Dr. Martin Luther King, who was, among other things, a Christian minister, applied for a gun permit, but the Alabama authorities found him unsuitable. A decade later, he won a Nobel Peace Prize. How's that "may issue" gun-permit policy working for you?

The NRA opposed these discretionary gun permit laws and proceeded to grant NRA charters to blacks who sought to defend themselves from Klan violence—including the great civil rights hero Robert F. Williams. A World War II Marine veteran, Williams returned home to Monroe, North Carolina, to find the Klan riding high—beating, lynching, and murdering blacks at will. No one would join the NAACP for fear of Klan reprisals. Williams became president of the local chapter and increased membership from six to more than two hundred. But it was not until he got a charter from the NRA in 1957 and founded the Black Armed Guard that the Klan got their comeuppance in Monroe.

Williams's repeated thwarting of violent Klan attacks is described in his stirring book, *Negroes With Guns*. In one crucial battle, the Klan besieged the home of a black physician and his wife, but Williams and his Black Armed Guard stood sentry and repelled the larger, cowardly force. And that was the end of it. As the Klan found out, it's not so much fun when the rabbit's got the gun.

The NRA's proud history of fighting the Klan has been airbrushed out of the record by those who were complicit with the KKK, which is to say, the Democrats.

In the preface to *Negroes With Guns*, Williams writes, "I have asserted the right of Negroes to meet the violence of the Ku Klux Klan by armed self-defense—and have acted on it. It has always been an accepted right of Americans, as the history of our Western states proves, that where the law is unable, or unwilling, to enforce order, the citizens can, and must act in self-defense against lawless violence."

Contrary to MSNBC hosts, I do not believe the shooting in Florida is evidence of a resurgent KKK. But wherever the truth lies in that case, gun control is always a scheme of the powerful to deprive the powerless of the right to self-defense.

Elizabeth Warren Dances with Lies
May 9, 2012

Elizabeth Warren, who also goes by her Indian name, "Lies on Race Box," is in big heap-um trouble. The earnest, reform-minded liberal running for Senate against Scott Brown, R-MA, lied about being part-Cherokee to get a job at Harvard. Harvard took full advantage of Warren's lie, bragging to the *Harvard Crimson* about her minority status during one of the near-constant student protests over insufficient "diversity" on the faculty. Warren also listed herself as an Indian in law school faculty directories and, just last month, said, "I am very proud of my Native American heritage."

Except, oops, she has no more evidence that she's an Indian than that buffoon out in Colorado, Ward Churchill.

The *Boston Globe* immediately leapt to Warren's defense, quoting a genealogist who found a marriage license on which Warren's great-great-uncle scribbled that his mother, Warren's great-great-great-grand-mother, was a Cherokee. This is not part of the official marriage license. (If I scribble "Kenyan" on Obama's birth certificate, does that make it true?)

But let's say it's true. That would make Warren a dotriacontaroon— 1/32nd Cherokee. That's her claim to affirmative action bonus points? *You don't know what it's like to be 1/32nd Cherokee, to never have anyone to talk to, spending so many evenings home alone, wondering if there was some other 1/32nd Cherokee out there, perhaps looking at the same star I was.*

Soon, however, the preponderance of the evidence suggested she wasn't even 1/32nd Cherokee. The census records for 1860 list the alleg-edly Cherokee great-great-great-grandmother, O. C. Sarah Smith Craw-ford, as "white." Also, Warren's family isn't listed in the Cherokee registry. (Unlike Democrat voter rolls, to be on the Cherokee list, proof is required.)

On the other hand, we have what her son scribbled on his marriage license—something, by the way, that none of his siblings claimed about their mother. So now we're down to Warren's reminiscence that her great-aunt used to point to a portrait of her great-great-grandfather and call him an Indian, noting his high cheekbones. Family lore is not proof. Proof is contemporary documentation, produced under penalty of perjury, such as a census record. My mother told me she found me under a rock, but I don't put that on job applications.

The universities that employed Warren rushed to claim that her fake Indian ancestry had nothing to do with it. They speak with forked tongue, causing heap-um laughter. (Indeed, Harvard was so desperate for diversity, it made a half-black dilettante president of the *Harvard Law Review*!)

To grasp what a sin against political correctness this is, consider the Jesuitical debates about blackness regularly engaged in at our universities. About the time Lies on Race Box was getting a job with Harvard as a fake Indian—valued for her fake hunting and tracking skills—a debate broke out at Northwestern University School of Law about whether a potential faculty hire was black enough. One professor wrote a heated three-page letter to the hiring committee complaining that the recruit "should not be considered a black candidate," explaining, "[n]ot all with dark skins are black," nor should they be considered "black in the U.S. context." (Flash to: my exact position on Obama.)

Warren has defended herself, claiming she did it only so she would be invited to powwows or what the great white father calls "meetings," saying she hoped "I would be invited to a luncheon, a group something that might happen with people who are like I am." What on Earth does "people who are like I am" mean? Let's invite Elizabeth because she's 1/32nd Cherokee. We really need the 1/32nd-Cherokee perspective around here. Maybe she has some old recipes that are 1/32nd Cherokee!

Then, the Warren campaign claimed it was sexist to question Warren about her bald-faced lie: "Once again, the qualifications and ability of a woman are being called into question by Scott Brown.... It's outrageous." First, Scott Brown has barely mentioned Warren's big, stinking lie. But, second, the only people who consider it a "qualification" to be 1/32nd Cherokee are university hiring committees. Possible Warren campaign speech: "I am a dotriacontaroon American. I want to be a voice for those who are 1/32nd Cherokee, but also 1/32nd Pequot, 1/32nd Mohawk—basically the senator for all dotriacontaroons. Isn't it time we had a senator who was 1/32nd Cherokee?"

Now it's beginning to look like her ancestors not only did not suffer but caused the suffering she's getting the benefit of. The great-great-great-grandfather married to the not-Cherokee O. C. Sarah Smith Crawford turns out to have been one of the white enforcers on the brutal Trail of Tears, helping round up Indians from their homes in order to march them to a less desirable part of the country.

What's next?

"Yes, and my other grandfather, Theophilus Connor ..."

BULL CONNOR?

"Yes, but I swear, James Earl Ray is not a BLOOD uncle. We're related only by marriage. At least that's what my cousin John Wayne Gacy used to always tell me."

Warren's lie is outrageous enough to someone like me, who isn't a fan of race-based affirmative action programs. Still, she is a liar, and she stole the credit of someone else's suffering. For liberals, it should be a mortal sin: Elizabeth Warren cheated on affirmative action.

Matthews a Few Race Cards Short of a Full Deck
September 5, 2012

Apparently, Monday, August 27, was opening day for Hysterical Liberal Sanctimony about Imagined Republican Racism. During this first round, the *New York Times*, the *Atlantic*, and the TV networks each put in a splendid showing. I'd need a book to cover it all. HOLD ON!

I HAVE ONE—*Mugged: Racial Demagoguery from the Seventies to Obama*, available in fine bookstores near you September 25, 2012.

Today, we will focus on the outstanding individual performance of the man who, since the departure of Contessa Brewer, is widely regarded by his colleagues as the stupidest on-air personality at MSNBC. Ladies and gentlemen, I give you Chris Matthews.

Appearing on *Morning Joe*, Matthews exploded at Republican National Committee chairman Reince Priebus, alleging that Mitt Romney's harmless birth certificate joke from a few days earlier was a "cheap shot," "awful," and an example of the Republicans playing "that card." (Discussing his hometown roots while campaigning in Michigan, Romney had cited the local hospitals where he and his wife were born, adding, "No one's ever asked to see my birth certificate.")

Even the liberals on the show were perplexed. Asked to clarify whether he considered the birth certificate joke "playing the race card," Matthews angrily said, "Yeah, there's no doubt he did with his birth certificate. No doubt. Why would he bring it up? Why would he say, 'I have no problem with my birth certificate'? What's that supposed to say?"

Mika Brzezinski: "Because he's an awkward joker?"

Joe Scarborough: "Because he misfired badly on the joke?"

But Matthews didn't have time for alternative explanations. Besides, he had already yelled at Joe and Mika, so the issue was obviously resolved. Chris quickly moved on to Romney's ads describing the Obama administration's change to welfare requirements as another example of racism.

Matthews said that Romney's (factually correct) claim that Barack Obama is weakening the work requirement for welfare was "playing that card," fuming at the RNC chair, "and you are playing that little ethnic card there." Priebus, like most people who haven't spent much time around Matthews, could only laugh awkwardly. Matthews raged, "You can—you play your games and giggle about it, but the fact is your side is playing that card. You start talking about work requirements, you know what game you're playing and everybody knows what game you're playing. It's a race card."

Asked by Scarborough if he really believed that the welfare ad was racist, Matthews said, "Of course it is. Welfare? Food stamps?"

On *Hardball* that night, Matthews continued his welfare rant: the Romney ad was "ethnically charged" and a "dog whistle." (The phrase "dog whistle" is a dog whistle for imaginary sightings of racism.) For the clincher, Matthews added: "Did you catch Romney following it up by saying this was Obama's effort to excite and shore up his base, passing out welfare checks? His base."

As everyone but Chris knows, the "base" Romney referred to consists not of individuals collecting welfare, but those distributing it, i.e. union-dues-paying government workers. Democrats' problem with welfare reform always was that if it worked, we would need fewer of these well-pensioned public employees, a fact repeatedly acknowledged by liberals themselves.

When welfare reform was first proposed in 1994:

- Will Marshall of the liberal Progressive Policy Institute said the reforms would sever Democratic ties to the liberal "base," which he described as: "Congress, the interest groups that cluster around them, the bureaucracies that work closely with them, the social service providers and experts and think tank types."
- Robert Kuttner of the über-liberal *American Prospect* magazine wrote that welfare reform would hurt Bill Clinton with "the Democratic base."
- Liberal journalist Jeff Greenfield of ABC News said that Clinton's becoming a third-way, New Democrat would risk "alienating a liberal base."

I'm sorry, gentlemen, but it is my sad duty to inform you: you're all racists.

The next night on *Hardball*, Matthews made his most dramatic announcement yet! It seems the mention of "Chicago" in relation to the president is also a racist dog whistle.

Matthews: "They keep saying Chicago, by the way, you noticed?"

Guest John Heilemann, like an orderly in a mental institution trapped alone with a patient, played along, responding, "Well, there's a lot of black people in Chicago"—while frantically jabbing at the alarm button.

For the love of Pete, can't we all acknowledge that a reference to "Chicago" in this context manifestly refers to corrupt, big-city, machine politics and 1920s gangsterism—not race? No one thinks Al Capone was an African American.

My advice to Chris is: pace yourself. It's a long way to Election Day. If you get too crazy too soon, you'll have nothing left for the fourth quarter.

White Liberals Tell Black Lies about Civil Rights
February 13, 2013

Liberals ignored my book *Mugged: Racial Demagoguery from the Seventies to Obama* throughout the fall. Now that I'm safely home from my book tour, they feel free to jabber on about their make-believe history of the civil rights movement with abandon.

In the hackiest of all hacky articles, Sam Tanenhaus, the man responsible for ruining the *New York Times Book Review*, has written a cover story in the *New Republic*, titled: "Original Sin: Why the GOP Is and Will Continue to Be the Party of White People." MSNBC has been howling this cliché for a decade—or, as MSNBC's Chris Matthews said of Tanenhaus's article, "a bold headline"!

Being interviewed by a giddy Matthews—who has no black friends, employees, or neighbors—Tanenhaus announced the startling fact that once, long ago, some Republicans supported civil rights! "In the 1950s, as I say in the piece you read, Republicans looked pretty good on civil rights under Eisenhower. We had the *Brown* decision, the Central High in Little Rock, where he did the tough thing and sent the troops in, and we had the first modern civil rights act."

It wasn't a "tough" decision for Eisenhower to send troops to Little Rock in 1957. In the presidential campaign the year before, the Republican platform had expressly endorsed the Supreme Court decision in *Brown v. Board of Education*. The Democratic platform did not. To the contrary, that year, ninety-nine members of Congress signed the "Southern Manifesto" denouncing the court's ruling in *Brown*. Two were Republicans. Ninety-seven were Democrats.

As president, Eisenhower pushed through the 1957 Civil Rights Act and the 1960 Civil Rights Act. He established the Civil Rights Commission. It was Eisenhower, not Truman, who fully desegregated the military. Meanwhile, the *Brown* decision was being openly defied by the Democratic governor of Arkansas (and Bill Clinton pal), Orval Faubus, who refused to admit black students to Little Rock Central High School.

Liberals act as if Eisenhower's sending federal troops to Little Rock was like Nixon going to China. No, it was like Nixon going to California.

Only someone who knows no history could proclaim, as Tanenhaus did, that the 1957 Act "wasn't great, it wasn't what LBJ gave us, but it was something." If Eisenhower's 1957 civil rights bill was weak, it was because of one man: Lyndon B. Johnson. As Robert Caro explains in his book *Master of the Senate: The Years of Lyndon Johnson,* it was LBJ who stripped the bill of its enforcement provisions. Even after that, the bill was still opposed by eighteen senators—all of them Democrats.

To the easily astounded Chris Matthews, Tanenhaus breathlessly remarked, "Not one Republican voted against that bill!"—as if the 1957 Civil Right Act was a Democratic idea and they were delighted to get any Republican support at all. Imagine a modern German historian saying, "Remember—it wasn't just Germans who opposed the Holocaust. The English and Americans did too!" Such a historian would be beaten bloody, quite rightly so.

The 1957 bill was sent to Congress by Eisenhower, passed with the intervention of Vice President Richard Nixon, and opposed exclusively by Democrats. Not "Southern Democrats," not "conservative Democrats," but Democrats, such as Wayne Morse of Oregon, Warren Magnuson of Washington, James Murray of Montana, Mike Mansfield of Montana, and Joseph O'Mahoney of Wyoming.

With absolutely no evidence (because there is none), Tanenhaus then asserted that Republicans decided "they were not going to be pro-civil rights.... They were going to side with the Southern oppressors." Cretin Matthews seconded this gibberish by saying Nixon was "playing the Southern Strategy electorally with Strom Thurmond and those boys."

Who exactly does Matthews imagine he means by "Strom Thurmond and those boys"? Every single segregationist in the Senate was a Democrat. Only one of them ever became a Republican: Strom Thurmond. The rest remained not only Democrats but quite liberal Democrats. These included such liberal luminaries as Harry Byrd, Robert Byrd, Allen Ellender, Albert Gore Sr., J. William Fulbright, Walter F. George, Russell Long, and Richard Russell.

Fulbright was Bill Clinton's mentor. Gore was "Al Jazeera" Gore's father. Sam Ervin headed Nixon's impeachment committee. The segregationists who were in the Senate in the '50s were rabid Joe McCarthy opponents. In the '60s, they opposed the Vietnam War and supported LBJ's Great Society programs. In the '90s, they got 100 percent ratings from NARAL Pro-Choice America.

These "Southern oppressors" were liberal Democrats when they were racists and remained liberal Democrats after they finally stopped being racists (in public). If Republicans had a racist "Southern strategy," it didn't work on the racists.

Nor did Nixon—or Reagan—ever win over segregationist voters. Republicans only began sweeping the South after the segregationists died. Even as late as 1980, when Reagan won a forty-four-state landslide, the old segregationists were still voting Democrat. Although Reagan handily won Southern states that had been voting Republican since the '20s, he barely won—or lost—the Goldwater states (many of which voted for Goldwater because he bucked the Republican Party and voted against the 1964 Civil Rights Act on purist libertarian grounds). According to numerous polls, Reagan swept Southern college students, while their elders voted Democrat. The *Washington Post* called the elderly "a bedrock of Carter's southern base."

As LBJ explained to fellow Democrats after doing a 180-degree flip on civil rights and pushing the 1964 Civil Rights Act (which resembled the 1957 Civil Rights Act he had gutted as a senator): "I'll have them niggers voting Democratic for two hundred years." That's according to a steward on Air Force One, who overheard him say it.

It's one thing to rewrite history to say the Holocaust was when the Swedes killed the Jews. But it's another to say that the Holocaust was when Jews killed the Germans. That's how liberals rewrite the history of civil rights in America. For the truth, get *Mugged*.

This Year's Duke Lacrosse Case
July 10, 2013

This week, instead of attacking a Hispanic senator, Marco Rubio, I will defend a Hispanic citizen, George Zimmerman, on trial for the murder of Trayvon Martin. (Zimmerman would make a better senator.)

It's becoming painfully obvious why no charges were brought against Zimmerman in this case—until Al Sharpton got involved. All the eyewitness accounts, testimony, ballistics, and forensics keep backing up Zimmerman. We should send a big, fat bill for the whole thing to Sharpton, courtesy of MSNBC.

With the prosecution's witnesses making the defense's case, the inquisitors' last stand is to claim that, if the races were reversed, the black guy would have been instantly charged with murder.

As explained in the *New York Times*: "Had Mr. Martin shot and killed Mr. Zimmerman under similar circumstances, black leaders say, the case would have barreled down a different path: Mr. Martin would have been quickly arrested by the Sanford Police Department and charged in the killing, without the benefit of the doubt." (Also, CNN could have dropped the "white" and referred to Zimmerman exclusively as "Hispanic.")

The people who say this are counting on the rest of us being too polite to mention that it is nearly impossible to imagine such a case in a world where half of all murders and a majority of robberies are committed by blacks. To reverse the races with the same set of facts, first, we're going to need a gated, mixed-race community, similar to the Retreat at Twin Lakes, that has recently experienced a rash of robberies by white guys. The only way to do that is to enter the Twilight Zone.

There were at least eight burglaries in the fourteen months before Zimmerman's encounter with Martin. Numerous media accounts admit that "most" of these were committed by black males. I'm waiting to hear about a single crime at Twin Lakes that was not committed by a young black male.

Just six months before Zimmerman's encounter with Martin, two men had broken into the home of a neighbor, Olivia Bertalan, while she was alone with her infant son. She had just enough time to call 911 before running upstairs and locking herself in a room. The burglars knew she was home but proceeded to rob the place anyway, even trying to enter the locked room where she held her crying child.

Bertalan had seen the burglars just before they broke into her house—one at the front door and one at the back. They were young black males. They lived in the Retreat by Twin Lakes. In another case, a black teenager strode up to Zimmerman's house and, in broad daylight, stole a bicycle off the front porch. The bike was never recovered.

Weeks before Zimmerman saw Martin, he witnessed another young black male peering into the window of a neighbor's house. He called the cops, but by the time they arrived the suspect was gone. A few days later, another house was burglarized. The thieves made off with jewelry and a new laptop. Roofers working across the street had seen two black teenagers near the house at the time of the robbery. When they spotted one of the teens the next day, they called the police. This time, the roofers followed the suspect so he wouldn't get away. The cops arrived and found the stolen laptop in his backpack. This was the same black teenager Zimmerman had seen looking in a neighbor's window.

The only reason it's hard to imagine the Zimmerman case with the races reversed is that it's hard to imagine a white teenager living in a mixed-race, middle-class community mugging a black homeowner. This is not a problem of society's reactions, but of the facts.

There is, however, at least one case of a black homeowner fatally shooting a white troublemaker. He was not charged with murder. In 2006, the ironically named John White was sound asleep at his nice

Long Island home when his teenage son woke him to say there was a mob of white kids shouting epithets in front of the house. The family was in no imminent danger. They could have called 911 and remained safely behind locked doors. But White grabbed a loaded Beretta and headed out to the end of the driveway to confront the mob. A scuffle ensued, and White ended up shooting one of the kids in the face, killing him.

White was charged and convicted only of illegal weapons possession—this was New York, after all—and involuntary manslaughter. He was sentenced to twenty months to four years in prison, but after serving five months was pardoned by Governor David Paterson. With all due compassion for the kid who was killed, the public was overwhelmingly on the father's side—a fact still evident in internet postings about the case. The kids were punks menacing a law-abiding homeowner. Even the prosecutor complained only that Paterson hadn't called the victim's family first. The local NAACP had campaigned aggressively on White's behalf. There were no threats to riot in case of an acquittal.

The centerpiece of White's self-defense argument was his recollection of his grandfather's stories about the Ku Klux Klan. George Zimmerman's memory of young black males committing crimes at Twin Lakes is somewhat more recent. John White wasn't jumped, knocked to the ground, repeatedly punched, and his skull knocked against the ground. He wasn't even touched, though he claimed the white teen was lunging at him when he shot. Talk about no reason to "follow," there was no reason for him to leave the safety of his locked home. White's son knew the kids by name. They could have waited for the cops.

So, yes, this case probably would be very different if Zimmerman's and Martin's races were reversed. It is only when the victim is black that we must have a show trial, a million-dollar reward paid to the victim's parents, and the threat of riots.

CHAPTER SEVEN

PC Police:
Shoot First, Hug Later

I t cannot be said often enough that the chief of staff of the United States Army, General George Casey, reacted to a Muslim Army major's massacre of thirteen Americans at Fort Hood while shouting "Allahu Akbar" by saying, "Our diversity…is a strength."

As long as the general has brought it up: never in recorded history has diversity been anything but a problem. Look at Ireland with its Protestant and Catholic populations, Canada with its French and English populations, Israel with its Jewish and Palestinian populations. Or consider the warring factions in India, Sri Lanka, China, Iraq, Czechoslovakia (until it happily split up), the Balkans, and Chechnya. Also look at the festering hotbeds of tribal warfare—I mean the "beautiful mosaic"—in Third World hellholes like Afghanistan, Rwanda, and South Central Latin America.

131

"Diversity" is a problem to be overcome, not an advantage to be sought. True, America does a better job than most at accommodating a diverse population. We also do a better job at curing cancer. But no one goes around mindlessly exclaiming, "Cancer is a strength!"

If that weren't bad enough, liberals view diversity as a weapon. Far from tolerating a diverse society, their reaction to a heterogeneous population is to create a rigid pecking order based on alleged victimhood—as described in the electrifying book, *Guilty: Liberal "Victims" and Their Assault on America*. In modern America, aggressors are sanctified, while the innocent never stop paying—including with their lives, as they did at Fort Hood. Points are awarded to officially sanctified "victims" for angry self-righteousness, acts of violence, and general irritability.

What happens when Muslims in Dearborn, Michigan, decide they want to have Sharia law? With General Casey's mindset, you don't get to pick and choose your multicultural contributions: *We'll take the Mexican food, but not the polygamy, please.* Enjoy those clitorectomies, liberal America!

Freeze! I Just Had My Nails Done!
March 16, 2005

How many people have to die before the country stops humoring feminists? Last week, a defendant in a rape case, Brian Nichols, wrested a gun from a female deputy in an Atlanta courthouse and went on a murderous rampage. Liberals have proffered every possible explanation for this breakdown in security except the giant elephant in the room—who undoubtedly has an eating disorder and would appreciate a little support vis-à-vis her negative body image.

The *New York Times* said the problem was not enough government spending on courthouse security ("Budgets Can Affect Safety inside Many Courthouses"). Yes, it was tax cuts for the rich that somehow enabled a two-hundred-pound former linebacker to take a gun from a five-foot-tall grandmother. Atlanta court officials dispensed with any spending issues the next time Nichols entered the courtroom when he was escorted by seventeen guards and two police helicopters. He looked like P. Diddy showing up for a casual dinner party.

I have an idea that would save money and lives: have large men escort violent criminals. Admittedly, this approach would risk another wave of nausea and vomiting by female professors at Harvard.* But there are also advantages to not pretending women are as strong as men, such as fewer dead people. Even a female math professor at Harvard should be able to run the numbers on this one.

Of course, it's suspiciously difficult to find any hard data about the performance of female cops. Not as hard as finding the study showing New Jersey state troopers aren't racist,** but still pretty hard to find. Mostly what you find on Nexis are news stories quoting police chiefs who have been browbeaten into submission, all uttering the identical mantra after every public safety disaster involving a girl cop. It seems

---

* *In response to Harvard president Larry Summers's remarks in January 2005 that men and women might have different innate abilities in math and science, MIT biology professor Nancy Hopkins, spoke for many women in the room when told the* Washington Post, *"I felt I was going to be sick.... My heart was pounding and my breath was shallow.... I was extremely upset."*

** *Throughout the 1990s, the nation was in a panic over jack-booted New Jersey state troopers, accused of stopping speeders on the turnpike...just because they were black! On orders from the state of New Jersey, statisticians from the Public Service Research Institute in Maryland performed a comprehensive study of all drivers on the turnpike, using high-speed cameras and radar detectors to clock the speeds of nearly 40,000 drivers. It conclusively proved: no racial profiling. No matter how they fiddled with the data, the results came back the same. In fact, based on likelihood of speeding, the New Jersey state troopers weren't stopping enough black drivers. The Bush Justice Department placed the study in a triple-lock safety deposit box, threw away the key, and it has never seen the light of day.*

that female officers compensate for a lack of strength with "other" abilities, such as cooperation, empathy, and intuition.

There are lots of passing references to "studies" of uncertain provenance, but which always sound uncannily like a press release from the Feminist Majority Foundation. (Or maybe it was the Pew Research Center for the People and the Press, which recently released a study claiming that despite Memogate, *Fahrenheit 9/11*, the Richard Clarke show, and the campaign against the Swiftboat veterans, the press is being soft on Bush.)

The anonymous "studies" about female officers invariably demonstrate that women make excellent cops—even better cops than men! (One study cited an episode of *She's the Sheriff*, starring Suzanne Somers.) A 1993 news article in the *Los Angeles Times*, for example, referred to a "study"—cited by an ACLU attorney—allegedly proving that "female officers are more effective at making arrests without employing force because they are better at de-escalating confrontations with suspects." No, you can't see the study or have the name of the organization that performed it, and why would you ask?

There are roughly 118 million men in this country who would take exception to that notion. I wonder if female officers "de-escalate" by mentioning how much more money their last suspect made.

These aren't unascertainable facts, like Pinch Sulzberger's SAT scores. The U.S. Department of Justice regularly performs comprehensive surveys of state and local law enforcement agencies, collected in volumes called *Law Enforcement Management and Administrative Statistics*.

The inestimable economist John Lott Jr. has looked at the actual data. And I'll give you the citation! John R. Lott Jr., "Does a Helping Hand Put Others at Risk? Affirmative Action, Police Departments and Crime," *Economic Inquiry*, April 1, 2000. It turns out that, far from "de-escalating force" through their superior listening skills, female law enforcement officers are vastly more likely to shoot civilians than their male counterparts. (Especially when perps won't reveal where they bought a particularly darling pair of shoes.) Unable to use intermediate force, like a bop on the nose, female officers quickly go to fatal force. According to Lott's analysis, each 1 percent increase in the number of white female officers in a police force increases the number of shootings of civilians by 2.7 percent.

Adding white female officers also increases the number of civilians accidentally shot by police. By contrast, adding males to a police force decreases accidental civilian shootings. Adding black males decreases civilian shootings by police even more. (And for my Handgun Control, Inc., readers: private citizens are much less likely to accidentally shoot someone than are the police, presumably because they do not have to pursue the suspect to make an arrest.)

In addition to accidentally shooting people, female law enforcement officers are also a lot more likely to be assaulted than male officers—as the whole country saw in Atlanta last week. Lott says, "Increasing the number of female officers by 1 percentage point appears to increase the number of assaults on police by 15 percent to 19 percent."

Of course there are many explanations for why female cops are more likely to be assaulted and to accidentally shoot people, such as that our patriarchal society encourages girls to play with dolls. But we must also consider the fact that women are smaller and weaker than men. In a study of public safety officers, female officers were found to have 32 percent to 56 percent less upper-body strength and 18 percent to 45 percent less lower-body strength than male officers. (But their outfits were 43 percent more coordinated.) Here's the cite! Frank J. Landy, "Alternatives to Chronological Age in Determining Standards of Suitability for Public Safety Jobs," *Technical Report* 1, January 31, 1992.

Another study I've devised involves asking a woman to open a jar of pickles.

Tellingly, feminists insist that strength tests be watered down so that women can pass them. Feminists simultaneously demand that no one suggest women are not as strong as men and then turn around and require that all the strength tests be changed. It's one thing to waste everyone's time by allowing women to try out for police and fire departments under the same tests given to men. It's quite another to require the tests to be brawned-down so no one ever has to tell Harvard professors that women aren't as strong as men.

Acknowledging reality wouldn't be all bad for women. For one thing, they won't have to confront violent felons on methamphetamine. So that's a benefit right there. Also, while a sane world would not employ five-foot-tall grandmothers as law enforcement officers, a sane world would also not give full-body cavity searches to five-foot-tall grandmothers at airports.

Speaking Truth to Dead Horses: My Oscar Predictions
March 1, 2006

Not many writers would have the confidence to include an Oscars prediction column that didn't run the table. However, like a Dick Morris prediction, my analysis is scintillating, even if the conclusions were often incorrect.

This is my first annual Oscar predictions column, for which I am uniquely qualified by not having seen a single one of the movies nominated in any category. I've never even watched an Oscar ceremony, except once when a friend called me about an hour into

Halle Berry's acceptance speech, and I managed to catch the last twenty minutes of it.

I shall grant my awards based on the same criteria Hollywood studio executives now use to green-light movies: political correctness. Also, judging by most of the nominees this year, I gather the awards committee prefers movies that are wildly unpopular with audiences.

The box office numbers for this year's favorite, *Brokeback Mountain*, are more jealously guarded than the nuclear codes in the president's black box. Hollywood liberals want the government to reveal everything we know about al-Zarqawi, but refuse to release the number of people who have seen *Brokeback Mountain*.

I shall summarize the plots of the five movies nominated for Best Picture below:

- *Brokeback Mountain* (gay)
- *Capote* (death penalty with bonus gay lead)
- *Crash* (racism)
- *Good Night, and Good Luck* (McCarthyism)
- *Munich* (Jew athletes at Munich had it coming)

Everyone says it's going to be *Crash*, but I think *Crash* is too popular with filmgoers. Moreover, Hollywood feels it has done enough for the blacks. Hollywood can never do enough for the gays. Gays in the military, gays in the Texas Rangers, gays on the range. It's like a brokeback record! As Pat Buchanan said, homosexuality has gone from "the love that dare not speak its name" to "the love that won't shut up."

So I say *Brokeback Mountain* for Best Picture.

But is the idea of gay cowboys really that new? Didn't the Village People do that a couple of decades ago? Am I the only person who saw John Travolta in *Urban Cowboy*?

Movies with the same groundbreaking theme to come:

- *Westward Homo!*
- *The Magnificent, Fabulous Seven*
- *Gunfight at the K-Y Corral*
- *How West Hollywood Was Won*

[*Actual Best Movie Winner*: Crash]

OK, back to predictions. The best director award will go to… Ang Lee, director of *Brokeback Mountain*. (For analysis, see above.) Also, this is gays directed by an Asian, which should satisfy the gaysians. Hands down: Ang Lee.

[*Actual Best Director Winner*: *Ang Lee*]

The nominees for Best Actor in a Leading Role are:

- Philip Seymour Hoffman, *Capote*
- Terrence Howard, *Hustle & Flow*
- Heath Ledger, *Brokeback Mountain*
- Joaquin Phoenix, *Walk the Line*
- David Strathairn, *Good Night, and Good Luck*

The winner in this category will be… Philip Seymour Hoffman. The awards committee can't give *everything* to *Brokeback Mountain*, and at least Truman Capote was gay. I personally would have chosen the lion in the Narnia movie, but he wasn't even nominated.

[*Actual Best Actor in a Leading Role*: *Philip Seymour Hoffman*]

The nominees for Best Actress in a Leading Role are:

- Judi Dench, *Mrs. Henderson Presents*

- Felicity Huffman, *Transamerica*
- Keira Knightley, *Pride & Prejudice*
- Charlize Theron, *North Country*
- Reese Witherspoon, *Walk the Line*

I hear Reese Witherspoon is very good in *Walk the Line*, but that's irrelevant—this is the Oscars! Felicity Huffman plays a pre-op transsexual in *Transamerica*. That strikes a chord in Hollywood. It's not exactly gay, but close enough! I say Huffman wins.

[*Actual Best Actress in a Leading Role: Reese Witherspoon*]

For Best Actress in a Supporting Role, Rachel Weisz ought to win for *The Constant Gardener* because it's about how drug companies are evil, which to me is the essence of quality acting. Plus, English accent = good acting. But Michelle Williams (*Brokeback Mountain*) is engaged to Heath Ledger, who played a gay guy in *Brokeback Mountain*. So I pick Weisz, with Williams as the dark-horse favorite.

[*Actual Best Actress in a Supporting Role: Rachel Weisz*]

The best original screenplay will be *Good Night, and Good Luck* as Hollywood's final tribute to the old Stalinists (Hollywood's version of "The Greatest Generation"). George Clooney has been mau-mauing the awards committee by going around boasting that conservatives called him a "traitor," although I believe the precise term was "airhead."

[*Actual Best Original Screenplay: Crash*]

Finally, my favorite category: Best Foreign Language Film. Here I am at a disadvantage because no one else has seen these movies either. The nominees are:

- *Don't Tell* (Italy)
- *Joyeux Noel* (France)
- *Paradise Now* (Palestine)

- *Sophie Scholl* (Germany)
- *Tsotsi* (South Africa)

After consulting with the Yale admissions committee, the Oscar will go to ... *Paradise Now*, a heartwarming story about Palestinian suicide bombers. How good is it? Al Jazeera gave it 4 1/2 pipe bombs! It's SyrianAir's featured in-flight movie this month. I don't want to spoil the ending for you, but let's just say there won't be a sequel.

Normally, the smart money is on the Holocaust movie, so any other year, *Sophie Scholl* would have been the clear favorite. Unfortunately for the makers of *Sophie Scholl*, their Holocaust movie came out the same year as a pro-terrorist movie, so they lose.

[*Actual Best Foreign Language Film*: Tsotsi]

For my final prediction, for the second year, there will be no mention of Dutch filmmaker Theo van Gogh, who was brutally murdered by an angry Muslim a little over a year ago on the streets of Amsterdam. (Now *that's* blacklisted!) I also predict this will be the lowest-rated Oscars ever. Remember to turn off your cell phones, no talking ... or sleeping.

[*There was no mention of filmmaker Theo van Gogh. It was third-lowest Nielsen ratings in Oscar history.*]

Ho Ho Ho, Merry Imus!
April 11, 2007

The only person happier than Larry Birkhead about the big announcement that he is the father of Anna Nicole Smith's baby is Don Imus. By the way, what's the word for a woman who gives birth to a child of uncertain paternity?

English speakers in America need a rule book to tell us what people can say what words when, and under which set of circumstances. The rule book will be longer than the Patriot Act and will require weekly updates as new words and circumstances are added. Perhaps a NASDAQ-style ticker would be more efficient.

Depending on which TV show you tune into, what Imus said was wrong because:

(1) his show goes out on FCC-regulated airwaves; (2) he regularly interviews people like Senators John Kerry, John McCain, and Joe Biden; (3) he spoke at the White House Correspondents' Dinner a few years ago; or (4) he's not black.

Perhaps sensing that such constantly scrolling rules have a whiff of fascism about them, the scowling Miss Grundys of the world think they have hit on the perfect omnibus rule. They instruct us to "be nice."* (There's a word for the grim Miss Grundys, but apparently I'm not allowed to use it. Sarah Silverman is. This will be all in the rule book.)

The requirement to always "be nice" would be the end of Chris Rock and Dave Chappelle, two of the funniest comedians in America. Let me rephrase that: it would be the end of all humor. Even Bob Hope cruelly implied that Democrats didn't support the troops when he joked to the troops in Vietnam: "The country is behind you 50 percent."

At least we'll still be able to watch the *Charlie Rose* show! Actually, for all anyone knows, Rose is calling women "nappy-headed hos" on TV every night since no one has ever seen his show.

In addition to ending all humor, we'll lose political debate. For Americans over four years old, people in the public sphere are engaged in serious arguments—over abortion, illegal immigration, how much

---

* *Peggy Noonan, "That's Not Nice," Wall Street Journal, March 10, 2007.*

money the government takes from you, and the preeminent battle of our time against Islamic fascists.

The "be nice" admonition is the sort of thing stupid girls say when they can't think of anything substantive to say. I, for one, promise to implement the "be nice" policy just as soon as the other side does.

Say, does anyone remember if Winston Churchill was "nice" in his public pronouncements about his fellow countrymen? No, I don't think he was! This is what Winston Churchill said about the Labour Party's Ramsay MacDonald:

"I remember when I was a child, being taken to the celebrated Barnum's Circus, which contained an exhibition of freaks and monstrosities, but the exhibit on the program which I most desired to see was the one described as 'The Boneless Wonder.' My parents judged that the spectacle would be too demoralizing and revolting for my youthful eye, and I have waited fifty years to see The Boneless Wonder sitting on the Treasury Bench."

And guess what public figure was constantly accused of making "outrageous" remarks, trading in "insults, trashings and character assassinations"? Of what public figure was it asked: "Who can examine this record of insults and say that here is a man of class?" That's right: Ronald Reagan. Those particular quotes are from *Washington Post* columnists Richard Cohen and Colman McCarthy.

Was Reagan "nice" to the Soviets? They certainly didn't think so. The Soviets constantly denounced Reagan as "rude," and our dear friends at the BBC upbraided Reagan for his "rude attacks" on Fidel Castro, Nicaragua, and the Soviet Union. *Post* columnist McCarthy charged that Reagan had "put down an entire nation—the Soviet Union—by calling it 'the focus of evil in the modern world.'"

Oh dear! Reagan wasn't "nice." No wonder he never accomplished anything.

One more item for the delusional Miss Grundys still obtusely citing Reagan as their model of "niceness": As governor of California, Reagan gave student protesters at Berkeley the finger. Remember that next time you ask yourself: "What would Reagan do?" (Although you will get a different answer than if you employ "the simple wisdom of Grandma— 'That's not nice.'")

People who are afraid of ideas whitewash Reagan like they whitewash Jesus. Sorry to break it to you, but the Reagan era did not consist of eight years of Reagan joking about his naps.

The reason people don't like what Imus said was because the women on the Rutgers basketball team aren't engaged in public discourse. They're not public figures, they don't have a forum, they aren't trying to influence public policy. They play basketball—quite well, apparently—and did nothing to bring on an attack on their looks or character. It's not the words Imus used: it would be just as bad if he had simply said the Rutgers women were ugly and loose.

People claim to object to the words alone, but that's because everyone is trying to fit this incident into a PC worldview. It's like girls who say, "It's not that you cheated on me; it's that you lied about it." No—it's that you cheated.

If Imus had called me a "towheaded ho" or Al Sharpton a "nappy-headed ho," it would be what's known as "funny." (And if he called Anna Nicole Smith a "flaxen-headed ho," it would be "absolutely accurate.") But he attacked the looks and morals of utterly innocent women, who had done nothing to inject themselves into public debate. Imus should apologize to the Rutgers women—and those women alone—and stop kissing Al Sharpton's ring.

This wasn't an insult to all mankind, and certainly not an insult to Al Sharpton. Now, if Imus had called the basketball players "fat, race-baiting black men with clownish hairstyles," well, then perhaps Sharpton would be owed an apology.

They Gave Your Mortgage to a Less Qualified Minority
September 24, 2008

On MSNBC this week, *Newsweek*'s Jonathan Alter tried to connect John McCain to the current financial disaster, saying, "If you remember the Keating Five scandal that (McCain) was a part of.... He's really getting a free ride on the fact that he was in the middle of the last great financial scandal in our country."

McCain was "in the middle of" the Keating Five case in the sense that he was "exonerated." The lawyer for the Senate Ethics Committee wanted McCain removed from the investigation altogether, but, as the *New York Times* reported: "Sen. McCain was the only Republican embroiled in the affair, and Democrats on the panel would not release him." So John McCain has been held hostage by both the Viet Cong and the Democrats.

Alter couldn't be expected to know that: as usual, he was lifting material directly from Kausfiles. What is unusual was that he was stealing a random thought sent in by Kausfiles's mother, who, the day before, had emailed. "It's time to bring up the Keating Five. Let McCain explain that scandal away." It's bad enough for Alter to be constantly ripping off Kausfiles. Now he's so devoid of his own ideas, he's ripping off the idle musings of Kausfiles's mother.

The Senate Ethics Committee lawyer who investigated McCain already had explained that scandal away—repeatedly. It was celebrated lawyer Robert Bennett, most famous for defending a certain horny hick president a few years ago.

In February this year, on Fox News's *Hannity & Colmes*, Bennett said, for the eight billionth time:

"First, I should tell your listeners I'm a registered Democrat, so I'm not on (McCain's) side of a lot of issues. But I investigated John McCain for a year and a half, at least, when I was special counsel to the Senate Ethics Committee in the Keating Five.... And if there is one thing I am absolutely confident of, it is John McCain is an honest man.* I recommended to the Senate Ethics Committee that he be cut out of the case, that there was no evidence against him."

Even if McCain had been implicated in the Keating Five scandal—and he wasn't—that would still have absolutely nothing to do with the subprime mortgage crisis currently roiling the financial markets. This crisis was caused by political correctness being forced on the mortgage lending industry in the Clinton era.

Before the Democrats' affirmative action lending policies became something they had to lie about, the *Los Angeles Times* reported that, starting in 1992, a majority-Democratic Congress "mandated that Fannie and Freddie increase their purchases of mortgages for low-income and medium-income borrowers. Operating under that requirement, Fannie Mae, in particular, has been aggressive and creative in stimulating minority gains."

Under Clinton, the entire federal government put massive pressure on banks to grant more mortgages to poor minorities. Clinton's secretary of Housing and Urban Development, Andrew Cuomo, investigated Fannie Mae for racial discrimination and proposed that 50 percent of Fannie Mae's and Freddie Mac's portfolio be made up of loans to low- to moderate-income borrowers by the year 2001.

Instead of looking at "outdated criteria," such as the mortgage applicant's credit history, banks were encouraged to consider nontraditional measures of credit-worthiness, such as having a good jump shot or having a missing child named "Caylee." Threatening lawsuits, Clinton's Federal Reserve demanded that banks treat welfare payments and

---

* *Bennett hasn't heard McCain talk about his political positions.*

unemployment benefits as valid income sources to qualify for a mortgage. That isn't a joke—it's a fact.

When Democrats controlled both the executive and legislative branches, political correctness was given a veto over sound business practices. In 1999, liberals were bragging about extending affirmative action to the financial sector. *Los Angeles Times* reporter Ron Brownstein hailed the Clinton administration's affirmative action lending policies as one of the "hidden success stories" of the Clinton administration, saying that "black and Latino homeownership has surged to the highest level ever recorded." Meanwhile, economists were screaming from the rooftops that the Democrats were forcing mortgage lenders to issue loans that would fail the moment the housing market slowed and deadbeat borrowers couldn't escape their loans by selling their houses.

A decade later, the housing bubble burst and, as predicted, food stamp–backed mortgages collapsed. Democrats set an affirmative action time bomb, and now it's gone off.

In Bush's first year in office, the White House chief economist, N. Gregory Mankiw, warned that the government's "implicit subsidy" of Fannie Mae and Freddie Mac (explicit, after the crash), combined with loans to unqualified borrowers, was creating a huge risk for the entire financial system. Representative Barney Frank denounced Mankiw, saying he had no "concern about housing." *How dare you oppose suicidal loans to people who can't repay them!*

As the *New York Times* reported at the time, Fannie Mae and Freddie Mac were "under heavy assault by the Republicans," but these entities still had "important political allies" in the Democrats. Now, at a cost of hundreds of billions of dollars, middle class taxpayers are going to be forced to bail out the Democrats' two most important constituent groups: rich Wall Street bankers and welfare recipients.

Political correctness has already ruined education, sports, science, and entertainment. But it took a Democratic president with a Democratic Congress for political correctness to wreck the financial industry.

CHAPTER EIGHT

America's Enemies, Foreign and Democratic

emocrats long to see American mothers weeping for their sons lost
in a foreign war, but only if the mission serves absolutely no
national security objectives of the United States. If we are building
democracy in a country while also making America safer—such as in
Iraq—Democrats oppose it with every fiber of their being. Rwanda,
Darfur, and Somalia—that's where Democrats are itching to send
troops. Americans in harm's way? Check. Does not further America's
national security's interests? Check.

When Clinton's "nation-building" in Somalia led to the brutal killing
of eighteen Americans, some of whose corpses were dragged through
the streets, Clinton cut and ran, like he was climbing out of a married
woman's bedroom window. Osama bin Laden told ABC News in 1998
that America's humiliating retreat from Somalia emboldened his

jihadists: "The youth were surprised at the low morale of the American soldiers and realized more than before that the American soldier was a paper tiger and after a few blows ran in defeat."

I know Democrats will never learn, but I wish the voters would.

NY Times: Better Dead than Read
July 12, 2006

When I told a *New York Observer* reporter that my only regret was that Timothy McVeigh didn't hit the *New York Times* building, I knew many would agree with me—but I didn't expect that to include the *New York Times*. And yet, the *Times* is doing everything in its power to help the terrorists launch another attack on New York City.

As with forced school busing, liberals seem to believe that the consequences of their insane ideas can be confined to the outer boroughs.

Last year, the *Times* revealed a top secret program tracking phone calls connected to numbers found in Khalid Sheikh Mohammed's cell phone. How much more probable cause do you need, folks? Shall we do this as a diagram? How about in the form of an SAT question—or is that a touchy subject for the publisher of the *Times*? "9/11 architect Khalid Sheikh Mohammed is to terrorist attacks as …"?

The *Times'* reaction to Abu Musab al-Zarqawi's death last month was to lower the U.S. flag at the *Times* building to half-staff. (Ha ha—just kidding! Everybody knows there aren't any American flags at the *New York Times*.)

And most recently, ignoring the pleas of the administration, 9/11 commissioners, and even certifiable liberal Representative Jack Murtha, the *Times* revealed another top secret program. This one had allowed the Treasury Department to track terrorists' financial transactions.

We're in a battle for our survival, and we don't even know who the enemy is. As liberals are constantly reminding us, Islam is a "Religion of Peace." One very promising method of distinguishing the "Religion of Peace" Muslims from the "Slit Their Throats" Muslims is by following the al Qaeda money trail.

But now we've lost that ability—thanks to the *New York Times*.

People have gotten so inured to ridiculous behavior on the Left that they are no longer capable of appropriate outrage when something truly treasonous happens. It is rather like Bill Clinton's rapes losing their impact because of the steady stream of perjury, obstruction of justice, treason, adultery, and general sociopathic behavior coming from that administration.

This is a phenomenon known in the self-help community as "Clinton fatigue" (not to be confused with the lower back pain associated with excessive sexual activity known as "Clinton back").

In December 1972, Ronald Reagan called President Richard Nixon after watching Walter Cronkite's coverage of the Vietnam War on CBS News, to say that "under World War II circumstances, the network would have been charged with treason." No treason charges were brought, but we still have to hear liberals carrying on about Nixon's monstrous persecution of the press. (Which was strange, considering how nicely the press treated him.)

Today, *Times* editors and columnists are doing what liberals always do when they're caught red-handed committing treason: they scream that they're being "intimidated" before hurling more invective. This is like listening to the Soviet Union complain about the intimidation coming from Finland.

Liberals love to play-act victims of some monstrous attack from the right wing as they insouciantly place all Americans in danger. Their default position is umbrage, bordering on high dudgeon. We've had to listen to them whine for fifty years about the brute Joe McCarthy, whose name liberals blackened to shelter Soviet spies.

In 1985, *Times* columnist Anthony Lewis accused the Reagan administration of trying to "intimidate[] the press." Channeling Lewis this week, Frank Rich claims the Bush administration has "manufactured and milked this controversy to reboot its intimidation of the press, hoping journalists will pull punches in an election year."

Rich's evidence of the brutal crackdown on the press was the statement of San Francisco radio host Melanie Morgan—who, by the way, is part of the press—proposing the gas chamber for the editor of the *Times* if he were found guilty of treason, which happens to be the punishment prescribed by law. (Once again Frank Rich finds himself in over his head when not writing about gay cowboy movies.)

I prefer a firing squad, but I'm open to a debate on the method of punishment. A conviction for treason would be assured under any sensible legal system.*

But however many Americans agree with Reagan on prosecuting treason, we can't even get President Bush to stop building up the liberal media by appearing on their low-rated TV shows (CNN's Larry King)— in the process, dissing TV hosts who support him and command much larger TV audiences (FNC's Sean Hannity). American consumers keep driving CNN's ratings down, and then Bush drives them back up!

This is how Bush "intimidates" the press? The level of intimidation I had in mind is more along the lines of how President Dwight D. Eisenhower "intimidated" Julius and Ethel Rosenberg at 8:00 in the morning, June 19, 1953.

---

* *On June 16, 2013, former Vice President Dick Cheney said on* Fox News Sunday *that he had recommended prosecuting the* New York Times *for violating the law making it a felony offence to publish information about communications intelligence in the U.S. He suggested that the law be taken off the books if it's not going to be enforced.*

If Only Bin Laden Had a Stained Blue Dress . . .
September 13, 2006

I f you wonder why it took fifty years to get the truth about Joe McCarthy, consider the fanatical campaign of the Clinton acolytes to kill an ABC movie based on the 9/11 Commission Report. They're enraged that the movie whitewashes only 90 percent of Clinton's cowardice and incompetence in the face of terrorism, rather than all 100 percent.

Throughout the Clinton administration, Islamic jihadists attacked America year after year. They blew up nearly everything except his proverbial "bridge to the twenty-first century." And, year after year, Clinton found an excuse not to fight back.

The first month Clinton was in office, Islamic terrorists with suspected links to al Qaeda and Saddam Hussein bombed the World Trade Center.

For the first time ever, a terrorist act against America was treated not as a matter of national security, but as a simple criminal offense. The individual bombers were tried in a civilian court. (The one plotter who got away fled to Iraq—that peaceful haven of kite-flying children, per Michael Moore, until Bush invaded and turned it into a nation of dangerous lunatics.)

In 1995 and 1996, various branches of the Religion of Peace—al Qaeda, Hezbollah, and the Iranian "Party of God"—staged car bomb attacks on American servicemen in Saudi Arabia, killing twenty-four members of our military in all. Each time, the Clinton administration came up with an excuse to do nothing.

Despite the Democrats' current claim that only the capture of Osama bin Laden will magically end terrorism forever, Clinton turned down

Sudan's offer to hand us bin Laden in 1996. That year, Mohammed Atta proposed the 9/11 attack to bin Laden.

Clinton refused the handover of bin Laden because—he said in taped remarks on February 15, 2002—"[bin Laden] had committed no crime against America, so I did not bring him here because we had no basis on which to hold him." Luckily, after 9/11, we can get him on that trespassing charge.

Although Clinton made the criminal justice system the entire U.S. counterterrorism strategy, there was not even an indictment against Osama filed after the bombing of either Khobar Towers (1996) or the USS *Cole* (2000). Indictments were only filed when Bush/Ashcroft came into office.

In 1998, the Clinton-haters ("normal people") finally forced Clinton into a military response to terrorism. Solely in order to distract from the Monica Lewinsky scandal, Clinton lobbed a few bombs in the general direction of Saddam Hussein and Osama bin Laden. In August 1998, three days after Clinton admitted to the nation that he did in fact have "sex with that woman," he bombed Afghanistan and Sudan, doing about as much damage as another Clinton fusillade did to a blue Gap dress.

The day of Clinton's scheduled impeachment, December 18, 1998, he bombed Iraq. This accomplished two things: (1) it delayed his impeachment for one day, and (2) it got a lot of Democrats on record about the monumental danger of Saddam Hussein and his weapons of mass destruction.

So don't tell me impeachment "distracted" Clinton from his aggressive pursuit of terrorists. Without the Clinton-haters, he never would have bombed anyone.

As soon as Clinton was no longer "distracted" by impeachment, he went right back to doing nothing in response to terrorism. Thus, in October 2000, al Qaeda bombed the USS *Cole*, killing seventeen sailors and nearly sinking the ship. Clinton did nothing.

According to Rich Miniter, author of *Losing Bin Laden*, Clinton's top national security advisors made the following classic Democrat excuses for doing nothing in response to the *Cole* attack:

- Attorney General Janet Reno "thought retaliation might violate international law and was therefore against it."
- CIA director George Tenet "wanted more definitive proof that bin Laden was behind the attack, although he personally thought he was."
- Secretary of State Madeleine Albright "was concerned about the reaction of world opinion to a retaliation against Muslims and the impact it would have in the final days of the Clinton Middle East peace process." (How did that turn out, by the way? Big success, I take it? Everybody over there all friendly with one another?)
- Secretary of Defense William Cohen "did not consider the Cole attack 'sufficient provocation' for a military retaliation."

This is only an abbreviated list of Clinton's surrender techniques to Islamic savagery. For a president who supposedly stayed up all night "working," Clinton sure spent a lot of time sitting on his butt while America was being attacked.

Less than a year after Clinton's final capitulation to Islamic terrorists, they staged the largest attack in history on U.S. soil. The September 11 attack, planning for which began in the '90s, followed eight months of President Bush—but eight years of Bill Clinton.

Clinton's own campaign advisor on Iraq, Laurie Mylroie, says Clinton and his advisors are "most culpable" for the intelligence failure that allowed 9/11 to happen.

Now, after five years of no terrorist attacks in America, Democrats are hoping we'll forget the consequences of the Democrat strategy of doing nothing in response to terrorism and abandon the Bush policies that have kept this nation safe since 9/11. But first, they need to rewrite history by censoring an ABC movie.

Frank Rich Declares Iraq "Box Office Poison"
December 20, 2006

L ast year, Osama bin Laden's deputy, Ayman al-Zawahri, wrote to the head of al Qaeda in Iraq, Abu Musab al-Zarqawi, telling him to "be ready, starting now" for America to run, reminding him how America cut and ran from Vietnam. Alas, al-Zarqawi never got to implement his Iraq takeover plan because the same troops that are allegedly losing the war right now killed him in June.

But al Qaeda in America is still fighting!

New York Times theater critic Frank Rich made headlines on the Drudge Report last week by announcing: "We have lost in Iraq." Of course, Rich was saying we had lost in Iraq more than six months before we went into Iraq.

The war began on March 20, 2003. Seven months earlier, in August 2002, Rich wrote that Bush did not have the support of the American people for war in Iraq and, without that, he would "mimic another hubristic Texan president who took a backdoor route into pre-emptive warfare."

Then, in April 2003, barely a month after we invaded, Rich said the looting of national museums by Iraqis showed "our worst instincts at the very dawn of our grandiose project to bring democratic values to the Middle East." About six months into the war, he wrote a column about Iraq titled: "Why Are We Back in Vietnam?" (You can imagine how writing those words must have brought back memories of Frank Rich's own valiant service in Vietnam.)

In January 2004, less than a year after the invasion, Rich wrote, "The greater debate has been over the degree to which the follies of Vietnam are now being re-enacted in Iraq." Historians noted that this is the first time Rich ever panned something containing the word "follies." A month later, he was again comparing Iraq to Vietnam, saying Bush had forced the comparison "by wearing the fly boy uniform of his own disputed guard duty" when he landed on the aircraft carrier. Did Frank Rich win three purple hearts in combat, or was it four? I always forget.

In May 2004, Rich accused Bush of throwing "underprepared and underprotected" American troops in harm's way in Iraq. OK, I was kidding before. The closest Frank Rich has come to serving in the military was reviewing a revival of *The Caine Mutiny*. Though he does know the words to "In the Navy" by heart.

Even after transitioning from musical reviewer to hard-bitten military analyst, Rich couldn't resist tossing in a quick dance review. He gleefully described "pictures of Marines retreating from Fallujah and of that city's citizens dancing in the streets to celebrate their victory over the American liberators."

This, too, reminded Rich of Vietnam. Right now I'm trying to think of something that doesn't remind liberals of Vietnam. I'm drawing a blank.

In September 2005, Rich wrote that the war in Iraq "resembles its Southeast Asian predecessor in its unpopularity, its fictional provocation, and its unknown exit strategy." (Interestingly, those were the exact same words he used years ago in his review of *Miss Saigon*.) He leeringly anticipated "a Tet offensive, Sunni-style" to tilt the election in Kerry's direction.

In October 2004, Rich said Bush had "bungled the war in Iraq and, in doing so, may be losing the war against radical Islamic terrorism as well." He didn't explain how killing tens of thousands of Islamic terrorists constituted "bungling" a war against them. Then again, what do I know about military analysis? I thought *The Goat, or Who Is Sylvia?* (Broadway play about a man who falls in love with his goat) was atrocious.

In May of this year, Rich said that "the public has turned on the war in Iraq"—the very war that he said the public opposed long before we ever went in. And in June he said the public knows "defeat when they see it, no matter how many new plans for victory are trotted out to obscure that reality"—though I might be confusing this statement with Rich's comment on the *Times'* plan to charge readers for his column.

Liberals are like people with stale breath talking into your face at a party. You try backing away from them or offering them gum, but then they start whimpering. They've been gassing on with the exact same talking points about how we're losing in Iraq since before we invaded.

It seems liberals have finally succeeded in exhausting Americans and, thereby, handing a victory to al Qaeda. The weakest members of the herd are rapidly capitulating, trying to preserve a modicum of honor by claiming that if *their* plans had been implemented, Iraq would be in tip-top shape and our troops would be home for Christmas.

Well, if my plans had been implemented, the anti-war crowd would be weeping about Iraqi civilian deaths so much they wouldn't have time to pretend they gave a damn about the loss of American lives.

But the plans that were implemented have: deposed a monster and put him on trial, resulting in his conviction and death; killed off rape-hobbyists Uday and Qusay; led to three democratic elections; eliminated al-Zarqawi and scores of other al Qaeda leaders fighting Americans; and kept the U.S. safe from Islamic terrorist attacks for five years now. The least I can do is not capitulate to the Left's endless nagging by turning against this war.

The Democratic Party: A Vast Sleeper Cell
January 3, 2007

Fortunately for liberals, the Iraqis executed Saddam Hussein the exact same week that former President Ford died, so it didn't seem strange that Nancy Pelosi was in mourning clothes. Reminiscences about Ford's presidency should remind Americans that Democrats are always lying in wait, ready to force a humiliating defeat on America.

More troops, fewer troops, different troops, "redeployment"—all the Democrats' little talking points are just a way of sounding busy. Who are they kidding? Democrats want to cut and run as fast as possible from Iraq, betraying the Iraqis who supported us and rewarding our enemies—exactly as they did to the South Vietnamese under President Ford.

Liberals spent the Vietnam War rooting for the enemy and clamoring for America's defeat, a tradition they have brought back for the Iraq War. They insisted on calling the Soviet-backed Viet Cong "the National Liberation Front of Vietnam," just as they call Islamic fascists killing Americans in Iraq "insurgents"—or "civilians." Ho Chi Minh was hailed as a "Jeffersonian Democrat," just as Michael Moore compares the Islamic fascists in Iraq to the Minutemen.

The book *The Trust: The Private and Powerful Family behind the New York Times* tells of how now-publisher Arthur "Pinch" Sulzberger told his father during the Vietnam War that if an American soldier ran into a North Vietnamese soldier, he would prefer for the American to get shot. "It's the other guy's country," the scion explained. Now, as publisher of the *Times*, Pinch does all he can to provide aid and comfort to the enemies currently shooting at American soldiers.

After a half-dozen years of Democrat presidents creating a looming disaster in Vietnam—including President Kennedy ordering the assassination of our own ally in the middle of the war and President Johnson ham-handedly choosing bombing targets from the Oval Office—Nixon became president in 1969, and the world was safe again.

Nixon began a phased withdrawal of American ground troops, while protecting the South Vietnamese by increasing the bombings of the North, mining North Vietnamese harbors, and attacking North Vietnamese military supplies in Cambodia. All this was hysterically denounced by American liberals, eager for the Communists to defeat America.

Despite the massive anti-war protests staged by the Worst Generation, their marches, their draft-card burnings, their takeovers of university buildings—even their bombings of U.S. property to protest the bombing of North Vietnamese property—Nixon's Vietnam policy was apparently popular with normal Americans. In 1972, he won reelection against "peace" candidate George McGovern in a forty-nine-state landslide.

In January 1973, the United States signed the Paris Peace accords, which would have ended the war with honor. In order to achieve a ceasefire, Nixon jammed lousy terms down South Vietnam's throat, such as allowing Viet Cong troops to remain in the South. But in return, we promised South Vietnam that, if the North attacked, we would resume bombing missions and military aid.

It would have worked, but the Democrats were desperate for America to lose. They invented "Watergate," the corpus delicti of which wouldn't have merited three column inches during the Clinton years, and hounded Nixon out of office. (How's Sandy Berger weathering that tough wrist-slap?)

Three months after Nixon was gone, we got the Watergate Congress and with it, the new Democratic Party. In lieu of the old Democratic Party, which lost wars out of incompetence and naiveté, the new Democratic Party would lose wars on purpose.

Just one month after the Watergate Congress was elected, North Vietnam attacked the South.

Even milquetoast, pro-abortion, détente-loving Gerald R. Ford knew America had to defend South Vietnam or America's word would be worth nothing. As Ford said, "American unwillingness to provide adequate assistance to allies fighting for their lives could seriously affect our credibility throughout the world as an ally." He pleaded repeatedly with the Democratic Congress simply to authorize aid to South Vietnam—no troops, just money.

But the Democrats turned their backs on South Vietnam, betrayed an ally, and trashed America's word. Within a month of Ford's last appeal to Congress to help the South Vietnamese, Saigon fell.

The entire world watched as American personnel desperately scrambled into helicopters from embassy rooftops in Saigon while beating back our own allies, to whom we could offer no means of escape. It was the most demeaning image of America ever witnessed until Britney Spears came along.

Southeast Asia was promptly consumed in a maelstrom of violence that seems to occur whenever these "Jeffersonian Democrats" come to power. Communist totalitarians swept through Laos, Cambodia, and all of Vietnam. They staged gruesome massacres so vast that none other than Senator George McGovern called for military intervention to stop a "clear case of genocide" in Cambodia.

Five years after that, Islamic lunatics in Iran felt no compunction about storming the embassy of what was once the greatest superpower on Earth and taking American citizens hostage for fourteen months. To this day, al Qaeda boosts the flagging morale of its jihadists by reminding them of America's humiliating retreat from Vietnam.

Democrats have never admitted error in rejecting Ford's pleas on behalf of South Vietnam. There are still dangerous foreigners trying to kill Americans and they need the Democrats' help.

Welcome Back, Carter
June 10, 2009

Well, I'm glad that's over! Now that our silver-tongued president has gone to Cairo to soothe Muslims' hurt feelings, they love us again! Muslims in Pakistan expressed their appreciation for President Barack Obama's speech by bombing a fancy hotel in Peshawar this week.

Operating on the liberal premise that what Arabs really respect is weakness, Obama listed Muslims' historical contributions to mankind, such as algebra (actually, that was the ancient Babylonians), the compass (that was the Chinese), pens (the Chinese again), and medical discoveries (would that be clitorectomies?).

But why be picky? All these inventions came in mighty handy on September 11, 2001! Thanks, Muslims!!

Obama bravely told the Cairo audience that 9/11 was a very nasty thing for Muslims to do to us, but on the other hand, they are victims of colonization. Except we didn't colonize them. The French and the British did. So why are Arabs flying planes into our buildings and not the Arc de Triomphe? (And gosh, haven't the Arabs done a lot with the Middle East since the French and the British left?!)

In another sharks-to-kittens comparison, Obama said, "Now let me be clear, issues of women's equality are by no means simply an issue for Islam." No, he said, "the struggle for women's equality continues in many aspects of American life." So on one hand, twelve-year-old girls are stoned to death for being raped in Muslim countries. But on the other hand, we still don't have enough female firefighters here in America.

Delusionally, Obama bragged about his multicultural worldview, saying, "I reject the view of some in the West that a woman who chooses to cover her hair is somehow less equal." In Saudi Arabia, Iran, Afghanistan, and many other Muslim countries, women "choose" to cover their heads on pain of losing them.

Obama rolled out the crucial liberal talking point against America's invasion of Iraq, saying Iraq was a "war of convenience," while Afghanistan was a "war of necessity." Liberals cling to this nonsense doggerel as a shield against their hypocrisy on Iraq. Either both wars were wars of necessity or both wars were wars of choice. (No war is ever "convenient.")

Neither Iraq nor Afghanistan—nor any country—attacked us on 9/11. Both Iraq and Afghanistan, as well as many other Muslim countries, were sheltering those associated with the terrorists who did attack us on 9/11—and who hoped to attack us again.

The truth is, all wars are wars of choice, including the Revolutionary War, the Civil War, both World Wars, the Korean and Vietnam Wars, the Gulf War, and the wars in Iraq and Afghanistan. OK, maybe the war on teenage obesity is a war of necessity, but that's the only one I can think of.

The modern Democrat Party chooses—really chooses, not like Saudi women "choosing" to wear hijabs—to fight no wars. But the Democrats couldn't say that immediately after 9/11, so they pretended to support the war in Afghanistan and then had to spend the next seven and a half years trying to come up with a distinction between Afghanistan and Iraq.

Maybe next they can tell us why fighting Hitler—who never invaded the U.S. and had no plans to do so—was a "necessity" in a way that fighting Saddam wasn't. (Obama on Hitler: "Nazi ideology sought to subjugate, humiliate and exterminate. It perpetrated murder on a massive scale." Whereas Saddam Hussein was just messing with the Kuwaitis, Kurds, and Shiites.)

Meanwhile, Muslims throughout the Middle East are yearning for their own Saddam Husseins to be taken out by U.S. invaders so they can be liberated, too. (Then we'll see how many women—outside of an American college campus—"choose" to wear hijabs.) The war-of-choice/war-of-necessity point must be as mystifying to a Muslim audience as a discussion of gay marriage.

Arabs aren't afraid of us; they're afraid of Iran. But our aspiring Jimmy Carter had no tough words for Iran. To the contrary, in Cairo, Obama endorsed Iran's quest for nuclear "power," while attacking—brace yourself—America for helping remove Iranian loon Mohammad Mossadegh.

The CIA's taking out Mossadegh was probably the greatest thing that agency ever did. This was back in 1953, before the Democrats turned the CIA into a collection of lawyers and paper-pushers.

Mossadegh was as crazy as a March hare (which is really saying something when your competition is Muammar Gaddafi, Ayatollah Ruhollah Khomeini, and Saddam Hussein). He gave interviews in pink pajamas while lying in bed. He wept, he fainted, and he set his nation on a path of permanent impoverishment by "nationalizing" the oil wells, where they sat idle after the British companies that knew how to operate them pulled out.

But he was earthy and hated the British, so left-wing academics adored Mossadegh. The *New York Times* compared him to Thomas Jefferson.

True, Mossadegh had been "elected" by the Iranian parliament—but only in the chaos following the assassination of the sitting prime minister. In short order, the shah dismissed this clown, but Mossadegh refused to step down, so the CIA forcibly removed him and allowed the shah's choice to assume the office. This "coup," as liberal academics term it, was approved by liberals' favorite Republican president, Dwight Eisenhower, and supported by such ponderous liberal blowhards as John Foster Dulles.

For Obama to be apologizing for one of the CIA's most magnificent accomplishments isn't just crazy, it's Ramsey Clark crazy.

Obama also said that it was unfair that "some countries have weapons that others do not" and proclaimed that "any nation—including Iran—should have the right to access peaceful nuclear power if it complies with its responsibilities under the Nuclear Non-Proliferation Treaty." Wait—how about us? If a fanatical Holocaust denier with messianic delusions can have nuclear power, can't the U.S. at least build one new nuclear power plant every thirty years?

I'm sure Iran's compliance will be policed as well as North Korea's was. Clinton struck a much-heralded "peace deal" with North Korea in 1994, giving them $4 billion to construct nuclear facilities and five hundred thousand tons of fuel oil in return for a promise that they wouldn't build nuclear weapons. The ink wasn't dry before the North Koreans began feverishly building nukes.

But back to Iran, what precisely do Iranians need nuclear power for, again? They're not exactly a manufacturing powerhouse. Iran is a primitive nation in the middle of a desert that happens to sit on top of a large percentage of the world's oil and gas reserves. That's not enough oil and gas to run household fans?

Obama's "I'm OK, You're OK" speech would be hilarious, if it weren't so terrifying.

Obama to Iran: Let Them Eat Ice Cream
June 24, 2009

On Iran, President Obama is worse than Hamlet. He's Colin Powell, waiting to see who wins before picking a side. Last week, massive protests roiled Iran over an apparently stolen presidential election, in which nutcase Mahmoud Ahmadinejad was declared the winner within two hours of the polls closing. (We await reports that ACORN was involved.)

Obama responded by saying that the difference between the loon Ahmadinejad and his reformist challenger, Mir Hossein Mousavi, "may not be as great as advertised." Yes, maybe the thousands of protesters on the streets of Tehran just liked Mousavi's answer to the "boxers or briefs" question better than Ahmadinejad's.

Then, in a manly rebuke to the cheating mullahs, Obama said, "You've seen in Iran some initial reaction from the supreme leader that indicates he understands the Iranian people have deep concerns about the election." The "supreme leader"? Did FDR ever give a speech referring to Adolf Hitler as "Herr Führer"? What's with Obama?

Even the French condemned the Iranian government's "brutal" treatment of the protesters—and French tanks have one speed in forward and five speeds in reverse. You might be a scaredy-cat if...*the president of France is talking tougher than you are.* More than a week ago, French president Nicolas Sarkozy said, "The ruling power claims to have won the elections...if that were true, we must ask why they find it necessary to imprison their opponents and repress them with such violence."

But liberals rushed to assure us that Obama's lily-livered response to the fierce crackdown on Iranian protesters was a brilliant foreign policy move. (They also proclaimed his admission that he still smokes "lion-hearted" and "statesmanlike.") As our own Supreme Leader B. Hussein Obama (peace be upon him) explained, "It's not productive given the history of U.S.-Iranian relations to be seen as meddling."

You see, if the president of the United States condemned election fraud in Iran, it would crush the spirit of the protesters when they discovered, to their horror, that the Great Satan was on their side. (It also wouldn't do much for Al Franken's election theft in Minnesota.) Liberals hate America, so they assume everyone else does, too.

When a young Iranian woman, Neda Agha Soltan, was shot dead in the streets of Iran during a protest on Saturday and a video of her death ricocheted around the World Wide Web, Obama valiantly responded by...going out for an ice cream cone. (Masterful!) Commenting on a woman's cold-blooded murder at the hands of the government in the streets of Tehran is evidently above Obama's "pay grade" (as he once told Pastor Rick Warren, when asked when he believes an unborn baby acquires human rights).

But if a U.S. president must stay absolutely neutral between freedom-loving Iranian students and their oppressors, then why is Obama speaking out in support of the protesters now? Are liberals no longer worried about the parade of horribles they claimed would ensue if the U.S. president condemned the mullahs?

Obama's tough talk this week proves that his gentle words last week about Ahmadinejad and the "supreme leader" constituted, at best, spinelessness and, at worst, an endorsement of the fraud. Moreover, if the better part of valor is for America to stand neutral between freedom and

Islamic oppression, why are liberals trying to credit Obama's ridiculous Cairo speech for emboldening the Iranian protesters?

The only reason that bald contradiction doesn't smack you in the face is that it is so utterly preposterous that Obama's Cairo speech accomplished anything—anything worthwhile, that is. Not even the people who say it believe it. The only reaction to Obama's Cairo speech in the Middle East is that the mullahs probably sighed in relief upon discovering that the U.S. president is a coward and an imbecile.

Two weeks ago, *New York Times* columnist Thomas Friedman was exulting over the "free and fair" national election in Lebanon, in which the voters threw out Hezbollah and voted in the "U.S.-supported coalition." (Apparently, America's support for democracy in Lebanon is not dangerous and misguided, as it would be in Iran.)

To justify his *Times*-expensed airfare to Beirut, Friedman added some local color, noting that "more than one Lebanese whispered to me: Without George Bush standing up to the Syrians in 2005…this free election would not have happened." That's what Lebanese voters said.

But Friedman also placed a phone call to a guy at the Carnegie Endowment for International Peace—which he didn't have to go to Lebanon for—to get a quote supporting the ludicrous proposition that Obama's Cairo speech was responsible for the favorable election results in Lebanon. "And then here came this man [Obama]," Mr. Carnegie Fund said, "who came to them with respect, speaking these deep values about their identity and dignity and economic progress and education, and this person indicated that this little prison that people are living in here was not the whole world. That change was possible."

I think the fact that their Muslim brethren are now living in freedom in a democratic Iraq might have made the point that "change was possible" somewhat more forcefully than a speech apologizing for Westerners who dislike the hijab.

Obama—and America—are still living off President Bush's successes in the war on terrorism. For the country's sake, may those successes outlast Obama's attempt to dismantle them.

Ahmadinejad: "Yep, I'm Nuclear!"
February 17, 2010

The only man causing President Obama more headaches than Joe Biden these days is Mahmoud Ahmadinejad (who, coincidentally, was right after Biden on Obama's VP short list). Despite Obama's personal magnetism, the Iranian president is moving like gangbusters to build nuclear weapons, leading to Ahmadinejad's announcement last week that Iran is now a "nuclear state."

Gee, that's weird—because I remember being told in December 2007 that all sixteen U.S. intelligence agencies had concluded that Iran had ceased nuclear weapons development as of 2003.

At the time, many of us recalled that the U.S. has the worst intelligence-gathering operations in the world. The Czechs, the French, the Italians—even the Iraqis have better intelligence. (The Iraqis were trained by the Soviets.) Burkina Faso has better intelligence—and their director of intelligence is a witch doctor. The marketing division of Walmart has more reliable intel than the U.S. government does.

After Watergate, the off-the-charts left-wing Congress gleefully set about dismantling this nation's intelligence operations on the theory that Watergate never would have happened if only there had been no CIA. Ron Dellums, a typical Democrat of the time, who—amazingly—was a member of the House Select Committee on Intelligence and chairman of the House Armed Services Committee, famously declared in 1975, "We should totally dismantle every intelligence agency in this country piece by piece, brick by brick, nail by nail."

And so they did.

So now, our "spies" are prohibited from spying. The only job of a CIA officer these days is to read foreign newspapers and leak classified information to the *New York Times*. It's like a secret society of newspaper readers. The reason no one at the CIA saw 9/11 coming was that there wasn't anything about it in the Islamabad Post. (On the plus side, at least we haven't had another break-in at the Watergate.)

CIA agents can't spy because that might require them to break laws in foreign countries. They are perfectly willing to break U.S. laws to leak U.S. intelligence to the *New York Times*, but not in order to acquire foreign intelligence.

So it was curious that after months of warnings from the Bush administration in 2007 that Iran was pursuing a nuclear weapons program, a National Intelligence Estimate on Iran was leaked, concluding that Iran had ceased its nuclear weapons program years earlier.

Republicans outside of the administration went ballistic over the suspicious timing and content of the Iran-Is-Just-Peachy report. Even the *New York Times*, of all places, ran a column by two outside experts on Iran's nuclear programs that ridiculed the NIE's conclusion. Gary Milhollin of the Wisconsin Project on Nuclear Arms Control and Valerie Lincy of Iranwatch.org cited Iran's operation of three thousand gas centrifuges at its plant at Natanz, as well as a heavy-water reactor being built at Arak, neither of which had any peaceful energy purpose. (If only there were something plentiful in Iran that could be used for energy!)

Weirdly, our intelligence agencies missed those nuclear operations. They were too busy reading an article in the *Tehran Tattler*, "Iran Now Loves Israel."

Ahmadinejad was ecstatic, calling the NIE report "a declaration of the Iranian people's victory against the great powers." The only people more triumphant than Ahmadinejad about the absurd conclusion of our vaunted "intelligence" agencies were American liberals.

In *Time* magazine, Joe Klein gloated that the Iran report "appeared to shatter the last shreds of credibility of the White House's bomb-Iran brigade—and especially that of Vice President Dick Cheney." Liberal columnist Bill Press said, "No matter how badly Bush and Cheney wanted to carpet-bomb Iran, it's clear now that doing so would have been a tragic mistake."

Naturally, the most hysterical response came from MSNBC's Keith Olbermann. After donning his mother's housecoat, undergarments, and fuzzy slippers, Keith brandished the NIE report, night after night, demanding that Bush apologize to the Iranians. "Having accused Iran of doing something it had stopped doing more than four years ago," Olbermann thundered, "instead of apologizing or giving a diplomatic response of any kind, this president of the United States chuckled."

Olbermann ferociously defended innocent-as-a-lamb Mahmoud from aspersions cast by the Bush administration, asking, "Could Mr. Bush make it any more of a mess…in response to Iran's anger at being in some respects, at least, either overrated or smeared, his response officially chuckling, how is that going to help anything?" Bush had "smeared" Iran!

Olbermann's Ed McMahon, the ever-obliging Howard Fineman of *Newsweek*, agreed, saying that the leaked intelligence showed that Bush "has zero credibility." Olbermann's even creepier sidekick, androgynous *Newsweek* reporter Richard Wolffe, also agreed, saying American credibility "has suffered another serious blow." Poor Iran! Olbermann's most macho guest, Rachel Maddow, demanded to know—with delightful originality—"what the president knew and when he knew it."

All this was on account of Bush's having disparaged the good name of a messianic, Holocaust-denying nutcase, despite the existence of a cheery report on Iran produced by our useless intelligence agencies. Olbermann, who knows everything that's on the Daily Kos and nothing else, called those who doubted the NIE report "liars" and repeatedly demanded an investigation into when Bush knew about the NIE's (laughable) report.

Even if you weren't aware that the U.S. has the worst intelligence in the world, and even if you didn't notice that the leak was timed perfectly to embarrass Bush, wouldn't any normal person be suspicious of a report concluding Ahmadinejad was behaving like a prince?

Not liberals. Our intelligence agencies concluded Iran had suspended its nuclear program in 2003, so Bush owed Ahmadinejad an apology.

February 11, 2010: Ahmadinejad announces that Iran is now a nuclear power.

Thanks, liberals!

Bill Kristol Must Resign
July 7, 2010

Republican National Committee chairman Michael Steele was absolutely right. Afghanistan is Obama's war, and, judging by other recent Democratic ventures in military affairs, it's not likely to turn out well.

It has been idiotically claimed that Steele's statement about Afghanistan being Obama's war is "inaccurate"—as if Steele is unaware Bush invaded Afghanistan soon after 9/11. (No one can forget that—even liberals pretended to support that war for three whole weeks.) Yes, Bush invaded Afghanistan soon after 9/11. Within the first few months we had toppled the Taliban, killed or captured hundreds of al Qaeda fight-ers, and arranged for democratic elections, resulting in an American-friendly government.

Then Bush declared success and turned his attention to Iraq, leaving minimal troops behind in Afghanistan to prevent al Qaeda from regrouping. Having some vague concept of America's national inter-est—unlike liberals—the Bush administration could see that a country of illiterate peasants living in caves ruled by "warlords" was not a primo target for "nation-building."

By contrast, Iraq had a young, educated, pro-Western populace that was absolutely ideal for regime change. If Saddam Hussein had been a peach, it would still be a major victory in the war on terrorism to have a Muslim Israel—and it sure wasn't going to be Afghanistan (literacy rate, 19 percent; life expectancy, forty-four years; working toilets, seven).

Fortuitously, Iraq also happened to be a state sponsor of terrorism; was attempting to build nuclear weapons (according to endless bipar-tisan investigations in this country and in Britain); nurtured and gave refuge to Islamic terrorists—including the 1993 World Trade Center bombers; was led by a mass murderer who had used weapons of mass destruction; paid bonuses to the families of suicide bombers; had vast oil reserves; and was situated smack dab in the center of a critically important region.

Having absolutely no interest in America's national security, the entire Democratic Party (save Joe Lieberman) wailed about the war in Iraq for five years, pretending they really wanted to go great guns in Afghanistan. What the heck: they had already voted for the war in Afghanistan in the wake of 9/11 when they would have been hanged as traitors had they objected.

The obsession with Afghanistan was pure rhetoric. Democrats have no interest in fighting any war, unless it is directly contrary to America's interests. (They're too jammed with their wars against Evangelicals,

Walmart, the Pledge of Allegiance, SUVs, and the middle class.) Absent Iraq, they'd have been bad-mouthing Afghanistan, too.

So for the entire course of the magnificently successful war in Iraq, all we heard from these useless Democrats was that Iraq was a "war of choice," while Afghanistan—the good war!—was a "war of necessity." *Bush took his eye off the ball in Afghanistan! He got distracted by war in Iraq! WHERE'S OSAMA?* and—my favorite—*Iraq didn't attack us on 9/11!*

Neither did Afghanistan. But Democrats were in a lather and couldn't be bothered with the facts. The above complaints about Iraq come— nearly verbatim—from speeches and press conferences by Obama, Joe Biden, and Obama's national security advisors Susan Rice and Richard Clarke. Also, the entire gutless Democratic Party. Some liberals began including them in their wedding vows.

Obama didn't ramp up the war in Afghanistan based on a careful calculation of America's strategic objectives. He did it because he was trapped by his own campaign speeches bashing the Iraq War while pretending to be a hawk on Afghanistan.

At this point, Afghanistan is every bit as much Obama's war as Vietnam was Lyndon Johnson's war. True, President Kennedy was the first to send troops to Vietnam. We had sixteen thousand troops in Vietnam when JFK was assassinated. Within four years, LBJ had upped that to four hundred thousand troops.

In the entire seven-year course of the Afghanistan War under Bush, from October 2001 to January 2009, 625 American soldiers were killed. In eighteen short months, Obama has nearly doubled that number to 1,124 Americans killed. (By the middle of 2013, American fatalities in Afghanistan had nearly doubled again to 2,167 troops.)

Republicans used to think seriously about deploying the military. President Eisenhower sent aid to South Vietnam but said he could not "conceive of a greater tragedy" for America than getting heavily involved there. But now I hear it is the official policy of the Republican Party to be for all wars, irrespective of our national interest.

As Michael Steele correctly noted, every great power that's tried to stage an all-out war in Afghanistan has gotten its butt handed to it. Everyone knows it's not worth the trouble to take a nation of rocks and brigands.

Based on Obama's rules of engagement for our troops in Afghanistan, we're apparently not even fighting a war. The greatest fighting force in the world is building vocational schools and distributing cheese crackers to children. There's even talk of giving soldiers medals for NOT shooting people (which I gather will be awarded posthumously). Naomi Campbell is rougher with her assistants than our troops are allowed to be with Taliban fighters.

What if Obama decides to invade England because he's still ticked off about that Churchill bust? Can Michael Steele and I object to that? Or would that demoralize the troops? Our troops are the most magnificent in the world, but they're not the ones setting military policy. The president is—and he seems to be basing his war strategy on the chants of MoveOn.org cretins.

Nonetheless, Bill Kristol and Liz Cheney have demanded that Steele resign as head of the RNC for saying Afghanistan is now Obama's war—and a badly thought-out one at that. (Didn't liberals warn us that neoconservatives want permanent war?) I thought the irreducible requirements of Republicanism were being for life, small government, and a strong national defense, but I guess permanent war is on the platter now, too.

Of course, if Kristol is writing the rules for being a Republican, we're all going to have to get on board for amnesty and a "National Greatness Project," too—other Kristol ideas for the Republican Party. Also, John McCain. Kristol was an early backer of McCain for president—and look how great that turned out! Inasmuch as demanding resignations is another new Republican policy, here's mine: Bill Kristol and Liz Cheney must resign immediately.

Libya Commemorates 9/11
September 12, 2012

When President Obama intervened in Libya last year, he claimed that "it's in our national interest to act." He supported removing the tyrant Muammar Gaddafi, who—in response to Bush's invasion of Iraq—had just given up his weapons of mass destruction and pledged to be America's BFF.

Apparently Gaddafi neglected to also tell Obama, "I've got your back."*

Obama said, "We must stand alongside those who believe in the same core principles that have guided us through many storms…our support for a set of universal rights, including the freedom for people to express themselves and choose their leaders; our support for the governments that are ultimately responsive to the aspirations of the people."

The Libyan mob was the equivalent of our Founding Fathers! If you overlook the part about it being murderous and Islamic.

Meanwhile, Michael Scheuer, former head of the CIA's bin Laden unit, said, "The people we are fighting for in Libya, the backbone of that movement, are former mujahedeen from around the world." We are "enabling people who may not be formally aligned with al-Qaida but who want the same things to grasp ever closer to power."

Scheuer said the media had taken "a few English-speaking Arabs who are pro-democracy and a few Facebook pages out of the Middle East

---

* *2008 Obama campaign catchphrase*

and extrapolated that to a region-wide love of secular democracy," adding, "It is as insane a situation as I've ever encountered in my life."

No wonder Obama's running for reelection on his foreign policy expertise!

Among Republicans, Newt Gingrich, Sarah Palin, Mike Huckabee, and Rick Santorum all called for aggressive action against Gaddafi, including enforcement of a no-fly zone. Santorum cited Reagan's 1986 bombing of Libya (after Gaddafi had killed American servicemen in Berlin), saying, "If you want to be Reaganesque, it seems the path is pretty clear."

Gingrich took all sides, first demanding, "Exercise a no-fly zone this evening. We don't need to have the United Nations. All we have to say is that we think that slaughtering your own citizens is unacceptable and that we're intervening. This is a moment to get rid of him. Do it. Get it over with."

Then, two weeks later, he said, "I would not have intervened."

Only Mitt Romney and Haley Barbour resisted calling for aggressive action against Gaddafi, with Romney merely criticizing Obama's deer-in-the-headlights response and Barbour stating more directly, "I don't think it's our mission to make Libya look like Luxembourg." No offense, he said, "but it is not ever going to look like what we'd like."

The *New York Times*' Thomas Friedman exulted that the Arab peoples "have come up with their own answer to violent extremism and the abusive regimes we've been propping up…. It's called democracy."

The *Washington Post*'s David Ignatius praised Obama's major shift in strategy in seeing the Libyan uprising as a "positive development" and refusing to provide aid to the embattled dictator. "My own instinct," he said, "is that Obama is right."

French liberal blowhard Bernard-Henri Levy announced that "Libya will go down in history as the anti-Iraq. Iraq was a democracy parachuted in by a foreign power in a country which hadn't asked for it. Libya was a rebellion which demanded help from an international coalition."

The *Charleston Gazette* (West Virginia) editorialized, "Most of the world is rejoicing because of the historic success in Libya. We're glad it was accomplished by Libya's people, not by a U.S. invasion ordered by right-wing American politicians."

I note that the American ambassador in Iraq has not been murdered and his corpse dragged through the streets. I also recall that, a few years ago, when Muslims around the globe erupted in rioting over some Dutch cartoons, one Muslim country remained utterly pacific: George W. Bush's Iraq.

Apparently U.S. invasions ordered by right-wing American presidents are the only ones that work in the Middle East. Fake uprisings orchestrated by Muslim fanatics are less propitious.

Learn your history, Americans. The American Revolution was not the revolt of a mob. It was a carefully thought-out plan for a republic, based on ideas painstakingly argued by serious men in the process of creating what would become the freest, most prosperous nation in world history.

The much-ballyhooed "Arab Spring," with mobs of men gang-raping American reporters, firing guns in the air, and publically murdering their erstwhile dictators, is more akin to the pointless bloodletting of the French Revolution.

That godless antithesis to the founding of America is the primogenitor of the horrors of the Bolshevik Revolution, Hitler's Nazi Party, Mao's Cultural Revolution, Pol Pot's slaughter, and America's periodic mob uprisings, from Shays's Rebellion to today's union thugs in Madison, Wisconsin, and Occupy Wall Street.

Americans did win freedom and greater individual rights with their revolution. By contrast, the French Revolution resulted in bestial savagery, a slaughter of all the Revolution's leaders, followed by Napoleon's dictatorship, followed by another monarchy, and then finally something resembling an actual republic eighty years later.

Violent mob uprisings have never led to a functioning democratic republic, but they're always a hit with liberals.

CHAPTER NINE

Muslims: Why You're Barefoot in an Airport Right Now

I f only Obama really were a Muslim, at least he'd be against abortion and gay marriage.

Guantanamo Loses Five-Star Rating
June 22, 2005

I f you still have any doubts about whether closing Guantanamo is the right thing to do, Jimmy Carter recently demanded that it be shuttered. With any luck, he'll try to effect another one of those daring rescue attempts! Here's a foolproof method for keeping America safe:

Always do the exact opposite of whatever Jimmy Carter says. (Instead of Guantanamo, how about we close down the Carter Center?)

Senator Dick Durbin says Guantanamo is reminiscent of the "Nazis, Soviets in their gulags or some mad regime—Pol Pot or others." (He then offered the typical Democrat "if/then" non-apology: i.e., "if my remarks offended anyone"... which seems entirely likely if any sentient, English-speaking adult heard them.) Amnesty International also called Guantanamo a "gulag." Senator Teddy Kennedy actually said he cannot condone allegations of near-drowning "as a human being." And Senator Patrick Leahy called it "an international embarrassment," as opposed to himself, a "national embarrassment."

On the bright side, at least liberals have finally found a group of people in Cuba they think deserve to be rescued.

In the interests of helping my country, I have devised a compact set of torture guidelines for Guantanamo.

It's not torture if:

- It's comparable to the treatment U.S. troops received in basic training;
- The same acts performed on a live stage have been favorably reviewed by Frank Rich of the *New York Times*;
- Andrew Sullivan has ever solicited it from total strangers on the internet;
- You can pay someone in New York to do it to you;
- Karen Finley ever got a federal grant to do it;
- It's no worse than the way airlines treat little girls in pigtails flying to see Grandma in Idaho.

The most unpleasant aspect of Guantanamo for the detainees came with the move from the temporary "Camp X-Ray." Apparently, wanton homosexual sex among the inmates is more difficult in their newer, more commodious quarters. (Suspiciously, detainees retailing outlandish tales of abuse to the ACLU often include the claim that they were subjected to prolonged rectal exams.) Plus, I hear the views of the Caribbean aren't as good from their new suites.

Even the tales of "torture" being palmed off by the detainees on credulous American journalists are pretty lame. The *Washington Post* reported that a detainee at Guantanamo says he was "threatened with sexual abuse." (Bonus "Not Torture" rule: if it is similar to the way interns were treated in the Clinton White House.)

"Sign or you will be tortured!"

"What's the torture?"

"We will merely threaten you with horrible things!"

"That's it?"

"Shut up and do as we say, or we'll issue empty, laughable threats guaranteed to amuse you. This is your last warning."

One detainee in Afghanistan told a hyperventilating reporter for Salon that he was forced to stand with his arms in the air for "hours." *Doctor, I still have nightmares about the time I was forced to stand with my arms up in the air...* Others claimed they were forced into uncomfortable, unnatural positions, sort of like the Democrats' position on abortion. Next, the interrogators will be threatening to over-sauce the chicken fricassee!

According to *Time* magazine, this is how the "gulag of our time" treats the inmates: "The best-behaved detainees are held in Camp 4, a medium-security, communal-living environment with as many as ten beds in a room; prisoners can play soccer or volleyball outside up to nine hours a day, eat meals together and read Agatha Christie mysteries in Arabic." So they're not exactly raping the detainees with dogs.

Why do Democrats take such relish in slandering their country? If someone was constantly telling vicious lies about you, would you believe he loved you? *"I love John Smith, and that's why I accuse him of committing serial rape and mass murder. Oh, he doesn't do that? Yes, but how dare you say I don't love John Smith!"*

And now back to our regular programming on Air America…

What Can I Do to Make Your Flight More Uncomfortable?
November 22, 2006

Six imams removed from a US Airways flight from Minneapolis to Phoenix are calling on Muslims to boycott the airline. If only we could get Muslims to boycott all airlines, we could dispense with airport security altogether.

Witnesses said the imams stood to do their evening prayers in the terminal before boarding, chanting "Allah, Allah, Allah"—coincidentally, the last words ever heard by hundreds of airline passengers on 9/11. Witnesses also said that the imams were talking about Saddam Hussein, and denouncing America and the War in Iraq. About the only scary preflight ritual the imams didn't perform was the signing of last wills and testaments. After boarding, the imams did not sit together and some asked for seat belt extensions, although none were obese. Three of the men had one-way tickets and no checked baggage.

Also, they were Muslims.

The idea that a Muslim boycott against US Airways would hurt the airline proves that Arabs are utterly tone-deaf. This is roughly the equivalent of Cindy Sheehan taking a vow of silence. How can we hope to deal with people with no sense of irony? The next thing you know, New York City cab drivers will be threatening to bathe daily.

I suspect the whole affair may have been a madcap advertising scheme cooked up by US Airways. It worked with me. US Airways is my official airline now. Northwest, which eventually flew the Allah-spouting Muslims to their destinations, is off my list. You want to really hurt a U.S. air carrier's business? Have Muslims announce that it's their favorite airline.

The clerics had been attending an imam conference in Minneapolis. (Imam Conference slogan: "What Happens in Minneapolis—Actually, Nothing Happened in Minneapolis.") But instead of investigating the conference, the government is investigating my new favorite airline. What threat could Muslims flying from Minnesota to Arizona be?

Three of the nineteen hijackers on 9/11 received their flight training in Arizona. Long before the attacks, an FBI agent in Phoenix found it curious that so many Arabs were enrolled in flight school. But the FBI rebuffed his request for an investigation on the grounds that his suspicions were based on the same invidious racial profiling that has brought US Airways under investigation and into my high esteem.

Lynne Stewart's client, the Blind Sheik, Omar Abdel-Rahman, is serving life in prison in a maximum-security lock-up in Minnesota. One of the six imams removed from the US Airways plane was blind, so Lynne Stewart was the one missing clue that would have sent all the passengers screaming from the plane.

Wholly apart from the issue of terrorism, don't we have a seller's market for new immigrants? How does a blind Muslim get to the top of the visa list? Is there a shortage of blind, fanatical clerics in this country that I haven't noticed? Couldn't we get a Burmese with leprosy instead? A four-year-old could do a better job choosing visa applicants than the U.S. Department of Immigration.

One of the stunt-imams in US Airways's advertising scheme, Omar Shahin, complained about being removed from the plane, saying, "Six scholars in handcuffs. It's terrible." Yes, especially when there was a whole conference of them! Six out of 150 is called "poor law enforcement." How did the other 144 go scott free?

Shahin's own "scholarship" consisted of denying that Muslims were behind the 9/11 attack for months afterwards. On November 4, 2001, the *Arizona Republic* cited Shahin's "skepticism that Muslims or bin Laden carried out attacks on the World Trade Center and Pentagon." Shahin complained that the government was "focusing on the Arabs, the Muslims. And all the evidence shows that the Muslims are not involved in this terrorist act."

In case your memory of that time is hazy, within three days of the attack, the government had excluded all but nineteen passengers as possible hijackers based on extensive interviews with friends and family of nearly every passenger on all four flights. Some of the hijackers' seat numbers had been called in by flight attendants on the planes before they crashed. By September 14, the Justice Department had released the names of all nineteen hijackers, names like Majed Moqed, Ahmed al-Ghamdi, Mohand al-Shehri, Ahmed Ibrahim A. al-Haznawi, and Ahmed al-Nami.

By early October, bin Laden had claimed credit for the attacks on a videotape. By November 4, 2001, the *New York Times* had run well over one hundred articles on the connections between bin Laden and the hijackers (even more detailed and sinister than the *Times*' flowchart on neoconservatives!). Also, if I remember correctly, al Qaeda had taken out full-page ads in *Variety* and the *Hollywood Reporter* thanking their agents for the attacks.

But now, on the eve of the busiest travel day in America, these "scholars" have ginned up America's PC victim machinery to intimidate airlines and passengers from noticing six imams chanting "Allah" before boarding a commercial jet.

Terrorists' Restless Leg Syndrome
November 26, 2008

I thought the rest of the world was going to love us if we elected B. Hussein Obama! Somebody better tell the Muslims.

As everyone but President-elect Obama's base knows, many of the Guantanamo detainees cannot be sent to their home countries, cannot be released, and cannot be tried. They need to be held in some form of extra-legal limbo the rest of their lives, sort of like Phil Spector.

And now they're Obama's problem. If Obama wants his detention of Islamic terrorists to be dramatically different from Bush's Guantanamo, my suggestion is that he cut off—so to speak—the expensive prosthetic limb procedures now being performed on the detained terrorists.

Far from being sodomized by U.S. forces—as Obama's base has been wailing for the past seven years—the innocent scholars and philanthropists held at Guantanamo are being given expensive, high-tech medical procedures at taxpayer expense. If we're not careful, multitudes of Muslims will be joining the fight against America just so they can go to Guantanamo and get proper treatment for their erectile dysfunction.

After being captured fighting with Taliban forces against Americans in 2001, Abdullah Massoud was sent to Guantanamo, where the one-legged terrorist was fitted with a special prosthetic leg, at a cost of $50,000–$75,000 to the U.S. taxpayer. Under the Americans with

Disabilities Act, Massoud would now be able to park his car bomb in a handicapped parking space!

No, you didn't read that wrong. The VA won't pay for your new glasses, but Abdullah got a $75,000 prosthetic limb. I would have gone with hanging at sunrise, but what do I know?

Upon his release in March 2004, Massoud hippity-hopped back to Afghanistan and quickly resumed his war against the U.S., aided by his new artificial leg. Just a few months later, in October 2004, Massoud masterminded the kidnapping of two Chinese engineers in Pakistan working on the Gomal Zam Dam project. This proved, to me at least, that people with disabilities can do anything they put their minds to. Way to go, you plucky extremist!

Massoud said he had nothing against the Chinese but wanted to embarrass Pakistani president Pervez Musharraf for cooperating with the Americans. You know, the Americans who had just footed a $75,000 bill for his prosthetic leg.

Pakistani forces stormed Massoud's hideout, killing all the kidnappers, including Massoud. So that was a wasted leg operation. As a result of the kidnapping, from which only one Chinese engineer escaped alive, the Chinese pulled all one hundred workers out of Pakistan. Work on the dam ceased. This was bad news for the people of Pakistan—but good news for the endangered Pakistani snail darter!

Several news accounts of Massoud's return to jihad after his release from Guantanamo mentioned his prosthetic leg. But none explained that he had acquired that leg in Guantanamo, courtesy of American taxpayers after he was captured trying to kill Americans on the battlefield in Afghanistan.

To the contrary, although Massoud's swashbuckling reputation as a jihadist with a prosthetic leg appears in many news items, where he got it is almost purposely hidden—even lied about.

Abdullah Massoud…had earned both sympathy and reverence for his time in Guantanamo Bay…. Upon his release, he made it home to Waziristan and resumed his war against the U.S. With his long hair, his prosthetic limb and impassioned speeches, he quickly became a charismatic inspiration to Waziristan's youth.
—New York Times

Explaining where he got the prosthetic leg might interfere with the *Times'* news accounts of innocent aid workers being brutalized in Guantanamo.

He lost his leg in a landmine explosion a few days before the fall of Kabul to the Taliban in September 1996. It didn't dampen his enthusiasm as a fighter and he got himself an artificial leg later, says Yusufzai.
—Indo-Asian News Service

He "got himself an artificial leg"? Where? At Costco?

He was educated in Peshawar and was treated in Karachi after his left leg was blown up in a landmine explosion in the Wreshmin Tangi gorge near Kabul in September 1996. He now walks with an artificial leg specifically made for him in Karachi.
—*Gulf News* (United Arab Emirates)

They can't lick leprosy in Karachi, but the *Gulf News* tells us Massoud got his artificial leg at one of their specialty hospitals.

How about in return for no more waterboarding, we have no more elaborate, expensive operations to help these jihadists return to the fight against America?

Muslims: "We Do That on First Dates"
April 29, 2009

Without any pretense of an argument, which liberals are neurologically incapable of, the mainstream media are now asserting that our wussy interrogation techniques at Guantanamo constituted "torture" and have irreparably harmed America's image abroad.

Only the second of those claims is true: President Obama's release of the Department of Justice interrogation memos undoubtedly hurt America's image abroad, as we are snickered at in capitals around the world, where they know what real torture is. The Arabs surely view these memos as a pack of lies. *What about the pills Americans have to turn us gay?*

The techniques used against the most stalwart al Qaeda members, such as Abu Zubaydah, included one terrifying procedure referred to as "the attention grasp."

As described in horrifying detail in the Justice Department memo, the "attention grasp" consisted of: "[G]rasping the individual with both hands, one hand on each side of the collar opening, in a controlled and quick motion. In the same motion as the grasp, the individual is drawn toward the interrogator." The end. There are rumors that Dick "Darth Vader" Cheney wanted to take away the interrogators' Altoids before they administered "the grasp," but Department of Justice lawyers deemed this too cruel.

And that's not all! As the torments were gradually increased, next up the interrogation ladder came "walling." This involves pushing the terrorist against a flexible wall, during which his "head and neck are supported with a rolled hood or towel that provides a C-collar effect to prevent whiplash." People pay to have a lot rougher stuff done to them at Six Flags Great Adventure. Indeed, with plastic walls and soft neck collars, "walling" may be the world's first method of "torture" in which all the implements were made by Fisher-Price.

As the memo darkly notes, walling doesn't cause any pain, but is supposed to induce terror by making a "loud noise": "[T]he false wall is in part constructed to create a loud sound when the individual hits it, which will further shock and surprise." If you need a few minutes to compose yourself after being subjected to that horrifying description, feel free to take a break from reading now. Sometimes a cold compress on the forehead is helpful, but don't let it drip or you might end up waterboarding yourself.

The CIA's interrogation techniques couldn't be more ridiculous if they were out of Monty Python's Spanish Inquisition sketch:

Cardinal! Poke her with the soft cushions!…

Hmm! She is made of harder stuff! Cardinal Fang! Fetch… THE COMFY CHAIR!

So you think you are strong because you can survive the soft cushions. Well, we shall see. Biggles! Put her in the Comfy Chair!…

Now—you will stay in the Comfy Chair until lunchtime, with only a cup of coffee at 11:00.

Further up the torture ladder—from Guantanamo, not Monty Python—comes the "insult slap," which is designed to be virtually painless but involves the interrogator invading "the individual's personal space." If that doesn't work, the interrogator shows up the next day wearing the same outfit as the terrorist. (Awkward.)

I will spare you the details of the CIA's other comical interrogation techniques and leap directly to the penultimate "torture" in their arsenal: the caterpillar.

In this unspeakable brutality, a harmless caterpillar is placed in the terrorist's cell. Justice Department lawyers expressly denied the interrogators' request to trick the terrorist into believing the caterpillar was a "stinging insect." Human rights groups have variously described being trapped in a cell with a live caterpillar as "brutal," "soul-wrenching," and, of course, "adorable."

If the terrorist manages to survive the non-stinging caterpillar maneuver—the most fiendish method of torture ever devised by the human mind that didn't involve being forced to watch *The View*—CIA interrogators had another sadistic trick up their sleeves. I am not at liberty to divulge the details, except to mention the procedure's terror-inducing name: "The Ladybug."

Finally, the most savage interrogation technique at Guantanamo was "waterboarding," which is only slightly rougher than the Comfy Chair. Thousands of our troops are waterboarded every year as part of their training, but not until it was done to Khalid Sheikh Mohammed—mastermind of the 9/11 attack on America—were liberal consciences shocked. (I think they were mostly shocked because they couldn't figure out how Joey Buttafuoco ended up in Guantanamo.)

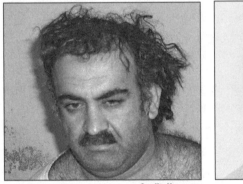 

Credit: Newscom   Credit: Corbis

As non-uniformed combatants, all of the detainees at Guantanamo could have been summarily shot on the battlefield under the Laws of War. Instead, we gave them comfy chairs, free lawyers, better food than is served in Afghani caves, prayer rugs, recreational activities, and top-flight medical care—including one terrorist who was fitted for an expensive artificial leg at Guantanamo, courtesy of the U.S. taxpayer—and released, whereupon he rejoined the jihad against America.

Only three terrorists—who could have been shot—were water-boarded. This is not nearly as bad as "snowboarding," which is known to cause massive buttocks pain and results in approximately ten deaths per year.

Normal human beings—especially those who grew up with my older brother, Jimmy—can't read the interrogation memos without laughing. At Al Jazeera, they don't believe these interrogation memos are for real. Muslims look at them and say: *THIS IS ALL THEY'RE DOING? We do that for practice. We do that to our friends.*

But the *New York Times* is populated with people who can't believe they live in a country where people would put a caterpillar in a terrorist's cell.

Muslim Suffers Bruised Ego in Fort Hood Tragedy
November 11, 2009

The massacre at Fort Hood last week is the perfect apotheosis of the liberal victimology described in my book *Guilty: Liberal "Victims" and Their Assault on America*. According to witnesses, Major Nidal Malik Hasan entered a medical facility at Fort Hood, prayed briefly, then shouted "Allahu Akbar" before he began gunning down American troops. Now I don't know which to be more afraid of: Muslims or government-run healthcare systems.

President Obama honored the victims by immediately warning Americans not to "jump to conclusions"—namely, the obvious conclusion that the attack was an act of Islamic terrorism. As conclusions go, it wasn't much of a jump. But the mainstream media waited for no information—indeed actively avoided learning any information—

before leaping to the far less obvious conclusion that the suspect's mass murder was set off by "stress." The day after the slaughter, the *New York Times* ran one editorial and two op-eds asserting as much.

Two days after the mass shooting, the *Times*' laughably predictable headlines about the Fort Hood bloodbath were:

- "Preliminary Inquiry Finds No Link to Terror Plot"
- "Painful Stories Take a Toll on Military Therapists"
- "When Soldiers' Minds Snap"

The *Los Angeles Times* jumped to the exact same conclusion, running an article on the massacre titled: "Fort Hood Tragedy Rocks Military as It Grapples with Mental Health Issues." *Time* magazine followed suit, posting an article titled: "Stresses at Fort Hood Were Likely Intense for Hasan."

Inasmuch as Major Hasan had never been deployed overseas, much less seen combat, liberals seem to have discovered the first recorded case of "pre-traumatic stress syndrome." Their point was: the real victim of Fort Hood was Major Hasan. Indeed, all Muslims were victims that day.

The media quickly set to work assembling lachrymose accounts of taunts Hasan had been subjected to in the military for being a Muslim, the most harrowing of which seems to have been his car being keyed at his off-base apartment complex. I suppose we should be relieved that liberals weren't claiming Hasan snapped because of the dimming prospects for a healthcare bill by the end of the year.

The evidence for the manifestly obvious conclusion we were supposed to avoid jumping to is rather more extensive. According to numerous eyewitness accounts, Hasan denounced the "War on Terror" as a war against Islam, said Muslims should attack Americans in retaliation for the War in Iraq, defended suicide bombers, and said he was "happy" when a Muslim murdered a soldier at a military recruiting center in

Arkansas earlier this year. (Stranger still, he wasn't auditioning for his own show on MSNBC when he made these statements.) Hasan shared a "spiritual advisor" with two of the September 11 hijackers, Imam Anwar al-Awlaki, whose unseemly enthusiasm for jihad got him banned from speaking in Britain, even by video link.

A few years ago, Hasan delivered an hour-long PowerPoint lecture to an audience of doctors at Walter Reed Army Medical Center, arguing that non-Muslims should be beheaded and have burning oil poured down their throats. He had tried to contact al Qaeda, and at least one U.S. intelligence official says the Army knew it. Despite being well aware of Hasan's disturbing conduct, the Army did nothing.

Far less offensive speech has been grounds for discipline or even removal from duties in the military. In the aftermath of the Tailhook scandal, for example, two Navy officers were reprimanded and reassigned after putting up a sign with the words of a nursery rhyme altered to include a vulgar sexual reference to liberal congresswoman Patricia Schroeder. But a Muslim Army doctor can go around a military installation somberly advocating the beheading of infidels, and the girls running the military treat him like he's Nicole Kidman and they're press junket reporters.

The Army's top brass, General George Casey, responded to the military's shocking decision to keep a terrorist-sympathizing Muslim in the Army by announcing: "Our diversity…is a strength," adding that "as great a tragedy as this was, it would be a shame if our diversity became a casualty as well." And I thought gays couldn't openly serve in the military.

On September 11, 2001, Muslims moved to the top of liberals' victim pantheon on the basis of having slaughtered three thousand Americans. Muslims were "victims" of Americans' displeasure with them for the biggest terrorist attack in world history. (The only American deserving of even more coddling than a Muslim is our first African-American president.) So, now any dyspeptic expression toward a Muslim is grounds for calling in a diversity coordinator. And when the "victim" attacks, as at

Fort Hood, the rest of us are supposed to feel guilty because Hasan's car got keyed once. As with all liberal "victims," it is the victim who is guilty.

Obama National Security Policy: Hope Their Bombs Don't Work
May 5, 2010

I t took Faisal Shahzad trying to set a car bomb in Times Square to get President Obama, Attorney General Eric Holder, and Secretary of Homeland Security Janet Napolitano to finally use the word "terrorism." (Not referring to Tea Party activists.)

This is a major policy shift for a president who spent a month telling Americans not to "jump to conclusions" after Army doctor Nidal Malik Hasan reportedly jumped on a desk, shouted "Allahu Akbar!" and began shooting up the Fort Hood military base. We know the president is taking terrorism seriously because, after last weekend, now Obama is even threatening to pronounce "Pakistan" correctly.

In a bit of macho posturing this week, Obama declared that Americans "will not be terrorized, we will not cower in fear, we will not be intimidated." First of all, having the Transportation Security Administration wanding infants, taking applesauce away from ninety-three-year-old dementia patients, and forcing all Americans to produce their containers with up to three ounces of liquid in Ziploc bags, shoes, and computers for special screening pretty much blows that "not intimidated" look Obama wants America to adopt.

"Intimidated"? How about "absolutely terrified"?

Second, it would be a little easier for the rest of us not to live in fear if the president's entire national security strategy didn't depend on average citizens happening to notice a smoldering SUV in Times Square or smoke billowing from the crotch of a fellow airline passenger. But after the car bomber, the diaper bomber, and the Fort Hood shooter, it has become increasingly clear that Obama's national defense strategy is: *Let's hope their bombs don't work!* (If only Dr. Hasan's gun had jammed at Fort Hood, that could have been another huge foreign policy success for Obama.)

The administration's fingers-crossed strategy is a follow-up to Obama's earlier and less successful "Let's Make Them Love Us!" project. In the past year, Obama has repeatedly apologized to Muslims for America's "mistakes." He has apologized to Iran for President Eisenhower's taking out the loon, Mohammad Mossadegh, before Mossadegh turned a comparatively civilized country into a Third World hellhole. (You know, like the ayatollahs have.) He has apologized to the entire Muslim world for the French and English colonizing them—i.e., building them flush toilets.

He promised to shut down Guantanamo. And he ordered the mastermind of 9/11, Khalid Sheikh Mohammed, to be tried in the same courthouse that tried Martha Stewart. There was also Obama's ninety-degree-bow tour of the Middle East. For his next visit, he plans to roll on his back and have his belly scratched like Fido. Despite favorable reviews in the *New York Times*, none of this put an end to Islamic terrorism.

So now, I gather, our only strategy is to hope the terrorists' bombs keep fizzling.

There's no other line of defense. In the case of the Times Square car bomber, the Department of Homeland Security failed, the Immigration and Naturalization Service failed, the CIA failed, and the TSA failed. (However, the Department of Alert T-Shirt Vendors came through with flying colors!) It took the combined work of a New York street vendor, the New York Police Department, and Shahzad's Rube-Goldberg bomb to prevent a major explosion in Times Square. (I do hope Shahzad is not offended by how Jewish that sounds. Oh well, Obama can apologize.)

Even after the NYPD de-wired the smoking car bomb and produced enough information to identify the bomb-maker, then tied it all up in a bow and handed it all to federal law enforcement…the government's crack No-Fly List failed to stop Shahzad from boarding a plane to Dubai. (To be fair, at the Emirates airline, being on a No-Fly List makes you eligible for pre-boarding.) Perhaps the Department of Homeland Security should consider creating a Really, REALLY No-Fly List.

Contrary to the wild excuses being made for the federal government on all the TV networks Monday night, it's now clear that this was not a wily plan of federal investigators to allow Shahzad to board the plane in order to nab his co-conspirators. It was a flub that nearly allowed Shahzad to escape.

Meanwhile, on that same Monday at JFK airport, approximately one hundred thousand passengers took off their shoes, coats, belts, and sunglasses for airport security. But the "highly trained federal force" the *New York Times* promised us on October 28, 2001, when the paper demanded that airport security be federalized, failed to stop the only guy they needed to stop at JFK last Monday—the one who planted a bomb in the middle of Times Square days earlier.

So why were a hundred thousand other passengers harassed and annoyed by the TSA? The federal government didn't stop the diaper bomber from nearly detonating a bomb over Detroit. It didn't stop a guy on the No-Fly list from boarding a plane and coming minutes away from getting out of the country. If our only defense to terrorism is counting on alert civilians, how about not harassing them before they board planes? We civilians might be a little more rested and alert if we hadn't just emerged from these totalitarian airport "security" procedures.

Both of the attempted bombers who sailed through airport security, I note, were young males of the Islamic faith. I wonder if we could develop a security plan based on that information?

Speaking of a "highly trained federal force," who's working at the INS these days? Who on earth made the decision to allow Shahzad to become a *U.S. citizen* last year? Our "Europeans Need Not Apply" immigration policies were absurd enough before 9/11. But after nineteen foreign-born Muslims, legally admitted to the U.S., murdered three thousand Americans in New York, Washington, and Pennsylvania in a single day, couldn't we tighten up our admission policies toward people from countries still performing stonings and clitorectomies?

Alert T-shirt vendors can't be everyplace.

CHAPTER TEN

Immigration: Addressing America's Chronic Shortage of Fertile, Unskilled Illiterates

W hy do we have to keep telling elected officials the same thing? We really don't want amnesty for illegal aliens. Americans made this resoundingly clear in 2007 when President Bush and John McCain, along with their pals Teddy Kennedy and Chuck Schumer, first tried to foist a "path to citizenship" on us. Amnesty was supported by the president's acolytes at the Fox News Channel as well as a nearly monolithic Democratic Party and its acolytes at ABC, NBC, CBS, CNN, MSNBC, MTV, Oxygen TV, the Food Network, the Golf Channel, the Home Shopping Network, the in-house "Learn to Gamble" channel at the MGM Grand in Las Vegas, and Comedy Central (unless that was just a sketch on the *Mind of [Carlos] Mencia*).

But ordinary Americans had a different idea. Their idea was: let's not reward lawbreakers with citizenship. The only "path to citizenship" the public wants involves making an application from Belgium, waiting a few years, and then coming over when it's legal. Americans were so emphatic on this point that they forced a sitting president to withdraw his signature second-term legislation.

So why did we get the exact same amnesty bill from Senator Marco Rubio in 2013? Rubio had campaigned as a Tea Party warrior. Back when he needed votes, he denounced his opponent, then-Governor Charlie Crist, for supporting the McCain plan.

"I think that plan is wrong," he said, denouncing amnesty "in any form, whether it's back of the line or so forth." An "earned path to citizenship," he said "is basically code for amnesty."

And then he got to Washington and his big legislative initiative was...a path to citizenship for illegal aliens! Yes, Rubio's plan to solve the problem of illegal immigration from Mexico is to bring them all here. Is it something in the water in D.C.? Whenever these Republicans need our votes, they're bellicose supporters of the people against the powerful on illegal immigration. Then they get elected and dedicate themselves to helping powerful business interests import millions of low-wage immigrant laborers.

Amnesty is so hated by Americans that even the Democrats are constantly being caught flat-footed on the issue. At a Democratic presidential debate in October 2007, Hillary Clinton took both sides of New York governor Elliot Spitzer's plan to give illegal aliens driver's licenses. First, Hillary said she supported the idea, but within two minutes said she opposed it. In response to a direct question, she refused to clarify her position on driver's licenses for illegal aliens.

The next day, Hillary issued a press release endorsing Spitzer's proposal. Elected Democrats throughout the state began denouncing the plan. Polls showed that 70 percent of New Yorkers opposed it. Even the *New York Times* would call driver's licenses for illegals "Mr. Spitzer's single most unpopular decision since he took office." (This was before the hookers.) Two weeks later, Hillary announced she was against it.

Guess who had that great idea first? Governor Jeb Bush of Florida! Bush ferociously pressed the legislature to approve driver's licenses for illegal aliens—four years AFTER the 9/11 terrorist attack, in which all four pilots had used Florida drivers licenses to board the planes. Fortunately, the state legislature ignored him. (And Jeb's supposed to be the smart one.)

So we return to an immigration system under which it is impossible for a French, German, or English person to immigrate here, but illegal aliens demand legal status so they can bring all twelve of their siblings to America, rather than just the seven already here.

America Nears El Tipping Pointo
December 5, 2012

I apologize to America's young people, whose dashed dreams and dim employment prospects I had laughed at, believing these to be a direct result of their voting for Obama. On closer examination, it turns out that young voters, aged 18–29, overwhelmingly supported Romney. But only the white ones.

According to Pew Research, 54 percent of white voters under thirty voted for Romney and only 41 percent for Obama. That's the same percentage Reagan got from the entire white population in 1980. Even the Lena Dunham demographic—white women under thirty—favored Romney.

Reagan got just 43 percent of young voters in 1980—and that was when whites were 88 percent of the electorate. Only 58 percent of today's under-thirty vote is white, and it's shrinking daily. What the youth vote shows is not that young people are nitwits who deserve lives of misery and joblessness, as I had previously believed, but that America is hitting the tipping point on our immigration policy.

The youth vote is a snapshot of elections to come if nothing is done to reverse the deluge of unskilled immigrants pouring into the country as a result of Ted Kennedy's 1965 Immigration Act. Eighty-five percent of legal immigrants since 1968 have come from the Third World. A majority of them are in need of government assistance.

Whites are 76 percent of the electorate over the age of thirty and only 58 percent of the electorate under thirty. Obama won the "youth vote" because it is the knife's edge of a demographic shift, not because he offered the kids free contraception (which they don't need, anyway, because it's hard to have sex when you're living with your parents at twenty-seven).

In 1980, Hispanics were only 2 percent of the population, and they tended to be educated, skilled workers who got married, raised their children in two-parent families, and sent their kids to college before they, too, got married and had kids. (In that order.)

That profile has nothing to do with recent Hispanic immigrants, who—because of phony "family reunification" rules—are the poorest of the world's poor. More than half of all babies born to Hispanic women today are illegitimate. As Heather Mac Donald has shown, the birthrate of Hispanic women is twice that of the rest of the population. Their unwed birthrate is one and a half times that of blacks.

That's a lot of government dependents coming down the pike. No amount of "reaching out" to the Hispanic community, effective "messaging," or Reagan's "optimism" is going to turn Mexico's underclass into Republicans. Any election analysis that doesn't deal with the implacable fact of America's changing demographics is bound to be wrong.

Perhaps the reason elections maven Michael Barone was so shockingly off in his election prediction this year was that, in the biggest mistake of his career, Barone has been assuring us for years that most of these Third World immigrants pouring into the country would go the way of Italian immigrants and become Republicans. They're hardworking! They have family values!

Maybe at first, but not after coming here, having illegitimate children, and going on welfare.

Charles Murray recently pointed out that—contrary to stereotype—Hispanics are less likely to be married, less likely to go to church, more supportive of gay marriage, and less likely to call themselves "conservative" than other Americans. Rather than being more hardworking than Americans, Hispanics actually work about the same as others or, in the case of Hispanic women, less.

It seems otherwise, Murray says, because the only Hispanics we see are the ones who are working—in our homes, neighborhoods, and businesses. "That's the way that almost all Anglos in the political chattering class come in contact with Latinos," he notes. "Of course they look like model Americans." (Black males would apparently like to work more. Nearly 20 percent of black males under thirty voted for Romney, more than three times what McCain got.)

An article by Nate Cohn in the current *New Republic* argues, as the title puts it: "The GOP Has Problems with White Voters, Too." As proof, Cohn cites Jefferson County, Colorado; Loudoun County, Virginia; Wake County, North Carolina; and Somerset County, New Jersey, all of which went Republican in presidential elections from 1968 through 2004, but which Romney lost in 2012.

Smelling a rat, I checked the demographic shifts in these counties from the 2000 to the 2010 census. In each one, there has been a noticeable influx of Hispanics (and Asians, who also vote Democrat), diminishing "the white vote" that Cohn claims Republicans are losing. Between the 2000 and 2010 census, for example, the white population of Jefferson County declined from more than 90 percent to the high seventies, while the Hispanic population more than doubled, from 6 percent to 14 percent.

In Loudoun County, whites plummeted from 83 percent to 69 percent of the population. Meanwhile, the Asian population tripled from

5 percent to 15 percent, and the Hispanic population doubled from 6 percent to 12 percent. Similarly, Wake County shifted from 74 percent white to 66 percent white in the past decade, while the Hispanic population doubled, from 5 percent to 10 percent, and the black population stayed even at about 20 percent. Somerset County is now just 62 percent white, while the Hispanic population grew by 63 percent and the Asian population grew by 83 percent since 2000.

These were the counties chosen by Cohn, not me, to show that Republicans are losing "the white vote." Except they're not so white anymore. With blacks, Asians, and Hispanics block-voting 93 percent, 73 percent, and 71 percent for Obama, Republicans have to do more than just win a majority of the white vote. They have to run the table.

Romney got a larger percentage of the white vote than Reagan did in 1980. That's just not enough anymore.

Ironically, Romney was the first Republican presidential candidate in a long time not conspiring with the elites to make America a dumping ground for the world's welfare cases. Conservatives who denounced Romney as a "RINO" were the ones doing the bidding of the real establishment: the soulless rich, who want cheap labor and couldn't care less if America ceases to be the land of opportunity that everyone wanted to immigrate to in the first place.

If Rubio's Amnesty Is So Great, Why Is He Lying?
April 17, 2013

hen Republicans start lying like Democrats, you can guess they are pushing an idea that's bad for America. During his William Ginsburg–like tour of the Sunday talk shows last weekend,

Senator Marco Rubio was the Mount Vesuvius of lies about his immigration bill.

Here is how Rubio explained the powerful border-enforcing mechanism in his bill on *Fox News Sunday*, which he denied was merely a "goal": "Basically, Homeland Security will have five years to meet that goal. If after five years, Homeland Security has not met that number, it will trigger the Border Commission, who will then take over this issue for them."

So the water torture awaiting the Department of Homeland Security if it fails to secure the border is ... *ANOTHER GOVERNMENT COMMISSION WILL BE CREATED! Take that, Homeland Security! Ha—we have you now!* The only thing more frightening than "another government commission" is a "strongly worded letter to the *New York Times*."

Rubio said his comprehensive immigration plan isn't amnesty because "amnesty is anything that says 'do it illegally, it will be cheaper and easier.'" But, he assures us, it's "cheaper, faster and easier for people to go back home and wait ten years"—as the law currently requires— "than it will be to go through this process that I've outlined."

Then why is he doing it? If it's "cheaper, faster and easier" for illegals to apply for citizenship under current law, what exactly does Rubio's plan accomplish? Is it to encourage illegals to go home and apply through normal channels? You know, since that's so much easier.

Why not just enforce the law on the books now? He dismisses enforcement of current law as trying to make "life miserable to them so that they'll self-deport," which he claims won't work. Does his plan make them just a little bit miserable so maybe some of them will "self-deport"? (Which doesn't work, according to him.) Or is he lying about it being "cheaper, faster and easier for people to go back home"?

Rubio keeps trotting out the canard about the bounty of taxes we're going to collect from millions more minimum-wage workers when illegals are legalized, stoutly asserting, "In order to keep this legal status, you must be gainfully employed and you must be paying taxes."

It's as if he's talking to someone who has never been to America and is unfamiliar with its tax system. By "paying taxes," Rubio means "filing a tax return and getting a payment back from the government in the form of the earned income tax credit." Another term for what Rubio calls "paying taxes" is "receiving welfare"—which newly legalized illegals will start receiving right away under Rubio's plan. The only tax they'll pay is the same tax they pay now: sales tax.

But, incomprehensibly, Rubio swore up and down that the newly legalized illegal immigrants won't get government benefits: "And then they don't qualify for any federal benefits. This is an important point. No federal benefits, no food stamps, no welfare, no Obamacare."

How on Earth does Rubio plan to enforce this "important point"?

Just three weeks ago, the U.S. Senate voted down a proposal to prevent illegal immigrants from receiving benefits under Obamacare. At the time, Democratic Senator Bob Menendez sneered at Republicans opposing Obamacare for illegals, saying, "This is not a great way to try to do your outreach to the Hispanic and immigrant community."

Forcing Republicans to spend the next two decades arguing that poor Hispanic children shouldn't have access to government benefits like healthcare and food programs sounds like a terrific way to win over the Hispanic vote! Good thinking, Republicans. Is it going to be easier or harder for Republicans to deny welfare to 20 million newly legalized illegal aliens than it is for them to simply say that people who have broken our laws should not be legalized in the first place?

Also, is Rubio planning to stop his newly legalized illegal aliens from having children? The children of illegal aliens become automatic citizens under our current insane interpretation of the Fourteenth Amendment. (It seems that, after the Civil War, what the framers of the Fourteenth

Amendment had at the top of their agenda was not invalidating the *Dred Scott* decision and confirming the citizenship of former slaves, but ensuring that, a century hence, the children of any foreigners who manage to sneak into the country illegally and give birth would become full-fledged U.S. citizens.)

As I've noted before, Hispanic women have a higher illegitimate birthrate than any other ethnic group in the country, including blacks. Currently, 71 percent of illegal immigrant households with children collect federal benefits. In California—which will be America if Rubio's plan goes through—82 percent of households headed by an illegal immigrant are on welfare, as are 61 percent of households headed by legal immigrants, according to the March 2011 Current Population Survey by the Center for Immigration Studies.

If you think Republicans are Hispandering now, wait until the children of 20 million illegal aliens start to vote. Rubio's amnesty isn't just bad for America, it's the end of America.

If the GOP Is This Stupid, It Deserves to Die
June 12, 2013

D emocrats terrify Hispanics into thinking they'll be lynched if they vote for Republicans, and then turn around and taunt Republicans for not winning a majority of the Hispanic vote.

This line of attack has real resonance with our stupidest Republicans. (Proposed Republican primary targets: Senators Kelly Ayotte, Jeff Flake, Lindsey Graham, and Marco Rubio.) Which explains why Republicans are devoting all their energy to slightly increasing their share of the Hispanic vote while alienating everyone else in America.

It must be fun for liberals to manipulate Republicans into focusing on hopeless causes. Why don't Democrats waste their time trying to win the votes of gun owners?

As journalist Steve Sailer recently pointed out, the Hispanic vote terrifying Republicans isn't that big. It actually declined in 2012. The Census Bureau finally released the real voter turnout numbers from the last election, and the Hispanic vote came in at only 8.4 percent of the electorate, not the 10 percent claimed by the pro-amnesty crowd. The sleeping giant of the last election wasn't Hispanics; it was elderly black women, terrified of media claims that Republicans were trying to suppress the black vote and determined to keep the first African-American president in the White House.

Contrary to everyone's expectations, 10 percent more blacks voted in 2012 compared to 2008, even beating white voters, the usual turnout champions. Eligible black voters turned out at rate of 66.2 percent, compared to 64.1 percent of eligible white voters. (Only 48 percent of all eligible Hispanic voters went to the polls.) No one saw the huge increase in black turnout coming, which is probably why Gallup had Romney up by five points before Hurricane Sandy hit and still up by one point in its last pre-election poll after the hurricane.

Only two groups voted in larger numbers in 2012 compared to 2008: blacks aged 45–64, and blacks over the age of 65—mostly elderly black women. In raw numbers, nearly twice as many blacks voted as Hispanics. Nine times as many whites voted as Hispanics. (Ninety-eight million whites, eighteen million blacks, and eleven million Hispanics.)

As Byron York has shown, even if Mitt Romney had won 70 percent of the Hispanic vote, he still would have lost. Keep in mind that no Republican presidential candidate in at least fifty years has won as much as half the Hispanic vote.

In the presidential election immediately after Reagan signed an amnesty bill in 1986, the Republican share of the Hispanic vote plummeted from

37 percent to 30 percent—and that was in a landslide election for the GOP. Combined, the two Bush presidents averaged 32.5 percent of the Hispanic vote—and they have Hispanics in their family Christmas cards. John McCain, the nation's leading amnesty proponent, won only 31 percent of the Hispanic vote, not much more than anti-amnesty Romney's 27 percent.

So, naturally, the Republican Party's entire battle plan going forward is to win slightly more votes from 8.4 percent of the electorate by giving them something they don't want.

The (pro-amnesty) Pew Research Hispanic Center has produced poll after poll showing that Hispanics don't care about amnesty. In a poll last fall, Hispanic voters said they cared more about education, jobs, and healthcare than immigration. They even care more about the federal budget deficit than immigration! (To put that in perspective, the next item on their list of concerns was "scratchy towels.")

Also, note that Pew asked about "immigration," not "amnesty." Those Hispanics who said they cared about immigration might care about it the way I care about it—by supporting a fence and E-Verify. Amnesty is a gift to employers, not employees.

Who convinced Republicans that Hispanics' wages aren't low enough and what they really need is an influx of low-wage workers competing for their jobs? Maybe the greedy businessmen now running the Republican Party should talk with their Hispanic maids sometime. Ask Juanita if she'd like to have seven new immigrants competing with her for the opportunity to clean other people's houses, so that her wages can be dropped from $20 an hour to $10 an hour.

A wise Latina, A. J. Delgado, recently explained on Mediaite.com why amnesty won't win Republicans the Hispanic vote—even if they get credit for it. Her very first argument was: "Latinos will resent the added competition for jobs."

But rich businessmen don't care. Big Republican donors—and their campaign consultants—just want to make money. They don't care about

Hispanics, and they certainly don't care what happens to the country. *If the country is hurt, I don't care, as long as I am doing better!* This is the very definition of treason.

Hispanic voters are a small portion of the electorate. They don't want amnesty, and they're hopeless Democrats. So Republicans have decided the path to victory is to flood the country with lots more of them!

It's as if Republicans convinced Democrats to fixate on banning birth control to win more pro-life voters. This would be great for Republicans because Democrats will never win a majority of pro-life voters, and about as many pro-lifers care about birth control as Hispanics care about amnesty.

But that still wouldn't be as idiotic as what Republicans are doing because, according to Gallup, pro-lifers are nearly half of the electorate. Hispanics are only 8.4 percent of the electorate. And it still wouldn't be as stupid as the GOP pushing amnesty because banning birth control wouldn't create millions more voters who consistently vote against the Democrats.

Listening to Republican National Committee Chairman Reince Priebus burble a few weeks ago on *Fox News Sunday* about how amnesty is going to push the Republicans to new electoral heights, one is reminded of Democratic pollster Pat Caddell's reason for refusing to become a Republican. No matter how enraged he gets at Democratic corruption, he says he can't bear to join such a stupid party as the GOP.

I Got Thirty Million Reasons
July 3, 2013

We keep hearing insistent claims that if Republicans don't pass amnesty *yesterday* it will be the end of the party.

Can I see the math on that? I can see why bringing in 30 million new Democratic voters would be good for the Democrats, but how does it help Republicans? Maybe conservatives shouldn't blindly trust the calculations of the guy who graduated fifth from the bottom of his class at the U.S. Naval Academy. (John McCain.)

If I were a Democrat, I would have tried to sneak this bill past Republicans by proposing amnesty only after reaching some easily rigged benchmarks. But, apparently, Chuck Schumer knows elected Republicans better than I do.

Step One: Everyone's amnestied.

Step Two: After they're amnestied, they can bring in all their relatives.

If Hispanics voted 50.1 percent for Democrats, amnesty would be a bad deal for Republicans. But, in fact, they vote 70 percent to 80 percent for Democrats. How did it become an urgent priority for Republicans to bring in 30 million new voters, 80 percent of whom will vote Democratic?

Democrats want 30 million new voters and they will say anything to get there:

- *It's a crisis! Illegal immigrants are "living in the shadows"!*

That's not a "crisis." At most—and this is highly dubious—it's a crisis for the illegal immigrants. But evidently, "living in the shadows" is at least better than living in Guadalajara. Otherwise, there's an easy solution.

We're always told, "You don't know what it's like to live in the shadows!" Yes, you're right, and that proves it's not a crisis. Sorry to sound legalistic, illegal aliens, but you broke the law and—look me in the eye—you know you broke the law. You hid in the backs of trucks, traveled across remote desert locations, ran from U.S. agents, and stole American IDs.

It's *supposed* to be uncomfortable to break the law. We aren't required to grant amnesty to people just because they've put themselves in the awkward position of being here illegally. (Or because the Democrats need 30 million new voters.) If illegals were Republicans, Chuck Schumer would be a "Minuteman," patrolling the Mexican border 24/7.

- *Oh boy! Are Hispanics ever going to take revenge on Republicans!*

The obvious retort is: If these people vote 80 percent against Republicans, how does it hurt Republicans if they can't vote? Is the claim that next time legal Hispanics vote against you, they'll have an angry glint in their eye? Voting machines don't register angry glints.

- *How could any decent person be against granting amnesty to lawbreakers?*

In common parlance, "the decent thing to do" is usually defined as "following the law." The fact that Democrats want 30 million new voters is not a good enough reason to ignore the law and screw over the millions of people who have been waiting twenty years to come here legally.

- *We already have "de facto amnesty."*

I gather Marco Rubio considers this his big showstopper, since he says it in every interview as if he's announcing the Kochen-Specker theorem. But if we already have de facto amnesty, why is this bill even necessary? Oh, that's right! The Democrats need 30 million new voters.

It's curious that Democrats don't hysterically demand amnesty for other lawbreakers, such as tax-cheats or polluters. Right now—hold on to your hat, Marco!—we have "de facto amnesty" for tax-cheats and polluters! (Also rapists and murderers and every other crime that doesn't have 100 percent enforcement.) And if we won't grant amnesty to tax-cheats and polluters, what about their children? Why punish the children? They did nothing wrong. Their parents *told them* they had lots of money for houses, clothes, and college tuition. How can you put a tax lien on the homes of innocent children? Think of how BP executives' children have suffered—the divorces, the deferred dreams, the broken families...

And by the way, polluters are also hard workers. They love their families and want the best for them, too. I bet illegal aliens who rape women and kill people in drunk-driving accidents love their families. Members of MS-13 work very hard at gang activities, such as, for example, when you cross them, they are very dogged about having you killed in a drive-by shooting. That shows a real stick-to-itiveness. But weirdly, Democrats are obsessed with amnesty only for the lawbreakers that will get them 30 million new voters. (Violent felons come next.)

Republicans don't have to be brave to vote against amnesty. They need to not be idiots.

This isn't a single issue. It's every issue. Presidential elections are decided by a few million votes. Giving the Democrats 30 million new voters means Republicans lose on everything—Obamacare, taxes, public sector unions, big government, abortion, gay marriage, racial preferences, and on and on and on. In another few years, the whole country will be California and no Republican will win another national election.

Maybe New Jersey governor Chris Christie supports amnesty (as he did, via his appointed senator), hoping to be the last Republican ever elected president. There's one for the history books! But if Christie says he's pro-life while giving the Democrats 30 million new voters, he's a liar. Hispanics favor abortion by 66 percent, compared to 50 percent of other voters. If he says he opposes Obamacare, court-mandated gay marriage, wants small government, and loves his country while voting to give the Democrats 30 million new voters, he's a liar. Hispanics support Obamacare by 62 percent, gay marriage by 59 percent, and big government by 75 percent. If he says he opposes bloated, expensive public sector unions, he's a liar. Look no farther than California for our future.

Instead of the elites bringing in another flood of low-wage immigrants to clean their homes and manicure their lawns (and vote Democrat!), how about we start getting some immigrants to compete with Florida senators and New Jersey governors?

CHAPTER ELEVEN

Guns and Crime:
Guns Do Kill People, Thank God

very liberal argument about crime employs the same trick. Liberals
will cite a statistic designed to create a specific image in your head,
when the reality is something entirely different. For example, they'll
say: *A gun in the home is X times more likely to kill you than to kill an
intruder.* (Also confidence-inspiring: the exact number is constantly
changing.) You're supposed to imagine some bumbling homeowner,
who thinks he's a hotshot with a gun, having it snatched away from him
by a criminal.

That never happens. Or, to be precise, criminals wrest firearms from
their owners in less than 1 percent of all defensive gun uses, according
to criminologist Gary Kleck. The principal way guns in the home kill
the owner is by suicide. But there is no evidence that the presence of a
gun increases the likelihood of suicide. More importantly, suicide is not

what we were picturing when liberals told us guns are more likely to be used to kill their owners than an intruder.

And then you also notice—why does the intruder have to be killed? Couldn't you just wing him? Couldn't you hold him at gunpoint until the police arrive? He might see the error of his ways, clean up, and go to Harvard Law School! By requiring that the attacker be killed, liberals have excluded 99 percent of cases where a gun is used to stop a criminal.

Similarly, liberals say murderers are X times more likely to get the death penalty when their victims are white than when the victim is black. Hearing that, most people imagine white racists across the land not caring when black people are murdered. The truth is nearly the opposite: That statistic merely reflects the fact that whites are *more* likely to get the death penalty than blacks. (A 2004 study by Cornell law professors John Blume, Theodore Eisenberg, and Martin T. Wells found that, from 1976 to 1998, blacks committed 51.5 percent of all murders in the U.S. but were only 41.3 percent of those sentenced to death from 1977 to 1999.)

The majority of black murder victims are killed by other blacks and most white murder victims are killed by whites. So looking at the race of the victims is just another way of looking at the race of the murderer. Death sentences are more likely when the victim is white only because their murderers are usually white—and whites are more likely to receive capital sentences.

One of the main reasons black murderers are less likely to get the death penalty than white murderers is that black-on-black killings tend to occur in places with large black populations. Black juries, it turns out, are far less likely than whites to vote for the death penalty. But the fact that blacks resist imposing capital sentences on other blacks is not the image created by the statement that the death penalty is more likely to be imposed when the victim is white.

Another good one is the claim that "more than three women are murdered by their husbands or intimate partners in this country every day." The important phrase in that sentence is: *intimate partners*. Always look for *intimate partners* in the domestic abuse statistics. It's like saying "Eighty-nine people are killed every day by puppies or cars." Can we separate out the puppies?

There's a cottage industry in putting out statistics that combine things that are not at all alike: *Every eleven seconds a woman in this country is raped, murdered, beaten, made fun of, not appreciated for her work, or told to talk more quietly.*

In 2010—a high-water mark for connubial murder, two women per thousand were killed by actual live-in husbands, according to Department of Justice, Bureau of Justice Statistics. Another 59.6 were killed by husbands from whom they were separated. Eight were killed by their boyfriends or lovers. Six and a half per thousand were killed by ex-husbands. And that year was unusually low for "partner" murders. In 2000, more than 116 women were killed by "intimate partners" whom they were not married to and living with. Less than two per thousand were killed by their live-in husbands.

Liberal crime statistics are like those "Spot the Difference" puzzles, where you examine two pictures to find some minor discrepancy, like a missing hair ribbon. You have to really scrutinize their statements to notice the sleight of hand involved.

One bogus study that made the rounds after the Newtown, Connecticut, shooting claimed that not a single public shooting in the last thirty years had been stopped by a civilian using a gun. Then you find out the reputable economists at *Mother Jones* magazine had that conclusion baked in the cake. Their study included only public shootings where at least four people were killed—in other words, cases in which the shooter was *not* stopped. It's like saying: *in order to prove that water does not prevent dehydration, we looked at every case in the last thirty years where someone died of thirst. In not one of those cases was water used to prevent dehydration.* Try drinking water next time.

By now, anyone who wants the truth knows that economist John Lott's studies prove beyond cavil that the only public policy to reduce casualties from public shootings are concealed-carry laws. With the cat out of the bag on that one, the Left's only retort is to neurotically refer to Lott as "discredited." In liberal lingo, "discredited" means, "Ignore this study; it didn't come out well for us."

Sometimes, word games won't do the trick and liberals are forced to lie outright. This was their approach with Troy Davis, a blindingly guilty cop-killer finally executed in 2011. As Davis's execution date approached, MSNBC and CNN provided urgent, around-the-clock coverage, confidently asserting that Davis was absolutely innocent. Seven of nine witnesses against him had recanted their testimony! Or so they claimed.

Now, two years later, after everyone has forgotten the details, Aaron Sorkin gets worked up about the case and writes a 2013 *Newsroom* episode repeating all the lies about the case. He deliberately used real names and real events to create this notion in people's minds: *Wow! Seven out of nine witnesses recanted! Troy Davis was innocent!* As set forth in the column below, there weren't nine witnesses against Davis, there were thirty-four.

And this will give you an idea of what liberals meant by "recanted." One such recantation was from Harriet Murray, the girlfriend of the homeless man, Larry Young, whom Davis was pistol-whipping when Officer MacPhail ordered him to stop, provoking Davis to murder MacPhail in a Burger King parking lot full of witnesses. Ms. Murray was sitting outside the restaurant, watching the whole melee. At trial she identified Davis as the man in the white shirt—numerous witnesses testified that the officer's murderer was wearing a white shirt—who pistol-whipped her boyfriend and then pumped bullets into Officer MacPhail.

In her "recantation," Ms. Murray recanted none of that. In fact, she repeated it. But the defense lawyer who drafted her affidavit slipped in the additional fact that the man who pistol-whipped her boyfriend and shot the police officer was "arguing with Larry." Other trial testimony indicated that the shooter had not argued with the homeless man before striking him. But as the court noted, this was such a minor variation from her original testimony, she may not have even realized it was different from what she had said at trial many years earlier. Nothing in the affidavit stated that she was recanting any of her testimony or that she had lied. She did not consider the affidavit important enough even to give Davis's lawyer time to notarize it. The affidavit was another "Spot the Difference" game, this time, intended to fool a witness.

That's not a recantation, it's a sneaky trick.

NY Times: Fraught Nexus of Lies, Stupidity, and Bigotry
June 22, 2011

Perhaps instead of taking potshots at me in its *Book Review* section, the *New York Times* could consider reviewing one of my eight massive *New York Times* bestsellers. With only one review several years ago and not in the book review section, the editors can rest assured that I know they don't like me.

Reviewing a book about the 1989 rape of the Central Park jogger last week, the reviewer sniped that "coarser pundits like Ann Coulter continue to exploit the case whenever possible."

The chapter on the Central Park rape in my most recent, smash *New York Times* bestseller, *Demonic: How the Liberal Mob Is Endangering America*, evidently "exploits" the case by citing facts. Based on those facts, I argue that the real trials reached more believable verdicts than the show trial held by the Left thirteen years later.

On April 19, 1989, a twenty-eight-year-old investment banker went for a run through Central Park, whereupon she was attacked by a violent mob, savagely beaten, raped, and left for dead. By the time the police found her at 1:30 a.m. that night, she had lost three-fourths of her blood, and the police couldn't tell if she was male or female. The homicide unit of the Manhattan DA's office initially took the case because not one of her doctors believed she would be alive in the morning.

Confessions were obtained in accordance with law, with the defendants' parents present at all police interrogations. All but one of the confessions was videotaped. After a six-week hearing solely on the admissibility of the confessions, a judge ruled them lawful.

At the trials, evidence was ruled on by the judge and tested in court. Witnesses were presented for both sides and subjected to cross-examination.

One witness, for example, an acquaintance of one of the defendants, testified that when she talked to him in jail after the arrests, he told her that he hadn't raped the jogger, he "only held her legs down while (another defendant) f—ked her." (That's enough for a rape conviction.)

In the opposite of a "rush to judgment," two multi-ethnic juries deliberated for ten days and eleven days, respectively, before unanimously finding the defendants guilty of most crimes charged—though innocent of others. The convictions were later upheld on appeal.

The only way liberals could get those convictions overturned was to change venues from a courtroom to a newsroom. So that's what they did.

The convictions were vacated based not on a new trial or on new evidence, but solely on the "confession" of Matias Reyes.

Coincidentally, this serial rapist and murderer had nothing to lose by confessing to the rape—and much to gain by claiming that he had acted alone, including a highly desirable prison transfer.

As with the tribunals during the French Revolution, the show trials were based on a lie, to wit, that Reyes's confession constituted "new evidence" that might have led to a different verdict at trial.

In fact, Reyes's admission that he had raped the jogger changed nothing about the evidence presented in the actual trials. It was always known that none of the defendants' DNA—a primitive science back in 1989—was found on the jogger. It was always known that others had participated in the attack on the jogger.

This is why prosecutor Elizabeth Lederer said in her summation to the jury: "Others who were not caught raped her and got away." The only new information Reyes provided was that he was one of those who "got away."

But thirteen years later, the show trial was relitigated in the backrooms of law offices and newsrooms by a remarkably undiverse group of Irish and Jewish, college-educated New Yorkers. They lied about the evidence in order to destroy trust in the judicial system, a favorite pastime of the Left.

Liberals despise the rule of law because it interferes with their ability to rule by mob. They portray themselves as the weak taking on the powerful, but it is the least powerful who suffer the most once the rule of law is gone. (Dominique Strauss-Kahn has now discovered that the most defenseless, penniless immigrant has the same legal rights as he, in an American court.)

Liberals' relentless attack on the judicial system is yet another example of their Jacobin lunacy in opposition to calm order. You will note that they never ask: Who did what in this case? All they want to know is which class of people are on trial. Social justice is the only justice that interests the Left because it's the only justice that can be delivered by the political agitation of a mob.

Thus, the book about the Central Park rape warmly reviewed in the *Times* was described as raising the "fraught nexus of race, class and gender." It was said to take a "tour through America's violently racist past and present."

What on Earth does any of that have to do with the evidence in this particular case?

Another way of determining the guilt or innocence of the convicted rapists would be to look at the facts of the case—the confessions, the corroborating evidence, the state of DNA testing in 1989, the jury verdicts, and Reyes's advantageously timed confession thirteen years later.

But looking at actual facts in a criminal trial, as I did, apparently constitutes a coarse exploitation of the case.

I suppose a writer who recounts truthful facts about the Holocaust "coarsely exploits" that crime, too. Rather than reciting gruesome facts about the Holocaust, I gather the *Times* would prefer a book that examines the general characteristics of Jews and Germans from 1850 to 1933—a study of the "fraught nexus" of race, religion, and nationality—before deciding whether the Jews deserved it.

Cop-Killer Is Media's Latest Baby Seal
September 21, 2011

For decades, liberals tried persuading Americans to abolish the death penalty, using their usual argument: hysterical sobbing. Only when the media began lying about innocent people being executed did support for the death penalty begin to waver, falling from 80 percent to about 60 percent in a little more than a decade. (Silver lining: that's still more Americans than believe in man-made global warming.)

Fifty-nine percent of Americans now believe that an innocent man has been executed in the last five years. There is more credible evidence that space aliens have walked among us than that an innocent person has been executed in this country in the past sixty years, much less the past five. But unless members of the public are going to personally review trial transcripts in every death penalty case, they have no way of knowing the truth. The media certainly won't tell them.

It's nearly impossible to receive a death sentence these days—unless you do something completely crazy like shoot a cop in full view of dozens of witnesses in a Burger King parking lot, only a few hours after shooting at a passing car while exiting a party.

That's what Troy Davis did in August 1989. Davis is the media's current baby seal of death row. After a two-week trial with thirty-four witnesses for the state and six witnesses for the defense, the jury of seven blacks and five whites took less than two hours to convict Davis of Officer Mark MacPhail's murder, as well as various other crimes. Two days later, the jury sentenced Davis to death.

Now, a brisk twenty-two years after Davis murdered Officer MacPhail, his sentence will finally be administered this week—barring any more of the legal shenanigans that have kept taxpayers on the hook for Davis's room and board for the past two decades. (The average time spent on death row is fourteen years. Then liberals turn around and triumphantly claim the death penalty doesn't have a deterrent effect. As the kids say: duh.)

It has been claimed—in the *New York Times* and *Time* magazine, for example—that there was no "physical evidence" connecting Davis to the crimes that night. Davis pulled out a gun and shot two strangers in public. What "physical evidence" were they expecting? No houses were broken into, no cars stolen, no rapes or fistfights accompanied the shootings. Where exactly would you look for DNA? And to prove what?

I suppose it would be nice if the shell casings from both shootings that night matched. Oh wait—they did. That's "physical evidence."

It's true that the bulk of the evidence against Davis was eyewitness testimony. That tends to happen when you shoot someone in a busy

Burger King parking lot. Eyewitness testimony, like all evidence, has gotten a bad name recently. But the "eyewitness" testimony in this case did not consist simply of strangers trying to distinguish one tall black man from another. For one thing, several of the eyewitnesses knew Davis personally.

The eyewitness testimony established the following:

- Two tall, young black men were harassing a vagrant in the Burger King parking lot, one in a yellow shirt and the other in a white Batman shirt. The one in the white shirt used a brown revolver to pistol-whip the vagrant. When a cop yelled at them to stop, the man in the white shirt ran, then wheeled around and shot the cop, walked over to his body, and shot him again, smiling.

- Some eyewitnesses described the shooter as wearing a white shirt, some said it was a white shirt with writing, and some identified it specifically as a white Batman shirt. Not one witness said the man in the yellow shirt pistol-whipped the vagrant or shot the cop.

- Several of Davis's friends testified that he was the one in a white shirt. Several eyewitnesses, both acquaintances and strangers, specifically identified Davis as the one who shot Officer MacPhail.

Now the media claim that seven of the nine witnesses against Davis at trial have recanted. First of all, the state presented thirty-four witnesses against Davis—not nine—which should give you some idea of how punctilious the media are about their facts in death penalty cases.

Among the witnesses who did not recant a word of their testimony against Davis were three members of the Air Force, who saw the shooting from their van in the Burger King drive-in lane. The airman who saw events clearly enough to positively identify Davis as the shooter explained on cross-examination, "You don't forget someone that stands over and shoots someone."

Recanted testimony is the least believable evidence since it proves only that defense lawyers managed to pressure some witnesses to change their stories, conveniently after the trial has ended. Even criminal lobbyist Justice William Brennan ridiculed post-trial recantations.

Three recantations were from friends of Davis, making minor or completely unbelievable modifications to their trial testimony. For example, one said he was no longer *sure* he saw Davis shoot the cop, even though he was five feet away at the time. All his remaining testimony still implicated Davis. One alleged recantation, from the vagrant's girlfriend (since deceased), wasn't a recantation at all, but rather reiterated all relevant parts of her trial testimony, which included a direct identification of Davis as the shooter.

Only two of the seven alleged "recantations" (out of thirty-four witnesses) actually recanted anything of value—and those two affidavits were discounted by the court because Davis refused to allow the affiants to testify at the post-trial evidentiary hearing, even though one was seated right outside the courtroom, waiting to appear. The court specifically warned Davis that his refusal to call his only two genuinely recanting witnesses would make their affidavits worthless. But Davis still refused to call them—suggesting, as the court said, that their lawyer-drafted affidavits would not have held up under cross-examination.

With death penalty opponents so fixated on Davis's race—he's black—it ought to be noted that all the above witnesses are themselves African American. The first man Davis shot that night was African American. I notice that the people so anxious to return this sociopathic cop-killer to the street to prove how much they love black people aren't the black people who live in his neighborhood.

There's a reason more than a dozen courts have looked at Davis's case and refused to overturn his death sentence. He is as innocent as every other executed man since at least 1950, which is to say, guilty as hell.

If I Were a Liberal . . .
October 26, 2011

I f I were a liberal, I would have spent the last week in shock that a Democratic audience in Flint, Michigan, cheered Vice President Joe Biden's description of policemen being killed. That's how liberals reacted to a Republican audience's cheering for Rick Perry during this exchange at the NBC debate:

NBC's Brian Williams: "Your state has executed 234 death row inmates, more than any other governor in modern times." (Applause.) "Have you struggled to sleep at night with the idea that any one of those might have been innocent?"

Governor Perry: "No, sir, I've never struggled with that at all. In the state of Texas, if you come into our state and you kill one of our children, you kill a police officer, you're involved with another crime and you kill one of our citizens, you will face the ultimate justice in the state of Texas, and that is you will be executed." (Wild applause.)

The airwaves bristled with righteous liberal indignation for the next week.

- CNN's Jack Cafferty: "Highly inappropriate" and "bloodthirsty."
- MSNBC's Chris Matthews: Republicans "look hot and horny for executions."

- CBS's David Letterman: "What kind of a person says, 'You know what, for president I want a heartless gunner. I want a guy who can kill 250 people without blinking an eye....'"
- CBS's Nancy Giles: "Applause at the number of people executed in Texas?... How could they not challenge the applause and maybe suggest that their invited audience take a step back from the bloodlust?"

But there hasn't been a peep about Biden's audience whooping and applauding last week in Flint when he said that without Obama's jobs bill, police will be "outgunned and outmanned." (Wild applause!) I suppose liberals would claim they were applauding because they believe Obama's jobs bill will prevent these murders. Which reminds me: Republicans believe the death penalty prevents murders!

Which belief bears more relationship to reality? In a case I have previously mentioned, Kenneth McDuff was released from death row soon after the Supreme Court overturned the death penalty in 1972 and went on to murder more than a dozen people.

William Jordan and Anthony Prevatte were sentenced to death in 1974 for abducting a teacher, murdering him, and stealing his car. They came under suspicion when they were caught throwing the murder weapon from the stolen vehicle in a high-speed car chase with the cops and because they were in possession of the dead man's wallet, briefcase, and watch.

The Georgia Supreme Court overturned their capital sentences in an opinion by Robert H. Hall, appointed by Governor Jimmy Carter. Hall said that the death sentences had to be set aside on the idiotic grounds that the jurors had overheard the prosecutor say that the judge and state supreme court would have the opportunity to review a death sentence, which might have caused them to take their sentencing role less seriously. (If the facts had been the reverse, the court would have overturned the death sentences on the grounds that the jurors did not take their sentencing decision seriously enough, under the misapprehension that no judge or court would second-guess them. Heads: liberals win; tails: crime victims lose.)

Prevatte was later released from "life in prison" and proceeded to murder his girlfriend. Jordan escaped and has never been found. As president, Carter appointed Hall to a federal court.

Darryl Kemp was sentenced to death in California in 1960 for the rape and murder of Marjorie Hipperson and also convicted for raping two other women. But he sat on death row long enough—twelve years—for the death penalty to be declared unconstitutional. He was paroled five years later and, within four months, had raped and murdered Armida Wiltsey, a forty-year-old wife and mother.

Kemp spent the next quarter-century raping (and probably murdering) a string of women. In 2002, his DNA was matched to blood found on the fingernails of Wiltsey's dead body. Although Kemp was serving a "life sentence" for rape in a Texas prison, he was months away from being paroled when he was brought back to California for the murder of Wiltsey. His attorney argued that he was too old for the death penalty. He lost that argument, and in 2009, Kemp was again given a capital sentence. He now sits on death row, perhaps long enough for the death penalty to be declared unconstitutional again, so he can be released to commit more rapes and murders.

Dozens and dozens of prisoners released from death row have gone on to murder again. No one knows exactly how many, but it's a lot more than the number of innocent men who have been executed in America, which, at least since 1950, is zero.

What is liberals' evidence that there will be more rapes and murders if Obama's jobs bill doesn't pass? Biden claims that, without it, there won't be enough cops to interrupt a woman being raped in her own home—

which would be an amazing bit of police work/psychic talent, if it had ever happened. (That's why Americans like personal firearms, liberals.)

Obama's jobs bill tackles the problem of rape and murder by giving the states $30 billion…for public school teachers. Only $5 billion is even allotted to the police.

Did Flint, in fact, use any money from Obama's last trillion-dollar stimulus bill to hire more police? No, Flint blew its entire $2.2 million on buying two electric buses. Even if what Flint really needed was buses and not cops, for $2.2 million, the city could have bought seven brand-new diesel buses and had $100,000 left over for streetlights. The "green buses" are more likely to increase crime by forcing people to spend a lot more time waiting at bus stops for those two buses. It's going to be a long wait: the "green" buses were never delivered because the company went out of business—despite a $1.6 million loan from the American taxpayer.

But if I were a liberal, I wouldn't acknowledge these facts, or any facts. I would close my eyes, cover my ears, and pretend to believe that tax-payer-funded "green" projects and an ever-increasing supply of public school teachers were the only things that separated us from a criminal dystopia. And when Republican audiences cheered for the death penalty that wasn't available to stop McDuff, Jordan, Prevatte, and Kemp, I would smirk and call them "bloodthirsty."

The Biggest Scandal in U.S. History
June 27, 2012

Forget executive privilege, contempt of Congress, "fast and furious," how many documents the government has produced, and who said what to whom on which date. The Obama administration has almost certainly engaged in the most shockingly vile corruption scandal in the history of the country, not counting the results of Season Eight on *American Idol*.

Administration officials intentionally put guns into the hands of Mexican drug cartels, so that, when the guns taken from Mexican crime scenes turned out to be American guns, Democrats would have a reason to crack down on gun sellers in the United States.

Democrats will never stop trying to take our guns away. They see something more lethal than a salad shooter and wet themselves. But since their party was thrown out of Congress for the first time in nearly half a century as a result of passing the 1994 "assault weapons ban," even liberals knew they were going to need a really good argument to pass any limitation on guns ever again.

So it's curious that Democrats all started telling the same lie about guns as soon as Obama became president. In March 2009, Secretary of State Hillary Clinton announced to reporters on a trip to Mexico: "Since we know that the vast majority—90 percent—of that weaponry [used by Mexican drug cartels], comes from our country, we are going to try to stop it from getting there in the first place." As she sentimentally elaborated on Fox News's *On the Record with Greta Van Susteren*: "The guns sold in the United States, which are illegal in Mexico, get smuggled and shipped across our border and arm these terrible drug-dealing criminals so that they can outgun these poor police officers along the border and elsewhere in Mexico."

Suddenly that 90 percent statistic was everywhere. It was like the fake statistic about the number of women beaten by their husbands on Super Bowl Sunday. CBS's Bob Schieffer asked Obama on *Face the Nation*: "It's my understanding that 90 percent of the guns that they're getting down in Mexico are coming from the United States. We don't seem to be doing a very good job of cutting off the gun flow. Do you need any kind of legislative help on that front? Have you, for example, thought about asking Congress to reinstate the ban on assault weapons?" At a Senate hearing, Senator Dianne Feinstein, D-CA, said: "It is unacceptable to have 90 percent of the guns that are picked up in Mexico—and used to shoot judges, police officers and mayors…come from the United States."

And then, thanks to Fox News—the first network to report it—we found out the 90 percent figure was complete bunkum. It was a fabrication told by William Hoover of the Bureau of Alcohol, Tobacco, Firearms, and Explosives (BATF) and then spread like wildfire by Democrats and the media. Mexican law enforcement authorities send only a fraction of the guns they recover from criminals back to the U.S. for tracing. Which guns do they send? The guns that have U.S. serial numbers on them. It would be like asking a library to produce all their Mark Twain books and then concluding that 100 percent of the books in that library are by Mark Twain. (You begin to see why the Left hates Fox News so much.)

Obama slowly backed away from the preposterous 90 percent claim. His National Security Council spokesman explained to Fox News that by "recovered," they meant "guns traceable to the United States." So, in other words, Democrats were frantically citing the amazing fact that almost all guns traceable to the U.S. were…traceable to the U.S.! Attorney General Eric Holder told reporters that even if the percentage is inaccurate, the "vast majority" of guns seized in crimes in Mexico come from the United States. (And he should know—he was sending them there!)

This was absurd. Most of the guns used by drug cartels are automatic weapons—not to mention shoulder-fired rockets—that can't be sold to most Americans. They are acquired from places like Russia, China, and Guatemala.

It seems that, right about the time the "90 percent" lie was unraveling, the Obama administration decided to give Mexican criminals thousands of American guns. Apart from the fact that tracking thousands of guns into Mexico is not feasible or rational, the guns dumped on Mexican criminal cartels didn't have GPS tracing devices on them, anyway. There is no conceivable law enforcement objective to such a program.

This is what we know:

1. Liberals thought it would be a great argument for gun control if American guns were ending up in the hands of Mexican criminals;
2. They wanted that to be true so badly, Democrats lied about it;
3. After they were busted on their lie, the Obama administration began placing thousands of American guns in the hands of Mexican criminals.

We also know that hundreds of people were murdered with these U.S.-supplied guns, including at least one American, U.S. Border Patrol agent Brian Terry. (But let's look on the bright side. The BATF was originally going to ship warheads to Iran until realizing the explosions might disable the tracking devices.)

Contrary to more Democrat lies, there was no program to dump thousands of guns in Mexico under George W. Bush. The Bush administration did have a program that put GPS trackers on about one hundred guns in order to actually trace them. That operation was ended almost as soon as it began because of the lack of cooperation from Mexican officials. You may as well say Holder's program was "started" by the first cop who ever put tracer dye on any contraband.

No one has explained what putting twenty-five hundred untraceable guns in the hands of Mexican drug dealers was supposed to accomplish. But you know what it might have accomplished? It would make the Democrats' "90 percent" lie retroactively true—allowing them to push for the same gun restrictions they were planning when they first concocted that lie. A majority of guns recovered from Mexican criminals would, at last, be American guns! But only because Eric Holder had put them there.

Unfortunately for the Democrats, some brave whistleblower inside the government leaked details of this monstrous scheme. As soon as Congress and the public demanded answers, Holder clammed up. He just says "oops"—and accuses Republicans of racism.

Guns Don't Kill People, the Mentally Ill Do
January 16, 2013

Seung-Hui Cho, who committed the Virginia Tech massacre in 2007, had been diagnosed with severe anxiety disorder as a child and placed under treatment. Virginia Tech was prohibited from being told about Cho's mental health problems because of federal privacy laws.

At college, Cho engaged in behavior even more bizarre than the average college student. He stalked three women and, at one point, went totally silent, refusing to speak even to his roommates. He was involuntarily committed to a mental institution for one night and then unaccountably unleashed on the public, whereupon he proceeded to engage in the deadliest mass shooting by an individual in U.S. history.

The 2011 Tucson, Arizona, shopping mall shooter, Jared Loughner, was so obviously disturbed that if he'd stayed in Pima Community College long enough to make the yearbook, he would have been named "Most Likely to Commit Mass Murder."

After Loughner got a tattoo, the artist, Carl Grace, remarked, "That's a weird dude. That's a Columbine candidate."

One of Loughner's teachers, Ben McGahee, filed numerous complaints against him, hoping to have him removed from class. "When I turned my back to write on the board," McGahee said, "I would always turn back quickly—to see if he had a gun."

On her first day at school, student Lynda Sorensen emailed her friends about Loughner, "We do have one student in the class who was disruptive today, I'm not certain yet if he was on drugs (as one person surmised) or disturbed. He scares me a bit. The teacher tried to throw him out and he refused to go, so I talked to the teacher afterward. Hopefully he will be out of class very soon, and not come back with an automatic weapon."

The last of several emails Sorensen sent about Loughner said, "We have a mentally unstable person in the class that scares the living cr** out of me. He is one of those whose picture you see on the news, after he has come into class with an automatic weapon. Everyone interviewed would say, Yeah, he was in my math class and he was really weird."

That was the summer before Loughner killed six people at the Tucson shopping mall, including a Republican-appointed federal judge and a nine-year-old girl, and critically wounded Representative Gabrielle Giffords, among others.

Loughner had run-ins with the law, including one charge for possessing drug paraphernalia—a lethal combination with mental illness. He was eventually asked to leave college on mental health grounds, released on the public without warning.

Perhaps if Carl Grace, Ben McGahee, or Lynda Sorensen worked in the mental health field, six people wouldn't have had to die that January morning in Tucson. But committing Loughner to a mental institution in Arizona would have required a court order stating that he was a danger to himself and others.

Innumerable studies have found a correlation between severe mental illness and violent behavior. Thirty-one to 61 percent of all homicides committed by disturbed individuals occur during their first psychotic episode. That's why mass murderers often have no criminal record. There's no time to wait with the mentally ill.

James Holmes, the accused Aurora, Colorado, shooter, was under psychiatric care at the University of Colorado long before he shot up a movie theater. According to news reports and court filings, Holmes told his psychiatrist, Dr. Lynne Fenton, that he fantasized about killing "a lot of people," but she refused law enforcement's offer to place Holmes under confinement for seventy-two hours.

However, Fenton did drop Holmes as a patient after he made threats against another school psychiatrist. And after Holmes made threats against a professor, he was asked to leave campus. But he wasn't committed. People who knew he was deeply troubled just pushed him onto society to cause havoc elsewhere.

Little is known so far about Adam Lanza, the alleged Newtown, Connecticut, elementary school shooter, but anyone who could shoot a terrified child and say to himself, "That was fun—I think I'll do it nineteen more times!" is not all there.

It has been reported that Lanza's mother, his first victim, was trying to have him involuntarily committed to a mental institution, triggering his rage. If true—and the media seem remarkably uninterested in finding out if it is true—Mrs. Lanza would have had to undergo a long and grueling process, unlikely to succeed.

As the *New York Times*' Joe Nocera recently wrote, "Connecticut's laws are so restrictive in terms of the proof required to get someone committed that Adam Lanza's mother would probably not have been able to get him help even if she had tried."

Taking guns away from law-abiding citizens without mental illnesses will do nothing about the Chos, Loughners, Holmeses, or Lanzas. Such people have to be separated from civil society, for the public's sake as well as their own. But this is nearly impossible because the ACLU has decided that being psychotic is a civil right.

Consequently, whenever a psychopath with a million gigantic warning signs commits a shocking murder, the knee-jerk reaction is to place yet more controls on guns. By now, guns are the most heavily regulated product in America.

It hasn't worked.

Even if it could work—and it can't—there are still subway tracks, machetes, fists, and bombs. The most deadly massacre at a school in U.S. history was at an elementary school in Michigan in 1927. It was committed with a bomb, by a mentally disturbed man.

How about trying something new for a change?

Why Does Anyone Need . . . ?
February 27, 2013

Having failed to convince Americans that taking guns away from law-abiding citizens will reduce the murder rate, Democrats have turned to their usual prohibitionary argument: "Why does anyone *need* an assault weapon?" "Why does anyone *need* a thirty-round magazine?" "Why does anyone *need* a semiautomatic?"

Phony conservative Democrat Joe Manchin, who won his U.S. Senate seat in West Virginia with an ad showing him shooting a gun, said, "I don't know anyone [who] needs thirty rounds in a clip."

CNN's Don Lemon, who does not fit the usual profile of the avid hunter and outdoorsman, demanded, "Who needs an assault rifle to go hunting?"

Fantasist Dan Rather said, "There is no need to have these high-powered assault weapons."

And prissy Brit Piers Morgan thought he'd hit on a real showstopper with, "I don't know why anyone needs an assault rifle." (Of course, where he comes from, policemen carry wooden sticks.)

Since when do Americans have to give the government an explanation for why they "need" something? If that's the test, I can think of a whole list of things I don't think anyone needs.

I don't know why anyone needs to burn an American flag at a protest. The point could be made just as well verbally.

I don't know why anyone needs to read about the private lives of celebrities. Why can't we shut down the gossip rags?

I don't know why anyone needs to vote. One vote has never made a difference in any federal election.

I don't know why anyone needs to bicycle in a city. They can walk or take the bus.

I don't know why anyone needs to have anal sex at a bathhouse. I won't stop them, but I don't know why anyone needs to do that.

I don't know why anyone needs to go hiking in national parks, where they're constantly falling off cliffs, being buried in avalanches, and getting lost—all requiring enormously expensive, taxpayer-funded rescue missions.

I don't know why Karen Finley needs to smear herself with chocolate while reading poems about "love." But not only do Democrats allow that, they made us pay for it through the National Endowment for the Arts.

In fact, I don't know why anyone needs to do any of the things that offend lots of people, especially when I have to pay for it. I don't mind paying for national monuments and the ballet, but if "need" is a legitimate argument, there's no end to the activities that can be banned.

Democrats are willing to make gigantic exceptions to the "need" rule for things they happen to personally like. Their position is: "I don't know why anyone needs to hunt; on the other hand, I do see why your tax dollars should be used to subsidize abortion, bicycle lanes, and the ballet."

They'll say that no one died in my examples (except abortion) (and bicycling) (and bathhouses) (and national parks), but the victims of mass shootings weren't killed by gun owners. They were killed by crazy people. How about keeping guns out of the hands of crazy people?

Liberals won't let us do that. But they can't explain why anyone needs to live on sidewalk grates, harass pedestrians, and crap in his pants. Those are "rights," straight from the pen of James Madison, and please stop asking questions.

"I don't see why anyone needs …" is code for: "I don't do it, so let's ban it." The corollary is: "I enjoy this, so you have to subsidize it." That's the difference between a totalitarian and a normal person. Liberals are obsessed with controlling what other people do.

As Senator Dianne Feinstein said this week, so-called "assault weapons" are a "personal pleasure" and "mothers and women" have to decide whether this personal pleasure "is more important than the general welfare."

The "general welfare" is every tyrant's excuse, going back to Robespierre and the guillotine. Free people are not in the habit of providing reasons why they "need" something simply because the government wants to ban it. That's true of anything—but especially something the government is constitutionally prohibited from banning, like guns.

The question isn't whether we "need" guns. It's whether the government should have a monopoly on force.

In liberals' ideal world, no one will even know you don't have to wait twenty-two minutes for the police when someone breaks into your home to defend yourself. No one will know there are toilets that can get the job done on one flush, that food tastes better with salt, and that you can drive over 55 mph and get there faster.

But we're all required to subsidize their hobbies—recycling, abortion, the "arts," bicycling, illegal alien workers, etc. Liberals ought to think about acquiring a new hobby: leaving people alone.

The Left's Continuing War on Women
March 27, 2013

The *New York Times* caused a sensation with its kazillion-word March 17 article by Michael Luo on the failures of state courts to get guns out of the hands of men in domestic violence situations.

The main purpose of the article was to tweak America's oldest civil rights organization, the National Rifle Association, for opposing some of the more rash anti-gun proposals being considered by state legislatures, such as allowing courts to take away a person's firearms solely on the basis of a temporary restraining order.

It's a new position for liberals to oppose the rights of the accused. Usually the *Times* is demanding that even convicted criminals be given weekend furloughs, early release, vegan meals, and sex-change operations. Another recent *Times* article about communities trying to keep sex offenders out of their neighborhoods quoted a liberal saying, "It's counterproductive to public safety, because when you have nothing to lose, you are much more likely to commit a crime than when you are rebuilding your life." The rights of the criminal always trump the rights of law-abiding citizens.

But that was about convicted child molesters. This is about guns, so all new rules apply.

As is usually the case when liberals start proposing gun restrictions, they assume the new rules will only apply to men. But temporary restraining orders aren't particularly difficult to get. It doesn't occur to liberals that an abusive man could also get one against his wife, thus disarming his victim.

Rather than helping victims of domestic abuse, this—and other *Times* proposals on guns—only ensures that more women will get killed. A gun in the hand of an abused woman changes the power dynamic far more than keeping a gun out of the hands of her abuser, who generally could murder his wife with his bare hands. The vast majority of rapists, for example, don't even bother using a gun because—as renowned criminologist Gary Kleck notes—they typically have a "substantial power advantage over the victim."

As the *Times* eventually admits around paragraph four hundred: "In fairness, it was not always clear that such an order (taking guns from the accused wife abuser) would have prevented the deaths." No kidding. In one case the *Times* cites, Robert Wigg ripped a door off its hinges and heaved it at his wife, Deborah, after having thrown her to the floor by her hair.

Deborah Wigg moved out, got an order of protection, and filed for divorce. But doors were not an impediment to Robert Wigg. He showed up at her new house and, in short order, broke down the door and murdered her. He happened to have used a gun, but he might as well have used his fists. Or an illegal gun, had the court taken away his legal guns. Or another door.

As her husband was breaking in, Deborah called her parents and she called 911. Her neighbors called 911, too. But the police didn't arrive in time. Even her parents got to the house before the cops did, only to find their daughter dead. The protection order didn't help Deborah Wigg; the police couldn't help; her neighbors and parents couldn't help. Only if she'd had a gun and known how to use it—after carefully disregarding everything Joe Biden has said on the subject—might she have been able to save her own life.

Numerous studies, including one by the National Institute of Justice, show that crime victims who resist a criminal with a gun are less likely to be injured than those who do not resist at all or who resist without a gun. That's true even when the assailant is armed.

Liberals' advice to domestic abuse victims is: lie back and enjoy it. The *Times*' advice is: get a restraining order. The NRA's advice is: blow the dirtbag's head off. Apparently a lot of abused women prefer not to lie back and take it. Looking at data from Detroit, Houston, and Miami, researchers Margo Wilson and Martin Daly found that the vast majority of wives who killed their husbands were not even indicted, much less convicted, because it was found they were acting in self-defense.

But the *Times* doesn't want abused women to have a fighting chance. Instead, it keeps pushing gun-control policies that will do nothing except disarm the victims.

Don't Knox This "Serious Network"
April 3, 2013

Just days after the Turner Broadcasting System CEO claimed that CNN "is a serious news network," it aired a childish report on *Anderson Cooper 360* about convicted murderer Amanda Knox that appears to have been written by her parents. Next up: "The Charles Manson story, reported by Squeaky Fromme."

Amanda, you may recall, was charged, along with her Italian boyfriend and another acquaintance, of sexually assaulting and murdering her English roommate, Meredith Kercher, in Perugia, Italy, in 2007. Amanda and her boyfriend, Raffaele Sollecito, were convicted, the convictions reversed, and then the reversal reversed. Among the evidence for her guilt is the fact that the murder weapon was found—freshly bleached—in the apartment of Amanda's boyfriend with the murder victim's DNA on the blade and Amanda's DNA on the handle.

CNN's case for Knox's innocence consists primarily of making snarky remarks about the prosecutor. This is going to be a long series if CNN plans on vindicating Knox by sneering at all those who say she is guilty—judges, forensic scientists, police, the other man also convicted of the murder—as well as the man Amanda falsely accused of the murder.

As CNN explained, the prosecutor, Giuliano Mignini, was a total jerk for diligently investigating Meredith's murder, proving he had caved to media pressure. Then—his jerkiest move—he briefly believed Amanda's lies. Thus, according to CNN's Drew Griffin, "As the media circus grew, so did the pressure on police to solve the case. On the night of Nov. 5, the police interrogated Amanda all night and into the next morning."

Actually, Amanda didn't show up that night at the police station until nearly 11:00 p.m., so "all night" means "until a few hours after she arrived." She and Raffaele came voluntarily. When she told the cops she was present during Meredith's murder and she knew who the murderer was, yes, they did want to chat a bit longer.

CNN's Griffin: "It was during this session Amanda confessed she was at the house that night. Her boss, Patrick Lumumba, was there as well. At that point Amanda Knox officially ceased to be a witness. She became the suspect." Manifestly, Amanda did not become "THE suspect": Patrick Lumumba did—for the sole reason that Amanda accused him of committing the murder. Griffin skipped over that detail with the strange statement: "Her boss, Patrick Lumumba, was there as well."

No, he wasn't. But Amanda said he was.

Until that night, Amanda had been lying to the police, claiming she was at her boyfriend Raffaele's apartment all night the evening Meredith was murdered. It was only when Amanda found out Raffaele was no longer backing her alibi that she turned around and accused an innocent man of murdering Meredith.

For anyone other than Amanda's parents and CNN producers, Amanda's going to the police and falsely accusing another man of the murder would raise suspicions. Griffin tries to soften the blow, claiming: "Almost immediately after police say she confessed to her crime, Amanda Knox recants."

Except she didn't. The next morning, she wrote out her confession from the night before. (Her story that night couldn't be used by the police precisely because Amanda had not been a suspect, only a witness, just like Meredith's other friends and roommates voluntarily providing information to the police.) Far from "almost immediately" recanting, Amanda again falsely accused Lumumba, in writing this time, and did not retract her story for the next two weeks as Lumumba sat in jail, waiting for the evidence to prove him innocent.

Griffin: "She tells her parents she broke under stress. In court, she would tell jurors how a police officer struck her from behind, how she was denied water, food, a translator, and how she says under pressure by police she was asked repeatedly to dream up, imagine scenarios for how it could have happened."

No. 1: The police had absolutely no reason to pressure Amanda into fingering Lumumba, who never would have been a suspect without Amanda accusing him. He had no connection to Meredith, other than employing her roommate, Amanda.

No. 2: Is CNN aware that there have already been lengthy proceedings in this case? Had they checked the record, they would have discovered that Amanda dropped her claim in court about the police hitting her, her lawyers never filed a complaint about it, and Amanda is currently being sued for slander by the police for having made the allegation. (Maybe it was Lumumba who hit her!)

Next, Griffin goes into full sneer-mode at the idiocy of police for believing Amanda.

Griffin: "That's not all that wouldn't make sense because it turns out virtually everything Amanda Knox told her interrogators the night of her so-called confession was a lie. Amanda Knox in this statement told police she was in the house the night of the murder and saw her boss, nightclub owner Patrick Lumumba, and Meredith Kercher go into Meredith's room, and she heard screams…. Police apparently didn't bother to check the facts about Lumumba."

The dolts! But wait—what on earth is CNN talking about? The police promptly investigated Lumumba's alibi—which, unlike Amanda's, held up—and tested the DNA. They released him the day after the DNA evidence came in, clearing him—but implicating another of Amanda's acquaintances, Rudy Guede. On balance, isn't CNN's heroine Amanda a little more to blame for the police suspecting Lumumba than the police are? Lumumba certainly thinks so. In court, Lumumba's lawyer called Amanda "Lucifer-like, demonic, satanic, diabolic," pursuing "borderline extreme behavior," and "devoted to lust, drugs and alcohol."

Guede, by the way, was later convicted, whereupon he said both Amanda and her boyfriend were involved in Meredith's murder. But as Alan Dershowitz has said, the American media just adore Amanda—at best, a liar and terrible person, at worst, a murderer—because she's pretty.

That's how a "serious news network" operates.

CHAPTER TWELVE

Courts:
The Third Branch of Liberalism

As an aperitif to the other judges discussed in this chapter, let's return to the honorable Frederica A. Massiah-Jackson of the Philadelphia Common Pleas Court. Whenever a judicial nomination comes up, please turn to this page of the book to remind yourself what Democrats consider a solid judicial nominee.

Bill Clinton nominated Massiah-Jackson to be a federal district court judge in 1997. Then-Philadelphia mayor and now frequent MSNBC guest Edward G. Rendell supported her nomination. The Philadelphia Bar Association commended her "judicial temperament." When Massiah-Jackson was forced to withdraw her nomination, the *New York Times* accused Senate Republicans of committing a "judicial mugging." (A glance at my *New York Times* to English dictionary reveals that "judicial mugging" means "routine questioning.") Massiah-Jackson, the *Times* said, "now returns to the state bench, battered but with her honor intact. Unfortunately, the same cannot be said of the Senate."

Why were Republicans so beastly to this stellar nominee? Here are a few details the *Times* didn't mention. As a judge on the Common Pleas Court, Massiah-Jackson was known for shouting obscenities from the bench and identifying undercover cops in open court. Among other notable rulings, Judge Massiah-Jackson sentenced the brutal rapist of a ten-year-old girl to the statutory minimum and then apologized to the rapist, saying, "I just don't think the five to ten years is appropriate in this case even assuming you were found guilty." She refused to allow the district attorney to present a victim impact statement, saying, "What would be the point of that?" After his release, the defendant was re-arrested for raping a nine-year-old boy.

In another case, after being informed that both the defendant and victim in a rape case had AIDS, Massiah-Jackson said: "Why are we having a trial? We are talking about life expectancy of three years for both of them. What's the difference?" In the end, Massiah-Jackson sentenced the rapist to one-year probation, giving him no prison time for a vicious rape and beating. She'd be sitting on the federal bench now, if Republicans had not swept Congress in the 1994 elections.

Fool Me Eight Times, Shame on Me
July 27, 2005

- "He's a scholarly man; he has a good education; he has been recommended by legal authorities; he has a good record in lower courts."

    —President Bush

- "This decision had the advantage of being acceptable to conservatives, plus Democrats won't be able to attack him. There is nothing to grab a hold of, to whack him on."
  —an administration official

- "Virtually every conservative who knows him trusts him and thinks he's a competent guy...."
  —Newt Gingrich

- "[He] has voiced opposition to many forms of abortion. He dislikes affirmative-action programs, contending that they amount to reverse discrimination. Also, he has vigorously defended...the Lord's Prayer in its public schools."
  —*Los Angeles Times*

- "He is a remarkable intellect and he's had great experience and he's had wide knowledge, and you all would enjoy an evening or more with him."
  —C. Boyden Gray

- "This guy is a complete S.O.B. of a conservative and you can't prove it."
  —P. J. O'Rourke

- "When you look at the man's record, his experience, his integrity and his ability to deal with tough questions of law in a way that the courts should, in a restrained way, not to attempt to legislate from the bench, I think he's a man in tune with the times."
  —Dick Thornburgh

- "His view is: 'Here's what it says state government can do—and if it doesn't say it can do it, then it can't do it.'"

  —lawyer who argued cases before the nominee

- "He is a 'stealth nominee.'…The right's not yelling; the left is trying to yell but can't find much to yell about."

  —Bob Beckel

- "This is a home run."

  —President Bush's chief of staff

He is David Hackett Souter, only the most recent reason Republican presidents—especially Republican presidents named "Bush"—have lost the right to say "Trust me" when it comes to Supreme Court nominations. The other reasons are: Earl Warren, William Brennan, Harry Blackmun, John Paul Stevens, Sandra Day O'Connor, and Anthony Kennedy.

Like John Roberts, Souter attended church regularly. Souter was also touted for his great intellect. He went to Harvard! And Harvard Law! (Since when does that impress right-wingers? So did Larry Tribe. It is one of the eternal mysteries of the world that liberals are good test-takers.)

At least when Souter was nominated, we needed a stealth nominee. The Senate was majority Democrat back then. The Judiciary Committee consisted of eight Democrats and six Republicans—two of whom were aggressively pro-abortion. A year later, faced with the same Democratic Senate, the current president's father nominated Clarence Thomas. Who would have thought the current Bush would be less macho than his father?

Roberts would have been a fine candidate for a Senate in Democratic hands. But now we have fifty-five Republican seats in the Senate—and Son of Read My Lips gives us another ideological blind date.

Fifty-five seats means every single Democrat in the Senate could vote against a Republican Supreme Court nominee—highly unlikely considering some of those Democrats are up for election next year— along with John McCain, Arlen Specter, Olympia Snowe, Susan Collins, and Lincoln Chafee. We would still win.

Of course it's possible that Roberts will buck all known human history when it comes to Supreme Court appointments—and be another Scalia or Thomas. (And we'll hear this news while attending a World Series game between the Cubs and, oh, say...the Detroit Tigers.) That will not retrospectively alter the fact that, right now, Bush and all the other Zarathustra Republicans cheering for Roberts haven't the first idea what kind of justice he will be. They are telling us their hopes and dreams.

I share their hopes and dreams! I also hope it doesn't rain in August. But I'm not throwing out all my umbrellas, and I won't be "proved wrong" in that decision even if the rain never comes. This much is a fact: right now, we don't know what kind of Justice Roberts will be. Republicans are desperately trying to convince themselves that Roberts will be different because they want to believe Bush wouldn't let us down on something so important. Somewhere in America, a woman is desperately trying to convince herself that her husband won't hit her again because he told her "things are going to be different this time." (And yes, that woman's name is Whitney Houston.)

Bush said "Trust me," and Republicans trust him. It shouldn't be difficult for conservatives to convince themselves that Roberts is our man. They've had practice convincing themselves of the same thing with Warren, Brennan, Blackmun, Stevens, O'Connor, Kennedy, and Souter.

This Is What "Advice and Consent" Means
October 5, 2005

I eagerly await the announcement of President Bush's real nominee to the Supreme Court. If the president meant Harriet Miers seriously, I have to assume Bush wants to go back to Crawford and let Dick Cheney run the country. Unfortunately for Bush, he could nominate his Scottish terrier Barney, and some conservatives would rush to defend him, claiming to be in possession of secret information convincing them that the pooch is a true conservative and listing Barney's many virtues—loyalty, courage, never jumps on the furniture…

Harriet Miers went to Southern Methodist University Dedman School of Law, which is not ranked at all by the serious law school reports and ranked No. 52 by *U.S. News & World Report*. Her greatest legal accomplishment is being the first woman commissioner of the Texas Lottery. I know conservatives have been trained to hate people who went to elite universities, and generally that's a good rule of thumb. But not when it comes to the Supreme Court.

First, Bush has no right to say "Trust me." He was elected to represent the American people, not to be dictator for eight years. Among the coalitions that elected Bush are people who have been laboring in the trenches for a quarter-century to change the legal order in America. While Bush was still boozing it up in the early '80s, Ed Meese, Antonin Scalia, Robert Bork, and all the founders of the Federalist Society began creating a farm team of massive legal talent on the Right. To casually spurn the people who have been taking slings and arrows all these years and instead reward the former commissioner of the Texas Lottery with a Supreme Court appointment is like pinning a medal of honor on some flunky paper-pusher with a desk job at the Pentagon—or on John Kerry—while ignoring your infantrymen doing the fighting and dying.

Second, even if you take seriously William F. Buckley's line about preferring to be governed by the first two hundred names in the Boston telephone book than by the Harvard faculty, the Supreme Court is not supposed to *govern* us. Being a Supreme Court justice ought to be a mind-numbingly tedious job suitable only for super-nerds trained in legal reasoning like John Roberts. Being on the Supreme Court isn't like winning a "Best Employee of the Month" award. It's a real job.

One website defending Bush's choice of a graduate from an undistinguished law school complains that Miers's critics "are playing the Democrats' game," claiming that the "GOP is not the party which idolizes Ivy League acceptability as the criterion of intellectual and mental fitness." (In the sort of error that results from trying to sound "Ivy League" rather than being clear, that sentence uses the grammatically incorrect "which" instead of "that." Websites defending the academically mediocre would be a lot more convincing without all the grammatical errors.) Actually, all the intellectual firepower in the law is coming from conservatives right now—and thanks for noticing! Liberals got stuck trying to explain *Roe v. Wade* and are still at work thirty years later trying to come up with a good argument.

But the main point is: au contraire! It is conservatives defending Miers's mediocre résumé who are playing the Democrats' game. Contrary to recent practice, the job of being a Supreme Court justice is not to be a philosopher-king. Only someone who buys into the liberals' view of Supreme Court justices as our rulers could hold legal training irrelevant to a job on the Supreme Court.

To be sure, if we were looking for philosopher-kings, an SMU law grad would probably be preferable to a graduate from an elite law school. But if we're looking for lawyers with giant brains to memorize obscure legal cases and to compose clearly reasoned opinions about ERISA pre-emption, the doctrine of equivalents in patent law, limitation of liability in admiralty, and supplemental jurisdiction under Section 1367—I think we want the nerd from an elite law school. Bush may as well appoint his chauffeur head of NASA as put Miers on the Supreme Court.

Third and finally, some jobs are so dirty, you can only send in someone who has the finely honed hatred of liberals acquired at elite universities to do them. Liberal insanity is an abstraction for normal, decent Americans living in the red states. By contrast, at the top universities, you come face to face with Satan's minions every day, and you learn all their little tropes and tricks.

Conservatives from elite schools have already been subjected to liberal blandishments and haven't blinked. These are right-wingers who have fought off the best and the brightest the blue states have to offer. The *New York Times* isn't going to mau-mau them—as it does intellectual lightweights like Jim Jeffords and Lincoln Chafee—by dangling fawning profiles before them. They aren't waiting for a pat on the head from Nina Totenberg or Linda Greenhouse. To paraphrase Archie Bunker on honest Italians, when you find a conservative from an elite law school, you've really got something.

However nice, helpful, prompt, and tidy she is, Harriet Miers isn't qualified to play a Supreme Court justice on *The West Wing*, let alone to be a real one. Both Republicans and Democrats should be alarmed that Bush seems to believe his power to appoint judges is absolute. This is what "advice and consent" means.

Democrats Stick Fork in Own Heads
November 3, 2005

Whata difference a week makes! Last week, liberals were expecting big things. On Friday, special prosecutor Patrick Fitzgerald was supposed to indict Karl Rove. Dick Cheney and Donald Rumsfeld were going to be named unindicted co-conspirators. Maybe Condoleezza Rice, too! Who knew? Maybe even Clarence Thomas and Antonin Scalia. It was going to be Fitzmas Day! (Which is much like Christmas except instead of having her baby in a manger, the woman has a late-term abortion.) Oh, it was hard to fall asleep on Fitzmas Eve!

But Friday came, and only Irve Lewis Libby was accused of committing any crimes. They were all crimes like perjury and obstruction of justice, personal to Libby, unrelated to the administration. Fitzmas sucked. Instead of GI Joe and Mr. Machine, all Democrats got was a lousy cardigan sweater.

With the Democrats still reeling from Friday's bad news, Bush gave them a right-hook by nominating the stunningly qualified Judge Sam Alito on Monday. (So I guess not *all* qualified candidates for the Supreme Court turned Bush down before he nominated Miers.) Not only is Alito qualified, but he also does not consider membership in the Federalist Society comparable to joining the Klan. In other words, this was just the sort of judicial nominee that would have terrified the White House a month ago.

Judge Alito's dear ninety-year-old mother—who evidently had not yet been briefed by White House political consultants to avoid stating positions popular with Americans—immediately said of her son, "Of course he's against abortion." As a judge on the Third Circuit Court of

Appeals, Alito voted to uphold a Pennsylvania statute passed by the legislature and signed into law by the governor that required women to notify their husbands before getting an abortion. (This was later deemed an "undue burden" by liberals' favorite "conservative" justice, Sandra Day O'Connor.)

There is no question about Alito's qualifications. Liberals can only oppose him for his record, which will alarm a narrow segment of lunatics commonly known as "the Democratic Party base." Now that timid Republicans have been forced to face their fears, it turns out that liberal America was always a paper tiger. Americans are not rising in righteous anger at a judicial nominee who upheld a law requiring husbands to be notified of their wives' abortions. The only people attacking Alito for his abortion ruling are the usual nuts: Planned Parenthood, NARAL, People for the American Way, and senators from New York and California (what CBS thinks of as "the American heartland").

So confident are the Democrats about the popularity of their stance on abortion that the day after Alito's nomination, Senate Democrats shut down the Senate so they wouldn't be forced to talk about Alito. Minority Leader Harry Reid dramatically invoked an obscure Senate rule to close the Senate for two hours, putatively in order to rehash old arguments about the Iraq War in closed session. In pursuit of more government transparency, Reid shut the doors, threw out the public, dimmed the lights, and turned off the TV cameras in the chambers of the U.S. Senate. That night, the cable news shows were fixated on Reid's weird stunt—and Senate Democrats narrowly avoided having to talk about Alito's abortion ruling for one more day.

If this is not a coincidence, let's see how long it takes Harry Reid to go on TV and state his position on a wife having to notify her husband before getting an abortion. Heck, I'd settle for seeing Harry Reid definitively adopt *any* position on abortion.

The nuts are perplexed. Why aren't Senate Democrats screaming from rooftops: "This is a judge who would force women to tell their husbands before having an abortion! Are you people listening?" Maybe the Democrats aren't running from their base. Maybe they're trying to help NARAL by preventing anyone from finding out what NARAL believes. Democrats would prefer for the American people to imagine that a group with the words "abortion" and "rights" in its name is some kind of benevolent little charity that holds bake sales. Believe me, you don't want liberals out there reminding the American people that it's a "constitutional right" to abort a baby five minutes before birth.

I gather that People for the American Way thinks it is "the American way" for wives not to tell their husbands about an abortion. But that's because they need to get out more. In a 2003 Gallup poll, 72 percent of respondents favored such spousal notification laws. To put it another way, only 28 percent of Americans hold the position that married men have absolutely no reproductive rights whatsoever. Upward of 60 percent of self-described "liberals" and "Democrats" favored husbands being notified of their wives' abortions.

If these poll results don't sound right to you, try crossing Central Park sometime. You'll find another part of Manhattan that's not the Upper West Side. Or do something wild and visit Queens—or Staten Island! You won't even have to leave New York City. See how normal people react to the idea of a woman not having to inform her husband that she's having an abortion.

In the past few years, the Democrats have had to run from big government, gun control, welfare, criminal rights, and gay marriage. With the Alito nomination, it looks like the Democrats are going to have to renounce the NARAL ladies or prepare for another bad day after the 2006 elections.

God Hates Judges
April 7, 2010

NOTE: The cause of a lot of bad Supreme Court law is bad lawyers, who think a strong back and willing heart can make up for not having the skills to argue a case before the Supreme Court. It's the Harriet Miers problem at the advocate level, rather than judge level. Incredibly important cases inadvertently land in the laps of mediocre lawyers, who will have to face the entire legal talent of the Harvard Law School in defending society's basic rules of decency against sophistical trickery. Those rulings remain on the books forever.

The Westboro cult's attack on a grieving father was one of those cases. The father turned down the gratis services offered by one of the most experienced Supreme Court advocates in the nation, deciding to stick with his country lawyer for the Supreme Court appeal. On the other side, there was a mountain of amicus briefs filed by the likes of the New York Times *and the* Wall Street Journal, *claiming first amendment protection as a defense to the intentional infliction of emotional distress. The strong back and willing heart went on to lose the case 8 to 1. Ironically, the sole dissent was written by Justice Samuel Alito, who replaced Bush's original strong-back/willing heart nominee, Harriet Miers.*

Before the argument, a local newspaper touted Phelps's country lawyer, saying he had achieved "the highest accomplishment a lawyer can reach—arguing a case in front of the United States Supreme Court." The lawyer himself added that "very few lawyers will ever be in front of the Supreme Court. There's no road map to get there."

It isn't an accomplishment to stand in the well of a courtroom and then lose your case 8 to 1, changing the law for the entire nation and thus enabling the wanton infliction of emotional distress on our fellow citizens.

There's a role for strong-back/good-heart lawyers, but it's not on the Supreme Court, or in front of it. We don't want Mariano Rivera playing shortstop. Once the Supreme Court rules, there is no "we'll get 'em next season."

I n an opinion that may have been written by Heidi Montag, a federal court of appeals recently threw out a jury verdict for intentional infliction of emotional distress in favor of Albert Snyder against protesters who had showed up at his son Matthew's funeral. Solely because Matthew was a Marine, a Kansas-based cult, whose members are almost entirely from a single family, traveled to Maryland in order to stand outside Matthew's funeral with placards saying things like, "God Loves Dead Soldiers," "God Hates You," "You're Going to Hell," "Semper Fi Fags," "Thank God for Dead Soldiers," "Thank God for IEDs," and "God Hates Fags."

But wait, it gets funnier. The cult's leader/father is Fred Phelps, who calls America a "sodomite nation of flag-worshipping idolaters." Since you won't read it anywhere else, Phelps has run for public office five times—always as a Democrat.

The Fred Phelps cult members travel around the country and hold vile signs outside military funerals because they believe that the reason American soldiers die in wars is that God hates the U.S. because it tolerates homosexuals. I'll leave it to others to speculate as to why the very thought of male homosexuality gets Fred Phelps into such a lather.

Snyder has appealed his case to the Supreme Court, and now the court will have to decide whether the tort of intentional infliction of emotional distress (IIED) can exist in a country with a First Amendment. The tort of IIED is not an obscure legal doctrine written in pig

Latin. It means what it says: speech or conduct specifically intended to inflict emotional distress. The standard description of IIED is that a reasonable man viewing the conduct would react by saying, "That's outrageous!"

The Second Restatement of Torts (1965) defines IIED as conduct "so outrageous in character, and so extreme in degree, as to go beyond all possible bounds of decency, and to be regarded as atrocious, and utterly intolerable in a civilized community." A classic example of IIED is to tell a mother her child is dead when he is not. As a respected New York judge, Judith Kaye, put it, "The tort is as limitless as the human capacity for cruelty." Inasmuch as IIED claims are based on all manner of insults, rudeness, name-calling, and petty affronts, the claim is often alleged but rarely satisfied.

But if a group of lunatics standing outside the funeral of a fallen American soldier with signs saying "GOD HATES FAGS!" does not constitute intentional infliction of emotional distress, then there is no such tort anymore. The protesters weren't publishing their views in a magazine, announcing them on a morning zoo radio program, proclaiming them on some fringe outlet like *Countdown With Keith Olbermann*. They weren't even standing on a random street corner. Their protest was held outside a man's funeral for the specific purpose of causing pain to the deceased's father and others left behind.

But the Fourth Circuit Court of Appeals noticed that the cult's malicious signs contained words, and that words are "speech"…which is protected by the First Amendment! (Or was it the Seventh?) Anyway, that was basically the end of the court's analysis.

True, speech is typically involved in inflicting emotional distress. Similarly, words are used in committing treason ("The Americans are over here!"), robbery ("Your money or your life!"), and sexual harassment ("Have sex with me or you're fired."). Copyright law prohibits speech that uses someone else's words, and insider trading and trade-secrets laws prohibit the use of words revealing protected information.

The fact that "speech" was involved in the Fred Phelps cult's assault on Matthew Snyder's funeral is a mundane and irrelevant fact. The question is: Did that speech constitute intentional infliction of emotional distress? *Hey, look! That reasonable man over there is nodding his head "yes."* If so, the First Amendment is as irrelevant as it is to a copyright law violation. In *Taylor v. Metzger*, for example, the New Jersey Supreme Court found that a single joking reference to the plaintiff as "jungle bunny" despite an apology, stated a cause of action for "intentional infliction of emotional distress."

The Fourth Circuit's fascination with the Supreme Court's decision in *Hustler v. Falwell* is utterly obtuse. That case involved Reverend Jerry Falwell's lawsuit for intentional infliction of emotional distress based on a trashy parody of him in the magazine published by Clinton advisor Larry Flynt. The court essentially held that not only can public figures not be defamed (*New York Times v. Sullivan*), but they cannot recover for intentional infliction of emotional distress caused by trashy magazine parodies. Oh well. Public figures generally have pretty good lives.

Albert Snyder was not a public figure. He was not injecting himself into the public eye in any way. He was a father attending his son's funeral. The Supreme Court has upheld shockingly restrictive bans on speech outside of abortion clinics: content-based restrictions on the speech of pro-lifers singing, "Jesus loves the little children, all the children of the world, red and yellow, black and white, they are precious in His sight, Jesus loves the little children of the world." Is abortion more sacrosanct than a son's funeral? Is singing "Jesus loves the little children" deserving of less First Amendment protection than placards saying, "God Loves Dead Soldiers"? *Hey, reasonable man over there— got a minute?*

Even the Fred Phelps cult's "epic" posted online and accusing the Snyders of raising their son badly, which would seem to have the strongest claim to First Amendment protection, might not be protected in other contexts. Last week in Massachusetts, nine teenagers were criminally charged with cyberbullying, based in part on malicious postings about the victim on their Facebook pages.

Thanks to idiot lawyers, who think it makes them sound smart to defend the indefensible, one of the biggest problems in society today is the refusal to draw lines. Here's a nice big, bright line: holding malevolent signs outside the funeral of an American son, defaming the deceased, constitutes intentional infliction of emotional distress.

CHAPTER THIRTEEN

"Keeping Abortion Safe" and Other Liberal Oxymorons

T he only way to understand the Left's positions on gays is to memorize each element separately. There's no logical framework, so this is the bizarre house of mirrors you enter:

- *Why isn't the Catholic Church stopping homosexual pedophiles from molesting children?*
- *Why are the Boy Scouts trying to stop homosexual pedophiles from molesting children?*
- *We hate the Catholic Church for allowing what we hate the Boy Scouts for trying to prevent!*

The Boy Scouts should agree to admit gay scoutmasters as soon as every liberal in the country signs an affidavit vowing to shun any trial lawyer who sues the Boy Scouts for molestation.

But enough about the gays. No matter what else liberals pretend to care about from time to time—gay marriage, wrecking healthcare, undermining national security, aiding terrorists, oppressing the middle class, freeing violent criminals—the single most important item on the Democrats' agenda is abortion. (Okay, fine, also trial lawyers and unionized government workers.) Liberals don't care about women, despite what you might think from observing the behavior of Anthony Weiner, Elliot Spitzer, Bob Filner, Bill Clinton, and Teddy Kennedy. They only care about destroying human life.

In June 2013, liberal America celebrated its new hero: Wendy Davis, the Texas legislator who spent thirteen hours filibustering a bill to ban abortions after twenty weeks. Yay, Wendy! About the same time, fifty thousand bumblebees killed by insecticide were honored in a memorial service in Wilsonville, Oregon. If the bumblebees had been unborn babies, Davis could have thrown a party!

When the Texas abortion bill finally passed, liberals somberly announced that, as a result of the law, three Planned Parenthood clinics in Texas would be forced to close. The clinic closings were confusing because just two years earlier, liberals had mocked conservatives, such as Senator Jon Kyl, for imagining that Planned Parenthood had anything to do with abortion. We were smirkingly informed by Senator Harry Reid and Comedy Central's Stephen Colbert that the bulk of Planned Parenthood's business consisted of cholesterol screenings and breast exams.

After the dramatic announcement of Planned Parenthood's clinic closings in response to the Texas abortion law, it apparently occurred to someone on the Left that they couldn't keep sneering about idiot right-wingers who thought Planned Parenthood performed a lot of abortions, then turn around and wail about clinics being forced to close in response to restrictions on abortion. Suddenly the news stories about Planned Parenthood's Texas clinics were rewritten to clarify that it was a law Texas passed *two years earlier* that forced the closings, not the recent law restricting abortions.

A story on the *Huffington Post*, for example, "clarified" that the closings were not about the abortion law:

> *"This piece was updated to clarify the reasons for the closure of each clinic. An original version implied that all were being closed in response to the signing of the new abortion law."*

> *"They are closing in response to a new package of abortion restrictions signed into law on Thursday and funding cuts to Texas' Women's Health Program that were passed by the Texas state legislature in 2011."*

The 2011 "funding cuts," incidentally, were also all about abortion.

Remove Dennis Kucinich's Feeding Tube!
November 13, 2003

N THE CURRENT battle over whether to remove the feeding tube from Florida woman Terri Schiavo, the basic positions are:

- She is in a permanent vegetative state; no, she's not.
- She is unconscious and does not react to stimuli; yes, she does.
- She will never get any better; yes, she will.
- She would not have wanted to be kept on a feeding tube; you don't know that.

The only thing everyone seems to agree on is that her husband is creepy. Terri's parents are fighting like mad to keep Terri alive. The husband, Michael Schiavo, is living with another woman with whom he has one child and is expecting another. Yet he has mounted a monumental crusade to have Terri's feeding tube removed.

Terri is not brain-dead and requires no extraordinary means to be kept alive. She is breathing, her heart is pumping, her organs are functioning. All she needs is food and water. (All three are technically true of Kate Moss, too.) But her husband wants to starve her to death.

As Larry King asked him, why not "walk away"?

That is the eternal mystery of this case. Assuming everything Michael says about Terri is true—she has no consciousness, she will never recover, and she would not want to live with feeding tubes—well, then, she's not in pain, bored, angry, or upset. Dennis Kucinich has been in a persistent vegetative state for twenty years—how about not feeding him? Why is Michael Schiavo so obsessed with pulling Terri's feeding tube? Why can't he just walk away?

Michael's answer to Larry King was this: "Why should I, Larry? This is Terri's wish. This is Terri's choice." As King pointed out, Terri's alleged "wish" was not memorialized anywhere in writing, only in Michael's memory. Michael responded to this point by invoking the courts: "It's been decided for six years of litigation that this was Terri's wish."

I note that "six years of litigation" is not enough to end the lives of child-molesting serial killers on death row. The same people who want to kill Terri believe that death-row cases are never final, no matter how many courts and juries have spoken over how many decades.

Moreover, it's not as if court after court has heard testimony on Terri's wishes and have unanimously agreed that Terri would have chosen death. One lone Florida circuit court judge, George Greer, credited Michael's testimony, finding "clear and convincing" evidence that Terri said she would not want to be kept alive on feeding tubes. Because Judge Greer was acting as the finder of fact, his finding is essentially unreviewable by any other court. Even the notorious Florida Supreme Court—which has a history of jumping in to try to save a dead man—refused to review the case.

Judge Greer's finding on Terri's wishes may be immune from legal review, but it's not immune from criticism. He's a finder of fact—he's not God. A few years ago, Judge Greer found that Helene Ball McGee did not have reasonable cause to believe domestic violence was imminent and denied her an order of protection. Two weeks later, Mrs. McGee was stabbed to death by her husband. So even Judge Greer can make mistakes.

The judge's pivotal "finding of fact" in the Schiavo case determining a life-or-death issue is based on something Terri allegedly said after watching a TV show. Michael didn't know his wife was bulimic, but he distinctly remembered Terri's remarks about a TV show. (It was an episode of *Melrose Place*, during which she said that Heather Locklear's shoes were "to die for.") After watching *Bambi*, I'm against deer hunting. Then I go out the next day and order venison. Maybe we could have a higher standard of proof before the government orders a woman to die.

Despite Michael's insistence that he has a vivid memory of Terri expressing her wishes regarding death, note this exchange on *Larry King Live*:

> KING: I have a thirty-five-year-old daughter. I've never asked her this question. I don't know if she has a living will. I hope she does. But if she doesn't, I don't know the answer to the question. Because most thirty-five-year-olds, I guess, don't talk about it.
>
> SCHIAVO: Nobody talks about death, Larry.

Michael apparently forgot to add—except for that one night I remember so clearly, Larry, when my wife, Terri, talked to me about death and expressed her firmly held desire not to be kept alive on a feeding tube. If you start making damning admissions on *Larry King Live*—with your lawyer sitting next to you, no less—you have a problem. Larry King can interview Louis Farrakhan and make him look like a charmer. As even the *New York Times* admits, Michael did not recall Terri's alleged desire to be taken off life support until after the million-dollar settlement was paid, most of it going for Terri's medical costs—and the remainder to him.

For the record: I want heroic measures taken to keep me alive, and I demand the immediate arrest of anyone trying to remove my life support.

What offhand comments might Terri have made if she had read in the *Baltimore Sun* about Rod Brandner, who indicated that he was coming out of a coma by squeezing his son's hand in response to questions less than two hours before his life support system was to be turned off? Or what if she had read the Associated Press news story on Chris Trickle, who lost 5 percent of his brain when he was shot in the head, but later came out of a nine-month coma to breathe on his own, eat three meals a day, and tell his girlfriend he loved her?

What would Terri have said after hearing that Gregory Dygas's mother refused to believe the doctors' assurances that Gregory was brain-dead and should be taken off life support, and six months later watched as Gregory sat up, talked, and watched television? What offhand remarks might Terri have made after reading about Terry Wallis, the Canadian man who just last summer awoke from a nineteen-*year* coma? (Or how about that case in Minnesota last year where the guy who'd been in a coma for decades suddenly reappeared and ran for Senate? What was his name? Mondale something?)

In the absence of a living will, I would think the courts ought to be erring on the side of life. But short of that, couldn't we at least all agree that the courts should not defer to the pull-the-plug demands from anyone who:

1. Expresses an unseemly enthusiasm for another person's death;
2. Was the only person present when the incident leading to the persistent vegetative state occurred;
3. Stands to make money off the person's death; or
4. Is wearing a "W.W.C.V.B.D." bracelet? (What would Claus von Bulow do?)

Forty-Nine Million to Five
June 3, 2009

Responding to the shooting death of late-term abortionist George Tiller, President Obama sent out a welcome message that this nation would not tolerate attacks on pro-lifers or any other Americans because of their religion or beliefs.

Ha ha! Just kidding. That was the lead sentence—with minor edits—of a *New York Times* editorial warning about theoretical hate crimes against Muslims eight months after 9/11. Why can't pro-lifers get the same oceans of ink devoted to assuring Americans that "most pro-lifers are peaceful"?

For years, we've had to hear about the danger that Americans might overreact to a terrorist attack committed by nineteen Muslims shouting "Allahu Akbar" as they flew commercial jets into American skyscrapers. We've never had a dozen pro-lifers shouting "Abortion kills a beating heart!" as they gunned down thousands of innocent citizens in Wichita, Kansas. Why aren't liberals rushing to assure us that "most pro-lifers are peaceful"? Unlike Muslims, pro-lifers actually are peaceful.

According to recent polling, a majority of Americans oppose abortion—a fact implicitly acknowledged by liberals' refusal to let us vote on the subject. In a country with approximately 150 million pro-lifers, five abortionists have been killed since *Roe v. Wade*. In that same thirty-six years, more than 49 million babies have been killed in the womb. Let's recap that halftime score, sports fans: 49 million to five.

Meanwhile, fewer than 2 million Muslims live in America and, while Muslims are less murderous than abortionists, I'm fairly certain they've killed more than five people in the United States in the last thirty-six years. For some reason, the number "3,000" keeps popping into my head. So in a country that is more than 50 percent pro-life—and 80 percent opposed to the late-term abortions of the sort performed by Tiller—only five abortionists have been killed. And in a country that is less than 0.5 percent Muslim, Muslims have killed thousands of Americans.

But the killing of about one abortionist per decade leads liberals to condemn the entire pro-life movement as "domestic terrorists."

Tiller bragged about performing sixty thousand abortions, including abortions of viable babies, able to survive outside their mother's womb. He made millions of dollars performing late-term abortions so gruesome that, in the entire country, only two other abortionists—not a squeamish bunch—would perform them.

Kansas law allows late-term abortions only to save the mother's life or to prevent "irreversible physical damage" to the mother. But Tiller was more than happy to kill viable babies, provided the mothers: (1) forked over $5,000; and (2) mentioned "substantial and irreversible conditions," which, in Tiller's view, included not being able to go to concerts or rodeos or being "temporarily depressed" on account of their pregnancies.

In return for blood money from Tiller's abattoir, Democrats ran a political protection racket for the late-term abortionist. In 1997, the *Washington Post* reported that Tiller attended one of Bill Clinton's White

House coffees for major campaign contributors. In addition to a $25,000 donation to Clinton, Tiller wanted to thank him personally for thirty months of U.S. Marshals' protection paid for by the U.S. taxpayer.

Kansas Democrats who received hundreds of thousands of campaign dollars from Tiller repeatedly intervened to block any interference with Tiller's abortion mill. Kathleen Sebelius, the governor of Kansas until Obama made her Health and Human Services secretary, received six-figure donations from Tiller. She vetoed one bill restricting late-term abortions and another one that would have required Tiller to turn over his records pertaining to "substantial and irreversible conditions" justifying his late-term abortions.

Kansas Attorney General Paul Morrison also got elected with the help of Tiller's blood money, replacing a Republican attorney general who was in the middle of an investigation of Tiller for various crimes including his failure to report statutory rapes, despite performing abortions on girls as young as eleven. But soon after Morrison replaced the Republican attorney general, the charges against Tiller were reduced and, in short order, he was acquitted of a few misdemeanors. In what is a not uncommon occurrence with Democrats, Morrison is now gone, having been forced to resign when his mistress charged him with sexual harassment and corruption.

Tiller was protected not only by a praetorian guard of elected Democrats, but also by the Evangelical Lutheran Church in America—coincidentally, the same church attended by Tiller's fellow Wichita executioner, the BTK killer. The official webpage of the ELCA instructs: "A developing life in the womb does not have an absolute right to be born." As long as we're deciding who does and doesn't have an "absolute right to be born," who's to say late-term abortionists have an "absolute right" to live?

I wouldn't kill an abortionist myself, but I wouldn't want to impose my moral values on others. No one is *for* shooting abortionists. But how will criminalizing those who make the difficult, often tragic, decision to shoot an abortionist be an effective means of reducing the shootings of abortionists?

Following the moral logic of liberals, I say: if you don't believe in shooting abortionists, then don't shoot one.

The Sun Never Sets on the British Welfare System
August 10, 2011

Those of you following the barbaric rioting in Britain will not have failed to notice that a sizable proportion of the thugs are white, something not often seen in this country. Not only that, but in a triumph of feminism, a lot of them are girls. Even the "disabled" (according to the British benefits system) seem to have miraculously overcome their infirmities to dash out and steal a few TVs.

Congratulations, Britain! You've barbarized your citizenry, without regard to race, gender, or physical handicap!

With a welfare system far more advanced than the United States, the British have achieved the remarkable result of turning entire communities of ancestral British people into tattooed, drunken brutes. I guess we now have the proof of what conservatives have been saying since forever: looting is a result of liberal welfare policies. And Britain is in the end stages of the welfare state.

In 2008, a nine-year-old British girl, Shannon Matthews, disappeared on her way home from a school trip. The media leapt on the case—only to discover that Shannon was one of seven children her mother, Karen, had produced with five different men. The first of these serial sperm-donors explained, "Karen just goes from one bloke to the next, uses them to have a kid, grabs all the child benefits and moves on."

Poor little Shannon eventually turned up at the home of one of her many step-uncles—whose ex-wife, by the way, was the mother of six children with three different fathers. (Is Father's Day celebrated in England? If so, how?)

The *Daily Mail* (London) traced the family's proud Anglo ancestry of stable families back hundreds of years. The Nazi war machine couldn't break the British, but the modern welfare state has.

A year earlier, in 2007, another product of the new order, Fiona MacKeown, took seven of her eight children (by five different fathers) and her then-boyfriend on a drug-fueled, six-month vacation to the Indian island of Goa. The trip was paid for—like everything else in her life—with government benefits. (When was the last time you had a free, six-month vacation? I'm drawing a blank, too.)

While in Goa, Fiona took her entourage on a side-trip, leaving her fifteen-year-old daughter, Scarlett Keeling, in the capable hands of a twenty-five-year-old local whom Scarlett had begun sleeping with, perhaps hoping to get a head start on her own government benefits. A few weeks later, Scarlett turned up dead, full of drugs, raped, and murdered.

Scarlett's estranged stepfather later drank himself to death, while her brother Silas announced on his social networking page, "My name is Si, n I spend most my life either out wit mates get drunk or at partys, playing rugby or going to da beach (pretty s**t really)." It's a wonder that someone like Silas, who has never worked, and belongs to a family in which no one has ever worked, can afford a cellphone for social networking. No, actually, it's not.

Britain has a far more redistributive welfare system than France, which is why France's crime problem is mostly a matter of Muslim immigrants, not French nationals. Meanwhile, England's welfare state is fast returning the native population to its violent eighteenth-century highwaymen roots. Needless to say, Britain leads Europe in the proportion of single mothers and, as a consequence, also leads the European Union in violent crime, alcohol and drug abuse, obesity, and sexually transmitted diseases.

Liberal elites here and in Britain will blame anything but the welfare state they adore. They drone on about the strict British class system or the lack of jobs or the nation's history of racism. None of that explains the sad lives of young Shannon Matthews and Scarlett Keeling, with their long English ancestry and perfect Anglo features.

Democrats would be delighted if violent mobs like those in Britain arose here—perhaps in Wisconsin! That would allow them to introduce yet more government programs staffed by unionized public employees, as happened after both the 1992 L.A. riots and the 1960s race riots (following the recommendations of the Kerner Commission). MSNBC might even do the unthinkable and offer Al Sharpton his own TV show. (Excuse me—someone's trying to get my attention…WHAT?)

Inciting violent mobs is the essence of the Left's agenda: promote class warfare, illegitimate children, and an utterly debased citizenry. Like the British riot-girls interviewed by the BBC, the Democrats tell us "all of this happened because of the rich people."

We're beginning to see the final result of that idea in Britain. The welfare state creates a society of beasts. Meanwhile, nonjudgmental elites don't dare condemn the animals their programs have created. Rioters in England are burning century-old family businesses to the ground, stealing from injured children lying on the sidewalks, and forcing Britons to strip to their underwear on the street.

I keep reading that it's because they don't have jobs—which they're obviously anxious to hold. Or someone called them a "kaffir." Or their social services have been reduced. Or their BlackBerries made them do it. Or they disapprove of a referee's call in a Manchester United game.

A few well-placed rifle rounds, and the rioting would end in an instant. A more sustained attack on the rampaging mob might save England from itself, finally removing shaved-head, drunken parasites from the benefits rolls that Britain can't find the will to abolish on moral or utilitarian grounds. We can be sure there's no danger of killing off the next Winston Churchill or Edmund Burke in these crowds.

But like Louis XVI, British authorities are paralyzed by their indifference to their own civilization. A half-century of berating themselves for the crime of being British has left them morally defenseless. They see nothing about England worth saving, certainly not worth fighting for. (Which is fortunate since most of their cops don't have guns.)

This is how civilizations die. It can happen overnight, as it did in Revolutionary France. If Britain of 1939 were composed of the current British population, the entirety of Europe would today be doing the "Heil Hitler" salute and singing the "Horst Wessel Song."

The Vagina Diatribes
March 14, 2012

Did I miss the deadline for alternative opinions on Sandra Fluke? What with liberal women who constantly talk about their vaginas suddenly pretending to be offended by the word "slut," and conservatives pretending to be as pussified as liberals about the nasty names they've been called, I never got an answer to the most pressing question about Sandra Fluke: Who are you again?

Was Fluke dragged out of obscurity after the women of America took a vote and chose her as our spokeswoman? *Please, Sandra, we know how deeply private, publicity-shy, and terribly busy with law school you are, but we need you to speak for us!*

I don't think that happened. Rather, Fluke is the latest in a long line of my absolute favorite liberal typology: hysterical drama queens.

From Murphy Brown to the Jersey Girls, Cindy Sheehan, Joe Wilson, and the New School's Jean Rohe, these fantasists inject themselves into a boiling-hot public debate and then claim victim status when anyone criticizes them.

At least since I've been keeping score, liberals had their first brush with the dark night of fascism in 1992, when Dan Quayle said of a fictional TV character, "It doesn't help matters when prime-time TV has Murphy Brown...mocking the importance of fathers by bearing a child alone and calling it just another lifestyle choice." Suddenly, it was 1939 Germany and multimillionaire Hollywood elites were the Jews.

At the Emmy Awards ceremony that year, the creator of *Murphy Brown*, Diane English, took the occasion to say: "I would like to thank our sponsors for hanging in there when it was getting really dangerous." Really dangerous? You want "really dangerous"? Try being a pedestrian crossing Ocean Avenue in Santa Monica when Diane English is on her way to the airport! (A year earlier, English's husband mowed down the matriarch of Santa Monica's Chez Jay, killing her, while driving Diane to the airport.)

Marge Tabankin, executive director of the Hollywood Women's Political Committee, said, "The community feels targeted. It's created a chill and fear reminiscent of the '50s. Let's face it: We feel we're being used as whipping boys." Yes, Hollywood liberals have got balls to spare, and that's why I admire them so much.

But the Academy Award winners of liberal martyrdom are the Dixie Chicks. In 2003, Chick Natalie Maines sucked up to a Bush-hating

London audience by saying, "Just so you know, we're ashamed the president of the United States is from Texas." What an odd coincidence that the only city Maines attacked Bush in was London! In a way, it was lucky for the band that, in their entire sixty-city world tour, Maines claimed to be embarrassed by Bush only in London and not, say, Lubbock, Texas.

But at least we had heard of Murphy Brown and the Dixie Chicks before they demanded we all stand in awe of their raw courage. Fluke was an absolute nobody who simply thrust herself into the limelight. She's more in the Jean Rohe tradition of the liberal drama queen.

Rohe, you will recall, was the student speaker at the 2006 New School commencement proceedings, who bravely insulted the official speaker, Senator John McCain. As Rohe described her decision to attack the invited speaker, every person she talked to the day before the ceremony hated McCain with blind fury. At two graduation ceremonies a day earlier, attacks on McCain had brought wild cheers from the audience.

Rohe's resolve to tell the audience what it wanted to hear was only hardened when she was told there would be media at the event. Sensing that fake heroism was within her grasp, Rohe explained, "It was something I didn't want to do, but knew I had to out of an obligation to my own values"—such as the value of being popular, of getting a standing ovation, and of being praised for her courage.

Liberals' idea of questioning authority is to check with the authorities to see if a "Question Authority" bumper sticker would be popular.

So, back to Fluke: Who is she, and how did she become the spokesperson for American womanhood? If we're allowed to submit names, I think we can do better than a Georgetown law student whose claim to fame is that she belongs to a college club on "reproductive justice."

Pursuing a typical path to liberal heroics, Fluke was an utter nobody whom the Democrats substituted in a last-minute witness-switch at a hearing on "religious liberty" to testify about contraception—as if her haircut isn't birth control enough. Despite her credentials as a heretofore unheard-of "birth control activist," the Oversight and Government Reform Committee declined to accept this eleventh-hour witness on the grounds that Fluke did not have appropriate credentials for any congressional hearing, much less one on religious liberty.

That was the Republicans' first foray into "silencing" Fluke's "voice."

Nancy Pelosi used an even less appropriate committee to ensure that Fluke's "voice" would be heard—the Democrats' Steering and Policy Committee, the normal function of which is to give House Democrats committee assignments. One longtime Democratic operative admitted privately that Fluke is the least-qualified witness ever to appear before a congressional committee.

As a result of the huge commotion the Democrats' made of Fluke's "testimony," she was ridiculed the same way people in ridiculous situations often are. She was called some mean names—"slut," "prostitute," "law student"…In full indignation, Fluke said her critics were trying "to silence women's voices." She said this on ABC, NBC, CBS, MSNBC, CNN, NPR, and a number of other national media outlets. Thus, Fluke became a liberal hero *even braver* than an actress standing up for abortion rights in front of a Bill Maher audience.

President Obama telephoned Fluke to make sure she was OK. He told her that her parents should be proud of her. Hillary Clinton said conservatives were trying to control women. Bill Clinton called her to see if she had any plans for the weekend. (Fluke seems to be holding up wonderfully under the nightmare of constant TV appearances. In fact, if I didn't know better, I'd think she's enjoying herself tremendously.)

I don't care what liberals believe. Just please stop telling me they're courageous for saying exactly what every non-Fox media outlet in America is dying to hear, or I'll throw up harder than Rick Santorum did when he read John F. Kennedy's speech.

Vulgarians on the Loose!
June 20, 2012

A Michigan legislator, Lisa Brown, gave a speech in the statehouse last week that would have made her right at home in a women's studies course at a local community college. But it was an odd way to address the Michigan House of Representatives.

Brown commented on a pending abortion bill by first announcing that she was Jewish, kept kosher, described her various sets of plates, and then saying that Jewish law makes abortion mandatory to save the life of the mother. (This had absolutely nothing to do with the bill being considered, but it may explain why there are no Jewish Tim Tebows.)

Then she said, "I have not asked you to adopt and adhere to my religious beliefs. Why are you asking me to adopt yours?" As her crescendo, she said, "And finally Mr. Speaker, I'm flattered that you're all so interested in my vagina, but 'no' means 'no'!"

It's not clear where Representative Brown got the idea that the Republican caucus was planning on date-raping her, but I think there's been a terrible misunderstanding. The bill under consideration merely ensured the safety of women having abortions—and, in a small way, the safety of the fetus, whom the U.S. Supreme Court has prohibited legislatures from protecting fully. Thus, the bill addressed insurance and health inspections of abortion clinics, and included a requirement that the abortionist confirm that the woman having the abortion was not being pressured by a third party to do so.

I have not polled all the Republicans in the Michigan statehouse yet, but the ones I've spoken to assure me that Representative Brown's vagina played a very small role in their deliberations. It's odd that she seems to think she's the object of so much Republican male fantasy. Why must a certain type of woman always start shouting about her vagina whenever the topic of abortion comes up?

Do what you want with your vagina. Pro-lifers just want to stop babies from being killed. It would be as though a slaveholder started talking about his anus every time the subject of abolishing slavery came up.

For making inappropriate remarks during a legislative session, Brown was prohibited from making floor speeches for one day. Being an hysterical drama queen who believes the Michigan Legislature was obsessed with her vagina, Representative Brown responded to the sanction by claiming she had been "silenced." A vulgar nut gets a one-day penalty, and suddenly she's Aleksandr Solzhenitsyn.

Representative Brown was not being silenced. She was being admonished for a crazy display of narcissism utterly irrelevant to the bill under discussion. I would never in a million years silence a woman because of her views on abortion, but I'd vote for a month of silence from this self-dramatizing freak.

The media are in full smirk mode, not at Representative Brown's perversely self-referential speech positing that Republican legislators were fantasizing about raping her ("'no' means 'no'!"), but at Republican bluenoses, whom they seem to think are shocked by the word "vagina."

Hey, does anyone else remember way back into the distant past three months ago when liberals were ablaze with indignation because Rush Limbaugh used the word "slut" to describe Sandra Fluke? That word had liberals fainting like Victorian virgins. In a letter to House Speaker John Boehner, seventy-five Democrats in Congress called the language used by Limbaugh "sexually charged," "patently offensive," "obscene and indecent," and called on Republican leaders to condemn it. The president of the United States even called Fluke to see if she was OK after having been called…the "s-word"!

But now, a whole several weeks later, you can't find a liberal female who isn't screaming "vagina." Thousands of these beasts appeared near the Michigan statehouse on Monday—as well as every show, every hour on MSNBC that night—to shout "vagina!" On one of the eight hundred TV shows Representative Lisa Brown did this week—which, ironically, were the exact same shows that had featured Fluke describing her trauma at having been called a "slut"—MSNBC's Lawrence O'Donnell gushed about the advances society has made.

Apparently, there was a time, long ago, when women did *not* prattle about their vaginas in public. He said, "It's easy, I think, for some of our audience tonight who are in their 30s or 20s to not be able to even comprehend what that world was like." Representative Brown somberly agreed, saying, "We have all, as women, come a long way."

Another guest, Eve Ensler, authoress of *The Vagina Monologues*, talked about the magic of thousands of women shouting "vagina" in public: "Many young women came up to thank both of us for giving them voice, for allowing them to be authentic, for allowing them to love their bodies, for allowing them to feel agency over their bodies and their rights, to know that they have choices, that what they decide to do with the reproductive decisions or abortion decisions or whatever they decide is their choice. It's their body."

That is, unless your little body hasn't been born yet, in which case, liberals think it can be torn to shreds and dumped in the garbage—a point they argue by shouting "vagina" and claiming Republican legislators want to date-rape them.

CHAPTER FOURTEEN

Higher Re-Education

n this chapter, we will consider the lives of more people you subsidize who can't be fired. On a single day, Monday, August 5, 2013:

- One tenured professor at Millikin University, Dr. James St. James, was told he would keep his job despite the revelation that, as a sixteen-year-old, he had murdered his mother, father, and sister;
- Another tenured professor, Donald Ratcliff at Wheaton College in Illinois, pleaded guilty to aggravated possession of child pornography (okay, this professor was fired—Wheaton is a Christian college, after all); and,
- A third tenured college professor, at Pasadena City College, Hugo Schwyzer, announced a leave of absence after

attempting suicide and being admitted to a psychiatric ward on account of a website publishing his graphic texting and masturbatory phone sex with a twenty-seven-year-old woman who regularly appeared naked on internet sex chats.

The last one was the big shocker. Schwyzer taught a course called "Navigating Pornography," offering young scholars the opportunity to explore sex and porn in a "safe space." Porn star James Deen had been a guest lecturer. (One may assume students were allowed to ask questions during Schwyer's lectures without raising their hands.) Who could have imagined that such a serious academic would have deep emotional problems?

But what about all the people who hired and employed Schwyzer? How many beds do we need to open up at the psychiatric ward? One more thought before you sign that college loan application: Ward Churchill was a full professor.

The Little Injun That Could
February 9, 2005

If Ward Churchill loses his job teaching at the University of Colorado, he could end up giving Howard Dean a real run for his money to head the Democratic National Committee.

Churchill already has a phony lineage and phony war record—just like John Kerry! (Someone should also check out Churchill's claim that he spent Christmas 1968 at Wounded Knee.) In 1983, Churchill met with Libyan dictator Muammar Gaddafi and later felt it necessary to announce that his group, the American Indian Movement, "has not requested arms from the Libyan government." In 1997, he was one of the "witnesses" who spoke at a "Free Mumia" event in Philadelphia on behalf of convicted cop-killer Mumia Abu-Jamal.

Come to think of it, Churchill could give Hillary a run for her money. All that's left for Churchill to do is meet with Al Sharpton and kiss Suha Arafat.

Churchill's claim that he is an Indian isn't an incidental boast, like John Kerry pretending to be Irish. It is the entire basis of his career. Churchill has been the co-director of the American Indian Movement of Colorado, the vice chairperson of the American Indian "Anti-Defamation" Council, and an associate professor and coordinator of American Indian Studies at the University of Colorado.

By Churchill's own account, a crucial factor in his political development was "being an American Indian referred to as 'chief' in a combat unit" in Vietnam, which made him sad. This is known to con men everywhere as a "two-fer."

In addition to an absence of evidence about his Indian heritage, there is no evidence that he was in combat in Vietnam. After the POW Network revealed that Churchill had never seen combat, he countered with this powerful argument: "They can say whatever the hell they want. That's confidential information, and I've never ordered its release from the Department of Defense. End of story." Maybe we should ask John Kerry to help Churchill fill out a Form 180.

In one of his books, *Struggle for the Land*, Churchill advances the argument that one-third of America is the legal property of Indians. And if you believe Churchill is a real Indian, he also happens to be part owner of the Brooklyn Bridge.

But his most famous oeuvre is the famed 9/11 essay in which he called the 9/11 World Trade Center victims "little Eichmanns" and said that "Arab terrorists"—which he put in quotes—had simply "responded to the massive and sustained American terror bombing of Iraq" by giving Americans "a tiny dose of their own medicine."

Having blurted out "Iraq" in connection with 9/11 in a moment of hysteria, Churchill had to backpedal when the anti-war movement needed to argue that Iraq had absolutely nothing whatsoever to do with Arab terrorism. He later attached an "Addendum" to the essay saying that the 9/11 attack was not only payback for Iraq, but also for various other of this country's depredations especially against "real Indians" (of which he is not one).

In light of the fact that Churchill's entire persona, political activism, curriculum vitae, writings, and university positions are based on his claim that he's an Indian, it's rather churlish of him to complain when people ask if he really is one. But whenever he is questioned about his heritage, Churchill rails that inquiries into his ancestry are "absolutely indefensible."

Churchill has gone from claiming he is one-eighth Indian "on a good day" to claiming he is "three-sixteenths Cherokee," to claiming he is one-sixty-fourth Cherokee through a Revolutionary War era ancestor named Joshua Tyner. (At least he's not posing as a phony Indian math professor.) A recent investigation by the *Denver Post* revealed that Tyner's father was indeed married to a Cherokee. But he married her after Joshua's mother—Churchill's relative—was scalped by Indians.

By now, all that's left of Churchill's claim to Indian ancestry is his assertion: "It is just something that was common knowledge in my family." (That, and his souvenir foam-rubber "tommyhawk" he bought at Turner Field in Atlanta.)

Over the years, there were other subtle clues the university might have noticed. Churchill is not in the tribal registries kept since the

1800s by the federal government. In addition, no tribe will enroll him—a verification process Churchill dismisses as "poodle papers" for Indians.

In 1990, Churchill was forced to stop selling his art as "Indian art" under federal legislation, sponsored by then congressman and actual Indian Ben Nighthorse Campbell (Republican), requiring Indian artists to establish that they are accepted members of a federally recognized tribe. Churchill responded by denouncing the Indian artist who had exposed him. (Hey, does anybody need two hundred velvet paintings of Elvis playing poker with Crazy Horse?)

In the early '90s, he hoodwinked an impecunious Cherokee tribe into granting him an "associate membership" by telling them he "wrote some books and was a big-time author." A tribal spokeswoman explained: he "convinced us he could help our people." They never heard from him again—yet another treaty with the Indians broken by the white man. Soon thereafter, the tribe stopped offering "associate memberships."

A decade ago, Churchill was written up in an article in *News From Indian Country*, titled, "Sovereignty and Its Spokesmen: The Making of an Indian." The article noted that Churchill had claimed membership in a scrolling series of Indian tribes, but over "the course of two years, NFIC hasn't been able to confirm a single living Indian relative, let alone one real relative that can vouch for his tribal descent claim."

When real Indians complained to Colorado University in 1994 that a fake Indian was running their Indian Studies program, a spokeswoman for the CU president said the university needed "to determine if the position was designated for a Native American. And I can't answer that right now." Apparently it was answered in Churchill's favor since he's still teaching.

If he's not an Indian, it's not clear what Churchill does have to offer a university. In his book, *A Little Matter of Genocide: Holocaust and Denial in the Americas, 1492 to the Present*, Churchill denounces Jews for presuming to imagine the Holocaust was unique. In the chapter titled "Lie for Lie: Linkages between Holocaust Deniers and Proponents of the Uniqueness of the Jewish Experience in World War II," Churchill calls the Third Reich merely "a crystallization" of Christopher Columbus's ravages of Churchill's people (if he were an Indian).

His research apparently consisted of watching the Disney movie *Pocahontas*, which showed that the Indians meant the European settlers no harm. (That's if you don't count the frequent scalpings.)

Even the credulous *Nation* magazine—always on red alert for tales of white male oppression—dismissed Churchill's 1988 book *Agents of Repression* about COINTELPRO-type operations against the American Indian Movement, saying the book "does not give much new information" and "even a reader who is inclined to believe their allegations will want more evidence than they provide." If the *Nation* won't buy your anti-U.S. government conspiracy theories, Kemosabe, it's time to pack up the teepee and hit the Trail of Tears.

In response to repeated complaints from Indians that a phony Indian was running CU's Indian Studies program, Churchill responded, "Guess what that means, guys? I'm not taking anyone's job, there wouldn't be an Indian Studies program if I wasn't coordinating it…. They won't give you a job just because you have the paper." This white man of English and Swiss-German descent apparently believes there are no actual Indians capable of performing his job at CU. (No wonder Indians aren't crazy about him.)

As long as we're all agreed that there are some people who don't deserve jobs at universities, can someone explain why Churchill does?

Tuition Soars Due to Knowledge Shortfall
May 3, 2006

E very sentient, literate adult knows that the current spike in gas prices is 90 percent due to forces completely beyond the control of Congress, the White House, or even "Big Oil" itself. The laws of supply and demand determine gas prices in the same way those laws determine the price of eggs, acid-washed blue jeans, and Kanye West downloads.

What determines the price of college tuition? It certainly isn't the quality of the product—as copiously demonstrated in David Horowitz's new book, *The Professors: The 101 Most Dangerous Academics in America.*

The two big topics on CNN last week were (1) high gas prices, and (2) the high cost of college tuition. (Also some story that I think was about an angry Hispanic lacrosse player who vanished from a cruise ship during Bush's low poll numbers.)

CNN reports that college tuition has risen an astonishing 40 percent since 2000. (And nearly 1,000 percent since 1970.) But the proposed solutions to the exact same problem—high prices—were diametrically opposed in the cases of gasoline and college tuition.

The only solution to high gas prices considered on CNN was to pay oil company executives less, perhaps by federal law or order of the president. But no one ever suggested that the solution to the high price of college—far, far outpacing inflation—was to pay professors less. In that case, the solution was for the government to subsidize college professors' salaries even more than it already does.

Why doesn't CNN report the crisis in college tuition the same way it covers high gas prices? To wit:

Coming up, soaring prices at the colleges. Who's to blame? How can you keep your child in college and cash in your wallet? And Harvard outrage, big education makes big bucks, but we pay the price. So should President Bush limit tuition costs?…

To our top story now. It seems like a summer ritual. Rising college administration salaries mean rising tuition prices. But this year, sticker shock at the tuition window is fueling more concern than ever. And it has many people asking where is it going to end?

JAMIE COURT, CONSUMER RIGHTS ADVOCATE: Every time you see the price of tuition go up, you can hear "ka-ching, ka-ching" in the bank accounts of college professors and administrators.

Other than the product being discussed, that's how CNN reports on gas prices.

Why not subsidize the oil companies and put a cap on the price of college? Oil companies provide a product essential to allowing three hundred million Americans to live, whereas colleges are designed to do nothing but turn young people into group-think liberal parasites.

As economist Richard Vedder of Ohio University has demonstrated, every time the government subsidizes college tuition through tuition tax credits, college tuition rises by the precise amount of the tuition tax credit. Can Congress please investigate the "shameful display of greed" by college professors?

Hardworking taxpayers who can't afford gas are forced to pay more in taxes because liberals think it's extremely important for young people to be taught that America is the worst country in the world and that bond traders in the World Trade Center on 9/11 deserved to die.

Maybe with a little less subsidized tuition, colleges couldn't afford luxuries like (fake-Indian) Indian studies professor Ward Churchill. He makes $120,000 a year as a department head at the University of Colorado, in addition to many speaking fees paid to him by other institutions of higher learning, all subsidized by taxpayers.

In addition to providing a vital product, former Exxon CEO Lee Raymond has a Ph.D. in chemical engineering.

Churchill doesn't have a Ph.D., not even one of those phony ones you have to buy on the internet before you can host your own show on Air America Radio. He does not produce a product that allows New Yorkers to eat without turning 90 percent of the city into farmland.

Rather, Churchill's highest academic achievement consists of having a B.A. in communications and graphic arts. At least those are the only parts of his résumé that haven't already been proved false. (And I believe it because no one would make that up.)

Churchill's written oeuvre consists of rants about how the Americans who died in the World Trade Center on 9/11 deserved it: "Well, really. Let's get a grip here, shall we? True enough, they were civilians of a sort. But innocent? Gimme a break.... If there was a better, more effective, or in fact any other way of visiting some penalty befitting their participation upon the little Eichmanns inhabiting the sterile sanctuary of the twin towers, I'd really be interested in hearing about it."

And thus, Churchill joined the ranks of Shakespeare, Tolstoy, Faulkner, and other great writers who employ the phrase, "Gimme a break." Perhaps he expresses himself better in graphic arts.

American taxpayers subsidize the most cretinous, idiotic, hate-filled lunatics in the universe—and liberals are demanding that we direct our hate toward people like Lee Raymond who allow us to go to the bathroom indoors.

How about Congress having weekly hearings on the price of college and the ridiculous salaries of professors like Churchill? Horowitz has already provided the witness list for the first two years.

Tase Him, Bro!
September 26, 2007

D emocrats should run Mahmoud Ahmadinejad for president. He's more coherent than Dennis Kucinich, he dresses like their base, he's more macho than John Edwards, and he's willing to show up at a forum where he might get one hostile question—unlike the current Democratic candidates for president who won't debate on Fox News Channel. He's not married to an impeached president, and the name "Mahmoud Ahmadinejad" is surely no more frightening than "B. Hussein Obama."

Plus: liberals agree with Ahmadinejad on the issues! We know that because he was invited by an American university to speak on campus.

Contrary to all the blather about "free speech" surrounding Ahmadinejad's appearance at Columbia, universities in America do not invite speakers who do not perfectly mirror the political views of their America-hating faculties. Rather, they aggressively censor differing viewpoints and permit only a very narrow category of speech on their campuses. Ask Larry Summers. If a university invites someone to speak, you know the faculty agrees with the speaker. Maybe not the entire faculty. Some Columbia professors probably consider Ahmadinejad too moderate on Israel.

Columbia president Lee Bollinger claimed the Ahmadinejad invitation was in keeping with "Columbia's long-standing tradition of serving as a major forum for robust debate."

Except Columbia doesn't have that tradition. This is worse than saying "the dog ate my homework." It's like saying "the dog ate my homework" when you're Michael Vick, and everyone knows you killed your dog. Columbia's "tradition" is to shut down any speakers who fall outside the teeny, tiny seditious perspective of its professors.

When Minutemen leader Jim Gilchrist and his black colleague, Marvin Stewart, were invited by the College Republicans to speak at Columbia last year, the tolerant, free speech–loving Columbia students violently attacked them, shutting down the speech. Imbued with Bollinger's commitment to free speech, Columbia junior Ryan Fukumori said of the Minutemen, "They have no right to be able to speak here."

Needless to say the university had not invited the Minutemen. (Unlike Ahmadinejad.) Most colleges and universities wouldn't buy a cup of coffee for a conservative speaker. Fees for speakers who do not hate America are raised from College Republican fundraisers and contributions from alumni and locals who think students ought to hear at least one alternative viewpoint in four years of college. Then college administrators turn a blind eye when liberal suck-ups physically attack the speaker. Bollinger, for example, refused to punish the students who stormed the stage and violently ended the Minutemen's speech.

So the one thing we know absolutely is that Bollinger did not allow Ahmadinejad to speak out of respect for "free speech" because Bollinger does not respect free speech.

Only because normal, patriotic Americans were appalled by Columbia's invitation to Ahmadinejad was Bollinger forced into the ridiculous position of denouncing Ahmadinejad when introducing him. Then why did you invite him? And by the way, I'll take a denunciation if college presidents would show up at my speeches and drone on for ten minutes about "free speech" before I begin.

At Syracuse University last year, when liberal hecklers tried to shut down a speech by a popular conservative author of (almost!) six books,

College Republicans began to remove the hecklers. But Dean of Students Roy Baker stopped them on the grounds that removing students screaming during a speech would violate the hecklers'"free speech." Liberals have a "free speech" right to prevent anyone from hearing a conservative's speech.

That's what colleges mean by "free speech." (And by the way, my fingers are getting exhausted from making air quotes every time I use the expression "free speech" in relation to a college campus.) "Tolerance of opposing views" means we have to listen to their anti-American views, but they don't have to hear pro-American views. (In Washington, they call this "the Fairness Doctrine.") Liberals are never called upon to tolerate anything they don't already adore, such as treason, pornography, and heresy. In fact, those will often get you course credit.

At Ahmadinejad's speech, every vicious anti-Western civilization remark was cheered wildly. It was like watching an episode of HBO's *Real Time with Bill Maher*. Ahmadinejad complained that the U.S. and a few other "monopolistic powers, selfish powers" were trying to deny Iranians their "right" to develop nukes.

Wild applause!

Ahmadinejad repeatedly refused to answer whether he seeks the destruction of the state of Israel.

Wild applause!

He accused the U.S. of supporting terrorism.

Wild applause!

Only when Ahmadinejad failed to endorse sodomy did he receive the single incident of booing throughout his speech.

Responding to a question about Iran's execution of homosexuals, Ahmadinejad said there are no homosexuals in Iran: "In Iran we don't have homosexuals, like in your country. In Iran we do not have this phenomenon. I don't know who's told you that we have it." I already knew that from looking at his outfit. If liberals want to run this guy for president, Columbia better get him to *Queer Eye for the Islamofascist Guy*.

Oh, Canada!
March 24, 2010

Since arriving in Canada I've been accused of thought crimes, threatened with criminal prosecution for speeches I hadn't yet given, and denounced on the floor of the Parliament (which was nice because that one was on my "bucket list").

Posters advertising my speech have been officially banned, while posters denouncing me are plastered all over the University of Ottawa campus. Elected officials have been prohibited from attending my speeches. Also, the local clothing stores are fresh out of brown shirts.

Welcome to Canada!

In advance of my visit, the provost of the University of Ottawa, average student IQ: 0, wrote to me—widely disseminating his letter to at least a half-dozen intermediaries before it reached me—in order to recommend that I familiarize myself with Canada's criminal laws regarding hate speech.

This marks the first time I've ever gotten hate mail for something I might do in the future.

Apparently Canadian law forbids "promoting hatred against any identifiable group," which the provost, François A. Houle advised me, "would not only be considered inappropriate, but could in fact lead to criminal charges." I was given no specific examples of what words and phrases I couldn't use, but I take it I'm not supposed to say, "F— you, François."

While it was a relief to know that it is still permissible in Canada to promote hatred against unidentifiable groups, upon reading François's letter, I suddenly realized that I had just been the victim of a hate crime! And it was committed by François A. Houle (French for "Frank A. Hole").

What other speakers get a warning not to promote hatred? Did François A. Houle send a similarly worded letter to Israel-hater Omar Barghouti before he spoke last year at U of Ottawa? (Ottawa: Indian for "Land of the Bed-Wetters.") How about Angela Davis, Communist Party member and former Black Panther who spoke at the University of Zero (University of Ottawa) just last month?

Or do only conservatives get letters admonishing them to be civil? Or— my suspicion—is it only conservative women who fuel François's rage? How about sending a letter to all Muslim speakers advising them to please bathe once a week while in Canada? Would that constitute a hate crime?

I'm sure Canada's Human Rights Commission will get to the bottom of François's strange warning to me, inasmuch as I will be filing a complaint with that august body, so I expect they will be reviewing every letter the university has sent to other speakers prior to their speeches to see if any of them were threatened with criminal prosecution, too.

Both writer Mark Steyn and editor Ezra Levant have been investigated by the Human Rights Commission for promoting hatred toward Muslims. Levant's alleged crime was to reprint the cartoons of Mohammed originally published in a Danish newspaper, leading practitioners of the Religion of Peace to engage in murderous violence across the globe. Steyn's alleged crime was to publish an excerpt of his book, *America Alone* in *Maclean's* magazine, in which he jauntily described Muslims as "hot for jihad."

Both of them also flew jet airliners full of passengers into skyscrapers in lower Manhattan, resulting in thousands of deaths. No, wait—that was somebody else.

Curiously, however, there was no evidence that either the cartoons or the column did, in fact, incite hatred toward Muslims. Nor was there the remotest possibility that they would.

By contrast, conservative speakers are regularly subjected to violent attacks on college campuses. Bill Kristol, Pat Buchanan, David Horowitz, and I have all been the targets of infamous campus attacks. That's why the Clare Boothe Luce Policy Institute (a sponsor of my Canada speeches) and the Young America's Foundation (a sponsor of many of my other college speeches) don't send conservatives to college campuses without a bodyguard.

You'd have to be a real A-Houle not to anticipate that accusing a conservative of "promoting hatred" prior to her arrival on a college campus would in actuality—not in liberal fantasies of terrified Muslims cowering in terror of Mark Steyn readers—incite real-world violence toward the conservative.

The university itself acknowledged that François's letter was likely to provoke violence against me by demanding—long after my speech was scheduled, but immediately after François disseminated his letter—that my sponsors pony up more than $1,200 for extra security.

Also following François's letter, the Ottawa University Student Federation met for seven and a half hours to hammer out a series of resolutions denouncing me. The resolutions included:

"Whereas Ann Coulter is a hateful woman";

"Whereas she has made hateful comments against GLBTQ, Muslims, Jews and women";

"Whereas she violates an unwritten code of 'positive-space'";

"Be it resolved that the SFUO express its disapproval of having Ann Coulter speak at the University of Ottawa."

At least the students didn't waste seven and a half hours on something silly, like their studies.

At the risk of violating anyone's positive space, what happened to Canada? How did the country that gave us Mike Myers, Martin Short, Dan Aykroyd, and Catherine O'Hara suddenly become a bunch of whining crybabies? (Want to hear my favorite Canadian joke? OK, here goes: François Houle! I never get tired of that one.)

After Tuesday night, the hatred incited by François's letter is no longer theoretical. The police called off my speech when the auditorium was surrounded by thousands of rioting liberals—screaming, blocking the entrance, throwing tables, demanding that my books be burned, and finally setting off the fire alarm.

Sadly, I missed the book burning because I never made it to the building. But, reportedly, a Canadian crowd hasn't been this excited since they opened a new Tim Hortons. Local reporters couldn't make out what the crowd was chanting, but it was something about "Molson" and a "sled dog."

I've given more than a hundred college speeches, and not once has one of my speeches been shut down at any point. Even the pie-throwing incident at the University of Arizona didn't break up the event. I said "Get them!," the college Republicans got them, and then I continued with my rambling, hate-filled diatribe—I mean, my speech.

So we've run this experiment more than a hundred times. Only one college speech was ever met with so much mob violence that the police were forced to cancel it: the one that was preceded by a letter from the university provost accusing me of hate speech. (To add insult to injury, François didn't even plan to attend my speech because Tuesday is his bikini wax night.)

If a university official's letter accusing a speaker of having a proclivity to commit speech crimes before she's given the speech—which then leads to Facebook postings demanding that Ann Coulter be hurt, a massive riot, and a police-ordered cancellation of the speech—is not hate speech, then there is no such thing as hate speech.

Either Francois goes to jail or the Human Rights Commission is a hoax and a fraud.

Repeal the Twenty-Sixth Amendment!
November 10, 2010

Jimmy Carter was such an abominable president we got Ronald Reagan, tax cuts, a booming economy, and the destruction of the Soviet Union.

Two years of Bill Clinton and a Democratic Congress got us the first Republican Congress in half a century, followed by tax cuts, welfare reform, and a booming economy—all of which Clinton now claims credit for. Obama's disastrous presidency has already produced Republican senators from Massachusetts, Wisconsin, and Illinois; New Jersey's wonder-governor, Chris Christie; and the largest House majority for Republicans since 1946.

We deserve more.

Clinton only threatened to wreck the health care system; Obama actually did it. We must demand repeal of the Twenty-sixth Amendment.

Adopted in 1971 at the tail end of the Worst Generation's anti-war protests, the argument for allowing children to vote was that eighteen-year-olds could drink and be conscripted into the military, so they ought to be allowed to vote. But eighteen-year-olds aren't allowed to drink anymore. We no longer have a draft. (Perhaps we could add a separate right to vote for members of the military, irrespective of age.)

As we have learned from Obamacare, young people are not considered adults until age twenty-six, at which point they are finally forced to get off their parents' healthcare plans. The old motto was: "Old enough to fight, old enough to vote." The new motto ought to be: "Not old enough to buy your own health insurance, not old enough to vote."

Eighteen- to twenty-six-year-olds don't have property, spouses, children, or massive tax bills. Most of them don't even have jobs because the president they felt so good about themselves for supporting wrecked the economy. The meager tax young people paid for car licensing fees in California threw them into such a blind rage in 2003 that they voted to recall the Democratic governor, Gray Davis. Wait until they start making real money and realize they share a joint-checking account arrangement with the government. Literally wait. Then we'll let them vote.

Having absolutely no idea what makes their precious cars run, young voters are the most likely to oppose offshore drilling. How about ten-year-olds? Why not give them the vote?

Then we'd have politicians wooing voters with offers of free Justin Bieber tickets instead of offers of a "sustainable planet" or whatever hokum the youth have swallowed hook, line, and sinker from their teachers, pop culture idols, and other authority figures. Like eighteen-year-olds, the ten-year-olds would be sublimely unaware that they're the ones who will be footing the bill for all these "free" goodies, paying and paying until they die young of old age.

What I always knew, science has now proved. Brain research in the last five years at Dartmouth and elsewhere has shown that human brains are not fully developed until age twenty-five. Young people are particularly deficient in their frontal lobes, which control decision-making, rational thinking, judgment, the ability to plan ahead, and to resist impulses.

Unfortunately, we didn't know that in 1971. Those of you who have made it to age twenty-six without dying in a stupid drinking game—and I think congratulations are in order, by the way—understand how insane it is to allow young people to vote.

It would almost be tolerable if everyone under the age of thirty just admitted he voted for Obama because someone said to him, "C'mon, it's really cool! Everyone's doing it!"

We trusted them, and now we know it was a mistake.

True, Reagan tied with Carter for the youth vote in 1980 and stole younger voters from Mondale in 1984, but other than that, young voters have consistently embarrassed themselves. Of course, back when Reagan was running for president, young voters consisted of the one slice of the population completely uninfected by the Worst Generation. Today's youth are the infantilized, pampered, bicycle-helmeted children of the Worst Generation.

They foisted this jug-eared, European socialist on us, and now they must be punished. Voters aged eighteen to twenty-nine years old comprised nearly a fifth of the voting population in 2008. They voted overwhelmingly for Obama, 66 percent to 31 percent.

And it only took twelve years of North Korean–style brainwashing to make them do it! At least their teachers haven't brainwashed them into burning books or ratting out their parents to the Stasi yet. (On the bright side, before any book-burning, their professors would be forced to teach them what a book is.) We may as well give public school teachers and college professors twenty votes apiece instead of allowing their toady students to vote.

The Re-Education Camp Effect can be seen in how these slackers living at home on their parents' health insurance voted in the middle of the Republican tidal wave this year. Youths aged 18–29 voted for the Democrats by sixteen points. The younger ones—kids aged 18–24—having just received an A in Professor Ward Churchill's college class on American Oppression—voted Democratic by a whopping ninteen points.

Young people voted for Obama as a fashion statement. One daughter of a friend of a friend of mine spent her whole college summer in 2008 working at a restaurant and then, with teary eyes, sent everything she made to the Obama campaign. Luckily, she doesn't have to worry about paying for tuition, rent, or food. Or property taxes, electric bills, plumbers, or electricians. After being exploited by the Left, she'll end up paying for it for the rest of her life, with interest. Which makes me laugh so hard!

Liberals fight tooth and nail to create an electorate disposed to vote Democratic by, for example, demanding that felons and illegal aliens be given the vote. Republicans need to fight for their own electorate: voters with fully functioning brains. Not old enough to buy your own health insurance, not old enough to vote.

CHAPTER FIFTEEN

Media: Does Barack Obama Have Nude Polaroids of Everyone in the Mainstream Media?

The one thing all veteran journalists agree on—besides how dreamy Obama is—is their contempt for the blogs. It frustrates them that people can get the news on their own now. *No—stop! You weren't supposed to go into that room!* As irritating as it is to see the elite media ignore the IRS scandal, the Benghazi scandal, and the spying-on-journalists scandal, most people use mainstream news only as an alert system so they know what to look up online. *Oh, there's a story about a black kid getting shot in Florida. I'll go online and find out what really happened.*

The old media did it to themselves with their blatant hypocrisy, double standards, and hide-the-news games. Any negative information about a Democrat would always come wrapped in a cocoon of denials: "Obama Administration Denies Claim You're Only Just Hearing about Now." Other facts, you simply will not hear, at all. In August 2009, for example, the media dramatically warned that people were bringing *guns* to protest the *first black president*, while zooming in on a rifle held by one protester, whose face was oddly obscured.

This photo induced the following hysteria on MSNBC:

- "Here you have a man of color in the presidency and white people showing up with guns.... There are questions about whether this has racial overtones...white people showing up with guns."

  —Contessa Brewer

- "[There's a lot of] anger about a black person being president. I'm not going to be surprised if we see somebody get a chance and take a chance and really try to hurt him."

  —Touré

- "Angry at government and racism, you put those two together...."

  —Dylan Ratigan

Then people went online and saw the exact same photo in a wide-shot—and the armed man turned out to be an African-American gun-rights supporter.

The hide-the-facts trick is a specialty of the *New York Times* (All the News That's Fit to Run by the Obama Press Office for Print). Usually, the *Times* prints what are technically all true facts but leaves out other crucial facts most people would consider important. *There was not one untrue statement in our report on the brutal, inhuman bombing of Dresden!* Yes, but you forgot to mention that Germany started the war.

Now we can get the full picture online.

The media's persistent lying can be exhausting. As communications director of Defenders of Republicans Unfairly Attacked by the Media and Then Immediately Sold Out by Their Fellow Republicans (DORUA-MATISOTFR), I will apparently have to point out every week for the rest of my life that Republicans in the audience at the Fox News-Google's 2012 Republican debate were not "booing a soldier." The audience was booing the soldier's demand that Republican presidential candidates commit to allowing gays to serve openly in the military, despite that policy having been adopted in a sleazy partisan vote in the twilight days of the heavily Democratic 2010 Congress.

The question and audience reaction went like this:

"In 2010, when I was deployed to Iraq ..."

(No booing.)

"I had to lie about who I was ..."

(No booing—despite the fact that not talking about your sex life with your co-workers is not lying about who you are. In fact, many Americans manage quite easily to go days and days without talking about their sex lives with co-workers.)

"because I'm a gay soldier ..."

(No booing, although we didn't ask and would prefer that you not tell.)

"and I didn't want to lose my job."

(No booing.)

To recap: so far, a remarkably boo-free interaction.

Finally, we got to the question: "My question is, under one of your presidencies, do you intend to circumvent the progress that's been made for gay and lesbian soldiers in the military?"

Then there was booing. And for good reason. It is beyond absurd to demand that Republican candidates pledge not to reconsider a recent rule change overturning a military policy that had been in effect from the beginning of warfare until the last few weeks of the 111th Congress. Of course there was booing for that! Only eight Republicans in the entire lame duck Senate had voted to end "Don't Ask, Don't Tell." It's safe to assume that no one running for president as a Republican supports this sexualization of the military, except maybe one of the nut candidates. (And John McCain wasn't running in 2012.)

This is not an anti-gay position; it's a pro-military position. The basic idea is that sexual bonds are disruptive to the military bond. A battalion of married couples facing a teeny, tiny unit of heterosexual men would be slaughtered.

But the main target of Republican booing at that question was the media. There were only eleven video questions from regular Americans during that entire debate. It was just like the media to waste 10 percent of voter questions on something that, in the grand scheme of things, is pretty insignificant. The Non-Fox Media certainly weren't going to admit the audience was booing anything other than "a soldier." Since it was a Fox News–sponsored debate, there was no one to point out that it was the media sponsor being booed.

And they wonder why we get our news from the internet.

Dan Rather: Fairly Unbalanced
September 22, 2004

I believe we now have conclusive proof that:

(1) Contrary to rumor, Dan Rather is not an honest newsman who was simply duped by extremely clever forgeries; and

(2) We could have won the Vietnam War.

A basic canon of journalism is not to place all your faith in a lunatic stuck on something that happened years ago who hates the subject of your story and has been babbling nonsense about him for years. And that's true even if you yourself are a lunatic stuck on something that happened years ago (an on-air paddling from Bush 41), who hates the subject of your own story (Bush II), and has been babbling nonsense about him for years, Dan.

CBS's sole source authenticating the forged National Guard documents smearing George W. Bush is Bill Burkett, who's about as sane as Margot Kidder was when they dragged her filthy, toothless butt out of somebody's shrubs a few years back. Burkett has compared Bush to Hitler and Napoleon, and rambles on about Bush's "demonic personality shortcomings." (This would put Burkett on roughly the same page as Al Gore.)

According to *USA Today*, an interview with Burkett ended when he "suffered a violent seizure and collapsed in his chair"—an exit strategy Dan Rather has been eyeing hungrily all week. Burkett admits to having nervous breakdowns and having been hospitalized for depression.

At a minimum, the viewing public should have been informed that CBS's sole source for the anti-Bush records was textbook crank Bill Burkett in order to help us evaluate the information. (*Oh no, not that guy again!*) The public would know to adopt the same skeptical eye it uses to watch the *CBS Evening News* itself.

Whoever forged these documents should not only be criminally prosecuted, but should also have his driver's license taken away for the stupidity of using Microsoft Word to forge 1971 documents. And yet this was the evidence CBS relied on to accuse a sitting president of a court martial–level offense fifty days before a presidential election.

A few days ago, Rather said he still believes the documents are genuine and that he wants to be the one to break the story if the documents are fake. (Dan might want to attend to that story after his exclusive report on the Japanese attack on Pearl Harbor.) Rather is also eagerly awaiting some other documents Burkett says he has that prove Bush is a brainwashed North Korean spy.

By now, there are only two possibilities: (1) Dan Rather knew he was foisting forgeries on the nation to try to change a presidential election, or (2) the "Kenneth, what's the frequency" guy inflicted some real brain damage when he hit Rather in the head back in 1986.

Liberals keep telling us to "move on" from the CBS scandal. That can only mean we're really onto something! They act surprised and insist this incident was a freak occurrence—an unfortunate mistake in the twilight of a great newsman's career.

To the contrary, such an outrageous fraud was inevitable given the mendacity and outright partisanship of the press. Burkett didn't come to CBS; CBS found Burkett. Rather's producer, Mary Mapes, called Joe Lockhart at the Kerry campaign and told him he needed to talk to Burkett. Lockhart himself is the apotheosis of the media-DNC complex, moving in and out of Democratic campaigns and jobs with the mainstream media, including at ABC, NBC, and CNN.

CBS was attempting to manipulate a presidential election. What if CBS had used better forgeries? What if—like Bush's thirty-year-old DUI charge—the media had waited seventy-two hours before the election to air this character assassination?

There is only one reason CBS couldn't wait until just before the election to put these forgeries on the air: it would have been too late. Kerry was crashing and burning…because of the Swift Boat Veterans for Truth. (Funny that the Swift Boat veterans haven't been able to get on CBS News.)

Despite a total blackout on the Swift Boat Veterans' charges against Kerry in the mainstream media, the Swifties had driven Kerry's poll numbers into the dirt long before the Republican National Convention—proving once again that it's almost impossible for liberals to brainwash people who can read. Even the *New York Times* had to stop ignoring the No. 1 book on its own bestseller list, *Unfit for Command*, in order to run front-page articles attacking the Swift Boat Veterans.

The *Today* show has given Kitty Kelley, author of a recent tabloid book on the Bush family, a chair next to Katie Couric until Election Day. In NBC's defense, they're more likely to get the truth in Kitty Kelley's book than in Doug Brinkley's *Tour of Duty*. But Katie hasn't had time to interview the Swift Boat veterans once.

Likewise, CBS showcased laughable forgeries obtained from a man literally foaming at the mouth in order to accuse the president of malfeasance, but would not put a single one of the 264 Vietnam veterans on the air to say what they knew about Kerry.

The Swift Boat Veterans for Truth show the role of the individual in history. It wasn't Republican strategists who finished Kerry off two months before the election. It was the Swift Boat veterans, who came along and kicked Kerry in the shins. No matter how much heat they took, they wouldn't back down. The veterans who served with Kerry told the truth, and the American people listened (as soon as they managed to locate a copy of *Unfit for Command* hidden on one of the back shelves at their local bookstores).

CBS was forced to run a fake story so early in the campaign that it was exposed as a fraud only because of the Swift Boat vets. These brave men, many of them decorated war heroes, have now not only won the election for Bush, they have ended Dan Rather's career.

It's often said that we never lost a battle in Vietnam, but that the war was lost at home by a seditious media demoralizing the American people. Ironically, the leader of that effort was Rather's predecessor at CBS News, Walter Cronkite, known here as "president of the Ho Chi Minh Admiration Society." It was Cronkite who went on air and lied about the Tet offensive, claiming it was a defeat for America. He told the American people the war was over and that we had lost. After seeing that broadcast, Ronald Reagan called President Nixon to say that CBS News officials should be tried for treason.

CBS News has already lost one war for America. The Swift Boat Vets weren't going to let them lose another.

Newsweek Dissembled, Muslims Dismembered!
May 18, 2005

When ace reporter Michael Isikoff was the first with detailed reporting on Paula Jones's accusations against a sitting president, Isikoff's then employer, the *Washington Post*, decided not to run it. The *American Spectator* got the story, followed by the *Los Angeles Times*.

When Isikoff had a detailed account of Kathleen Willey's nasty sexual encounter with President Clinton in the Oval Office, backed by eyewitness and documentary evidence, *Newsweek* decided not to run it. Matt Drudge scooped *Newsweek*.

When Isikoff had the scoop of the century, a thoroughly sourced story about the president of the United States having an affair with an intern and then pressuring her to lie under oath about it, *Newsweek* decided not to run the story. Again, Matt Drudge broke the news.

So, apparently, it's possible for Michael Isikoff to have a story that actually is true, but for his editors not to run it.

Why no pause for reflection when Isikoff had a story about American interrogators at Guantanamo flushing the Quran down the toilet? Why not sit on this story for, say, even half as long as NBC News sat on Lisa Meyers's highly credible account of Bill Clinton raping Juanita Broaddrick?

Newsweek seems to have very different responses to the same reporter's scoops. Who's deciding which of Isikoff's stories to run and which to kill? I note that the ones that Matt Drudge runs have turned out to be more accurate than the ones *Newsweek* runs. Maybe *Newsweek* should start running everything past Drudge.

Somehow *Newsweek* missed the news a few weeks ago about Saudi Arabia arresting forty Christians for "trying to spread their poisonous religious beliefs." But give the American media a story about American interrogators defacing the Quran, and journalists are so appalled there's no time for fact-checking—before they dash off to see the latest exhibition of *Piss Christ*.

Assistant Managing Editor Evan Thomas justified *Newsweek*'s decision to run the incendiary anti-U.S. story about the Quran, saying that "similar reports from released detainees" had already run in the foreign press—"and in the Arab news agency al-Jazeera."

Is there an adult on the editorial board of *Newsweek*? Al Jazeera also broadcast a TV miniseries last year based on the *The Protocols of the Elders of Zion*. (I didn't see it, but I hear James Brolin was terrific!) Al Jazeera has run programs on the intriguing question, "Is Zionism worse than Nazism?" (Take a wild guess where the network came out on this one.) It runs viewer comments about Jews being descended from pigs and apes. How about that one for a *Newsweek* cover story, Evan? You're covered—al Jazeera has already run "similar reports"!

Ironically, among the reasons *Newsweek* gave for killing Isikoff's Lewinsky bombshell was that Evan Thomas was worried someone might get hurt. It seems that Lewinsky could be heard on tape saying that if the story came out, "I'll (expletive) kill myself."

But *Newsweek* couldn't wait a moment to run a story that predictably ginned up Islamic savages into murderous riots in Afghanistan, leaving hundreds injured and sixteen dead. Who could have seen that coming? These are people who stone rape victims to death because the family "honor" has been violated and who fly planes into American skyscrapers because—wait, why did they do that again?

Come to think of it, I'm not sure it's entirely fair to hold *Newsweek* responsible for inciting violence among people who view ancient Buddhist statues as outrageous provocation. (Bumper sticker idea for liberals: news magazines don't kill people, Muslims do.) But then I wouldn't have sat on the story of the decade because of the empty threats of a drama queen gassing with her friend on the telephone between spoonfuls of Häagen-Dazs.

No matter how I look at it, I can't grasp the editorial judgment that requires killing Isikoff's stories about a sitting president molesting the help and obstructing justice, while rushing to print with Isikoff's not particularly credible story about Americans desecrating a Quran at Guantanamo.

Even if it were true, why not sit on it? There are a lot of reasons the media have withheld even true facts from readers. These include:

- A drama queen nitwit idly claims she'd kill herself if a story becomes public. (Evan Thomas's reason for holding the Lewinsky story.)
- The need for "more independent reporting." (*Newsweek* President Richard Smith explaining why *Newsweek* sat on the Lewinsky story even though the magazine had Lewinsky on tape describing the affair.)
- "We were in Havana." (ABC President David Westin explaining why *Nightline* held the Lewinsky story.)
- Unavailable for comment. (Michael Oreskes, *New York Times* Washington bureau chief, in response to why, the day the *Washington Post* ran the Lewinsky story, the *Times* had only a photo of Clinton meeting with the Israeli president on its front page.)

How about the media adding to the list of reasons not to run or not to run a news item: "Protecting ourselves before the American people rise up and lynch us for our relentless left-wing, anti-American propaganda."

Murder Spree by People Who Refuse to Ask for Directions
January 14, 2009

I n a front-page article on January 2 of this year, the *New York Times* took a brief respite from its ongoing canonization of Barack Obama and returned to its series on violent crimes committed by returning GIs, or, as I call it: "U.S. Military, Psycho Killers."

The *Treason Times'* series about Iraq and Afghanistan veterans accused of murder began in January last year but was quickly discontinued as readers noticed that the *Times* doggedly refused to provide any statistics comparing veterans with any other group. So they waited a year, hoping readers wouldn't notice they were still including no relevant comparisons for the implicit claim that veterans are especially murderous.

Forget comparing veteran murderers to the population at large. The germane comparison is between veterans and the general population of young males. The general population includes housewives, grandmothers, and little old men in nursing homes. But violent crime is committed almost exclusively by young men.

Consequently, any group composed primarily of young men will contain a mammoth number of murderers compared to the entire population.

Consider the harmless fantasy game, *Dungeons and Dragons*. After a number of murders were committed in the '80s by *Dungeons and Dragons* enthusiasts, some people concluded the game led to murderous tendencies. Another explanation is that it's a game that happens to be played almost exclusively by young men.

For its series about how America's brave enlisted men are really a bunch of psychopathic cutthroats, the *Times* triumphantly produced

121 homicides committed by veterans of the Iraq and Afghanistan wars. Perhaps the *Times'* next major exposé could be on how a huge percentage of murderers are people who won't ask for directions or share the TV remote.

Let's compare murders by veterans to murders by other eighteen- to thirty-five-year-olds in the U.S. population at large. From 1976 to 2005, eighteen- to twenty-four-year-olds—both male and more gentle females—committed homicide at a rate of 29.9 per 100,000.

Since 9/11, about 1.6 million troops have served in either Iraq or Afghanistan. That makes the homicide rate among veterans of these wars 7.6 per 100,000—or about one-third the homicide rate for their age group (18 to 35) in the general population of both sexes.

But fewer than 200,000 of the 1.6 million troops who served in Iraq and Afghanistan have been women, and the murder rate for the general population includes both males and females. Inasmuch as males commit nearly 90 percent of all murders, the rate for males in those age groups is probably nearly double the male/female combined rates, which translates, conservatively, to about 35 to 55 murderers per 100,000 males aged 18 to 35.

So comparing the veterans' murder rate to only their male counterparts in the general population, we see that Iraq and Afghanistan veterans are about five to ten times *less* likely to commit a murder than non-veterans.

But as long as the *Times* has such a burning interest in the root causes of murder, how about considering the one factor more likely to create a murderer than any other? That is the topic we're not allowed to discuss: single motherhood.

As I describe in my new book, *Guilty: Liberal "Victims" and Their Assault on America*, controlling for socioeconomic status, race, and place of residence, the strongest predictor of whether a person will end up in prison is that he was raised by a single parent. (The second strongest factor is owning a Dennis Kucinich bumper sticker.)

By 1996, 70 percent of inmates in state juvenile detention centers serving long-term sentences were raised by single mothers. Seventy percent of dropouts, suicides, runaways, teenage births, juvenile delinquents, and child murderers involve children raised by single mothers. Girls raised without fathers are more sexually promiscuous and more likely to end up divorced. A 1990 study by the left-wing Progressive Policy Institute showed that, after controlling for single motherhood, the difference in black and white crime disappeared.

Various studies come up with slightly different numbers, but all the figures are grim. A study cited in the far left-wing *Village Voice* found that children brought up in single-mother homes "are five times more likely to commit suicide, nine times more likely to drop out of high school, 10 times more likely to abuse chemical substances, 14 times more likely to commit rape (for the boys), 20 times more likely to end up in prison, and 32 times more likely to run away from home."

With new children being born, running away, dropping out of high school, and committing murder every year, it's not a static problem to analyze. But however the numbers are run, single motherhood is a societal nuclear bomb.

Even in liberals' fevered nightmares, predatory mortgage dealers, oil speculators, and Ken Lay could never do as much harm to their fellow human beings as single mothers do to their own children, to say nothing of society at large.

Think I'm being cruel? Imagine an America with 60 to 70 percent fewer juvenile delinquents, teenage births, teenage suicides, and runaways, and you will appreciate what the sainted "single mothers" have accomplished.

But the *Times* won't run that series because liberals cheer for the dissolution of traditional marriage in America. They detest the military, so they cite a few anecdotal examples of veterans who have committed murder and hope that no one asks for details.

Olbermann's Plastic Ivy
March 4, 2009

Fortunately, we have Keith Olbermann to point out that Rush Limbaugh did not accurately quote the preamble to the Constitution in his CPAC speech last weekend. I'm not sure what scam Olbermann imagined Rush was trying to put over on the American people by saying conservatives believed in the "preamble to the Constitution" and then quoting words from the Declaration of Independence—but Olbermann put an end to that cruel deception!

These small-time opportunities to show off by correcting someone else's teeny, tiny mistakes are the lifeblood of Olbermann's MSNBC show, *Countdown*. Olbermann is no more capable of not correcting Representative Charlie Rangel when he said "inferred," but meant "implied," than an obsessive compulsive could pass a sink without washing his hands.

There is utterly no purpose to these lame "gotchas," except that Olbermann is so desperately insecure that he is willing to waste valuable airtime in order to convince other status-conscious idiots that he is, like, *scary-smart*.

Olbermann relentlessly attacked low-level Bush administration employee Monica Goodling for not going to a name-dropping college, saying—approximately one million times—that she got her law degree "by sending 100 box tops to Religious Lunatic University." I would venture to say that the students at Goodling's law school at Regent University are far more impressive than those at the Cornell agriculture school—the land-grant, non-Ivy League school Keith attended.

I wouldn't mention it, except that Olbermann savages anyone who didn't go to an impressive college. As it happens, he didn't go to an impressive college, either.

If you've ever watched any three nights of his show, you know that Olbermann went to Cornell. But he always forgets to mention that he went to the school that offers classes in milking and bovine management. Indeed, Keith is constantly lying about his nonexistent "Ivy League" education, boasting to *Playboy* magazine, for example: "My Ivy League education taught me how to cut corners, skim books and take an idea and write 15 pages on it, and also how to work all day at the Cornell radio station and never actually go to class."

Except Keith didn't go to the Ivy League Cornell; he went to the Old MacDonald Cornell.

The real Cornell, the School of Arts and Sciences (average SAT: 1325; acceptance rate: 1 in 6 applicants), is the only Ivy League school at Cornell and the only one that grants a Bachelor of Arts degree. Keith went to an affiliated state college at Cornell, the College of Agriculture and Life Sciences (average SAT: about that of pulling guards at the University of South Carolina; acceptance rate: 1 of every 1 applicants).

Olbermann's incessant lying about having an "Ivy League education" when he went to the non-Ivy League ag school at Cornell would be like a graduate of the Yale locksmithing school boasting about being a "Yale man."

Among the graduates of the Ivy League Cornell are Ruth Bader Ginsburg, Thomas Pynchon, Paul Wolfowitz, E. B. White, Sanford I. Weill, Floyd Abrams, Kurt Vonnegut, Douglas Ginsburg, Janet Reno, Henry Heimlich, and Harold Bloom.

Graduates of the ag school include David LeNeveu of the Anaheim Ducks, Mitch Carefoot of the Phoenix RoadRunners, Darren Eliot, former professional hockey player, and Joe Nieuwendyk, multiple Stanley Cup winner. One begins to understand why Harvard students threw a chicken on the ice during Cornell's famous rout of Harvard at a 1973 hockey game.

If you actually want to pursue a career related to agriculture, there is no better school than the Cornell ag school. I have nothing but admiration for the farmers and aspiring veterinarians at the ag school. They didn't go there just to have "Cornell" on their résumés. In addition to the farmers, there are some smart kids who go to the ag school—as there are at all state universities. But most people who majored in "communications" at an ag school don't act like Marshall Scholars or go around mocking graduates of Regent University Law School.

The sort of insecurity that would force you to always say "trebled" instead of "tripled" could only come from a communications major with massive status anxiety, like Keith. Without even looking it up, I am confident that Harvard, Yale, and Princeton do not offer degrees in "communications." I know there is no "communications" major at the Ivy League Cornell. "Communications" is a major, along with "recreation science," most commonly associated with linemen at USC. But at least the linemen can throw a football, which Keith cannot because his mother decided he was not physically robust enough to play outdoors as a child.

It may seem cruel to reveal the true college of someone who already wakes up in the middle of the night in a cold sweat worried that he's a fraud. But I believe that by pointing out that Olbermann actually is a fraud, I am liberating him.

You may not realize it now, Keith, but you will look back on this day and say, "That was the best thing that ever happened to me!" Finally, you can stop pretending that you went to the hard-to-get-into Cornell. Now you won't have to quickly change the subject whenever people idly remark that they didn't know it was possible to major in "communications" at an Ivy League school. No longer will you have to aggressively bring up Cornell when it has nothing to do with the conversation.

Relax, Keith. Now you can let people like you for you.

Watching MSNBC Is Torture
May 6, 2009

The media wail about "torture," but are noticeably short on facts. Liberals try to disguise the utter wussification of our interrogation techniques by constantly prattling on about "the banality of evil." Um, no. In this case, it's actually the banality of the banal.

Start with the fact that the average Gitmo detainee has gained twenty pounds in captivity. Some prisoners have been heard whispering, "If you think Allah is great, you should try these dinner rolls."

In terms of "torture," there was "the attention grasp," which you have seen in every department store where a mother was trying to get control of her misbehaving child. If "the attention grasp" doesn't work, the interrogators issue a stern warning: "Don't make me pull this car over." Farther up the parade of horribles was "walling," which I will not describe except to say Elliot Spitzer paid extra for it. And for the most hardened terrorists, CIA interrogators had "the caterpillar." Evidently, the terrorists have gotten so fat on the food at Guantanamo, now they can't even outrun a caterpillar.

Contrary to MSNBC hosts who are afraid of bugs, water, and their own shadows, waterboarding was most definitely not a "war crime" for which the Japanese were prosecuted after World War II—no matter how many times Mrs. Jonathan Turley, professor of cooking at George Washington University, says so. All MSNBC hosts and guests were apparently reading *Little Women* rather than military books as children and therefore can be easily fooled about Japanese war crimes. (MSNBC: the Official Drama Queen Network of the 2012 Olympics.)

Japanese war crimes were things like: waterboarding PLUS killing the prisoner, or waterboarding PLUS amputating the prisoner's healthy arm. American-style waterboarding would be a reward in a Japanese POW camp.

What the Japanese did to their POWs made even the Nazis blanch. The Japanese routinely beheaded and bayoneted prisoners; forced prisoners to dig their own graves and then buried them alive; amputated prisoners' healthy arms and legs, one by one, for sport; force-fed prisoners dry rice and then filled their stomachs with water until their bowels exploded; and injected them with chemical weapons in order to observe, time, and record their death throes before dumping them in mass graves.

To claim that the Japanese—architects of the Bataan Death March— were prosecuted for "waterboarding" would be like saying Ted Bundy was executed for engaging in sexual harassment. While only 4 percent of British and American troops captured by German or Italian forces died in captivity, 27 percent of the Allies' POWs captured by the Japanese died in captivity. Japanese war crimes were so atrocious that even rape was treated as only a secondary war crime in the Tokyo trial (similar to what happens in an R. Kelly trial).

The Japanese "water cure" was to "waterboarding" as practiced at Guantanamo what a knifepoint mugging is to bumping someone on the sidewalk. Their version of "waterboarding" was to fill the prisoner's stomach with water until his stomach was distended—and then pound on his stomach, causing the prisoner to vomit. Or they would jam a stick into the prisoner's nose so he could breathe only through his mouth and then pour water in his mouth so he would choke to death. Or they would "waterboard" the prisoner with saltwater, which would kill him.

Meanwhile, the alleged "torture" under the Bush administration consists of things like:

- "failing to respect a Serbian national holiday"; or

- "forgetting to wear plastic gloves while handling a Quran."

Finding out who started the tall tale about "waterboarding" being treated as a war crime after World War II would take the talents of a forensic historian, someone like Christina Hoff Sommers.

After years of hearing the feminist "fact" that emergency room admissions for women beaten by their husbands soared by 40 percent on Super Bowl Sundays, Sommers traced it back to an unsubstantiated rumination erupting from a feminist rap session. But the lunatic claim was passed around with increasing credibility until it ended up being cited as hard fact in the *New York Times*, the *Boston Globe*, and on *Good Morning America*.

One of the earliest entries in the "waterboarding as war crimes" myth must be this October 2006 article in the *Washington Post*, citing a case raised by Senator Teddy Kennedy—and heaven knows Kennedy understands the horrors of a near-drowning: "Twenty-one years earlier, in 1947, the United States charged a Japanese officer, Yukio Asano, with war crimes for carrying out another form of waterboarding on a U.S. civilian. The subject was strapped on a stretcher that was tilted so that his feet were in the air and head near the floor, and small amounts of water were poured over his face, leaving him gasping for air until he agreed to talk."

Even if that description of what Asano did were true—and it isn't—the only relevant word in the entire paragraph is "civilian."

Any mistreatment of a civilian is a war crime. So every other part of that paragraph is utterly irrelevant to the treatment of prisoners of war, much less non-uniformed enemy combatants at Guantanamo, who could have been shot on sight under the laws of war.

What Americans need to understand is that under liberals' own "laws of war," they will invent apocryphal incidents from history in order to give aid and comfort to America's enemies.

Like, Is Sarah Palin Totally Conceited?
September 15, 2010

I n the October issue of *Vanity Fair* now on newsstands, Michael Gross reverts to junior high school to issue gossip-girl digs at Sarah Palin. Next up in *Vanity Fair*: "Sarah Palin Super Stuck Up; Thinks She's All That." Gross dramatically reveals, for example, that her speech in Wichita, Kansas, was "basically the same speech she gave 18 hours earlier to the Tea Party group in Independence (Mo.)."

A politician repeated lines in a speech? You must be kidding! *Hello, Ripley's? No, you cannot put me on hold. This is a worldwide exclusive. I'm sitting on a powder keg here.*

Gross also apparently believes *Vanity Fair* readers will be tickled, rather than appalled by this story about Palin: "Sometimes when she went out in public, people were unkind. Once, while shopping at Target, a man saw Palin and hollered, 'Oh my God! It's Tina Fey! I love Tina Fey!' When other shoppers started laughing, the governor parked her cart, walked out of the store, and drove away." (That jackass was lucky Sarah didn't have her moose rifle with her.)

A random encounter with a rude, abusive jerk in public is supposed to make her look bad? Liberals have really lost their minds about Palin. They'd laugh if someone hit her with a baseball bat.

Gross also includes a strange exegesis about Palin's tipping. It seems an unnamed bellman at an unnamed Midwestern hotel "waited up until past midnight for Palin and her entourage to check in—and then got no tip at all for 10 bags."

First of all, what does Gross's imaginary bellboy think the entire Palin family and their assistants and aides were doing until after midnight? Bowling? Playing beer-pong at a local pub? They've been traveling—with kids—all day, arriving after midnight, and the only thing he can think about is how he had to stay up late before going home to sleep in his own bed. Assuming the story is true, which I do not, why is it Palin's fault no tip was given? According to the bellboy, there must have been at least half a dozen people in her group. Palin is the "talent." Other than Trig, she's the last person who should be held responsible for the tip.

Gross was just getting warmed up with the bellboy. "The same went for the maids who cleaned Palin's rooms in both places." In a worldwide exclusive, he reveals: "no tip whatsoever." I think most normal people reading that aren't thinking about Palin, they're thinking, "Wait—do I tip maids?"

I don't on principle, unless I've stayed several nights or left a dead body in the room. Even then, it depends on the size of the body. I also don't leave a tip for the guy who put batteries in the TV remote, the hotel buyer who chose the nice soaps, or the interior decorator who designed the room. That's what I'm buying: a clean, functional room for one night.

Also fantastic is Gross's conspiracy theory on why no one in Alaska will talk to him about Palin. In part, this is the typical, head-up-the-butt New York reporter's view of Alaska. Gross assumes everyone in the state personally knows Sarah Palin and if they don't talk to him . . . they must be hiding something! Thus, according to Gross, "They don't want *her* to find out they have talked with a reporter, because of a suspicion that bad things will happen to them if she does."

Why else wouldn't people talk to him? *It's me—Michael Gross from Manhattan! Everyone in Alaska should want to hang with me!* The fact that they don't is evidence of a conspiracy. Another explanation is that not everyone in Alaska, not even everyone in Wasilla, personally knows Sarah Palin. Nor are they in awe of Manhattan or *Vanity Fair*. In other words, maybe Alaska is remarkably like other places.

Most psychotically insane is Gross's rumination on why the Palins would leave their home on, I quote, "the anniversary of Sarah's resignation." This is the kind of "anniversary" celebrated only by Keith Olbermann and other Palin obsessives. It is not yet, as we go to press, an anniversary celebrated by Hallmark.

The fact that Michael Gross imagines the date Palin resigned is an "anniversary" anyone else in the world would notice proves only that he is a head case. He discusses the Palins' absence on this momentous day (in his own mind) with his fellow obsessive, Joe McGinniss—the man who moved into the house next door to the Palins for more convenient stalking.

On and on the two nutcases speculate about why the Palins are gone—because, you see, THERE MUST BE AN EXPLANATION! Perhaps "the Palins would want assurance that no curiosity seekers would trespass," Gross offers. But why, he asks himself, "make such a long flight"?

In the climactic scene of the article, Gross asks McGinniss, "Wouldn't it be easier to hire a guard?" Before giving the reply, Gross notes that McGinniss has put himself "in the frame of mind of his subject—where everything is fungible, and everyone is suspect." So McGinniss speaks with authority. And he says: "A guard would have a story he could sell."

Yeah, like the Midwestern bellboy. But the reader is supposed to be gasping at the strangeness of the Palins, not the strangeness of the two reporters, standing alone, staring at the Palins' empty house on an imaginary "anniversary," postulating theories on why the Palins aren't there.

It turns out the Palins had simply flown to Todd's parents' house for the weekend. No "curiosity seekers" showed up at the house to gawk—other than the two reporters, who are utterly oblivious to the fact that the only paranoids in this story are them.

Media: Halliburton Paid Dick Cheney to Commit Rape in Iraq
August 3, 2011

A front-page story by James Risen in the *New York Times* on Wednesday, February 13, 2008, reported on a "troubling trend" of sexual assaults committed by American employees of military contractors in Iraq. The centerpiece of his story was Jamie Leigh Jones, who claimed to have been brutally gang-raped in 2005 while working in the Green Zone. (Risen also interviewed other women claiming to have been sexually assaulted in Iraq and—for journalistic balance—their attorneys.)

Jones infamously claimed that days after arriving in Iraq with KBR, then a subsidiary of Halliburton, she had been drugged and gang-raped by fellow employees. After reporting the rape, she said she was held by machine gun–toting guards in a tiny shipping container by KBR managers, with no food or water for twenty-four hours, as retaliation.

You may have heard about Jones's sensational allegations—they were reported on ABC's *20/20*; CNN; CBS News's *The Early Show*, MSNBC, National Public Radio, in every major U.S. newspaper, and lots of international media.

All she had to do was mention the words "rape" and "Halliburton," and journalists went wild! Jones told her tale before congressional committees, on numerous TV shows—and in a book she is actually writing, titled *The Jamie Leigh Story: How My Rape in Iraq and Cover-up Made Me a Crusader for Justice*. (Scheduled for release the third Tuesday after never.)

Then senator Barack Obama demanded a State Department investigation into Jones's claims.

But no one jumped on Jones's story with more self-righteousness than Senator Al Franken. He used her story to jam through a grandstandy "anti-rape" amendment to an appropriations bill. Rape would be stopped by prohibiting defense contractors from including mandatory arbitration clauses in employment contracts! (Coincidentally, banning arbitration would also help mountebank trial lawyers like John Edwards collect massive damages awards from illiterate jurors.)

The thirty Republican senators who voted against Franken's pro-trial lawyer amendment were promptly denounced as "pro-rape" across the internet, on liberal talk radio, and in mass phone calls to their offices.

And then a few weeks ago, the *Times* ran a microscopic, one-paragraph Associated Press story on page thirteen of a Saturday paper, reporting that a jury looked at the facts and found that...Jones made the whole story up. Maybe Republican senators should consider sponsoring a bill punishing false rape allegations by employees of defense contractors.

When the time came to put up or shut up, Jones's "gang-rape" claim simply disappeared. DNA evidence showed she'd had sex with only one man, and he claimed it was consensual. In fact, the whole crime disappeared: after a police investigation, no criminal charges were brought whatsoever.

Instead, Jones's lawyer brought a civil suit against KBR and its employees—with a much lower burden of proof—alleging only a routine he-said, she-said date-rape case. Jones's claim that she had been drugged with Rohypnol was demolished by tests taken by a female military doctor the day after the alleged attack. Rohypnol is detectable for seventy-two hours, but there was no trace of it, or any "date rape" drug, in her system.

Jones said the attack was so brutal that her breast implants were ruptured and her pectoral muscles torn, requiring massive reconstructive surgery. This was contradicted not only by the female doctor who examined her the next day, but also by her own plastic surgeon back in Houston.

Her claim that KBR management had held her at gunpoint in a shipping container vanished when it turned out she had only remembered that part of the story two years after it supposedly happened (coincidentally, just as the media frenzy began). Perhaps the Rohypnol made her forget something else: KBR employees, including security guards, don't carry guns, much less machine guns.

Having showcased Jones's original, false accusation in a fifteen-hundred-word article splashed across its front page, as soon as her story unraveled, the *Times* stared at its shoes and said nothing. In another six months, liberals will once again be citing Jones's case as evidence of the "troubling trend" of sexual assaults by military contractors.

If only Jones had accused Bill Clinton or any member of the Kennedy family of rape, the mainstream media might have greeted her allegations with a little more skepticism. But she accused employees of a company with a tertiary, long-ago, six-degrees-of-separation relationship with Dick Cheney. This was no time for fact-checking!

Still, wasn't it the tiniest bit suspicious to anyone in the media that Jones claimed KBR management responded to her rape claim by locking her in a shipping container? Why would a company that already had a PR problem stick its neck out to protect accused rapists? Isn't it more likely that a corporation would sell out even innocent employees accused of rape? Surely, it must have occurred to company honchos that she'd eventually get back to the U.S.

From the beginning, Jones's story was that she woke up remembering nothing of the night before … and then suddenly realized she must have been slipped the "date rape" drug Rohypnol, beaten, and gang-raped! How do you go from total amnesia to deciding that you were the star of your own Lifetime made-for-TV movie? I don't remember off-hand what I was doing last Tuesday, but this does not lead me to assume I was gang-raped.

Even before leaving for Iraq with KBR at the age of twenty, Jones had made rape accusations against, not one, but two other men. A few years earlier, she told a doctor her boyfriend had raped her, and right before leaving for Iraq she accused a KBR supervisor of raping her. She was already 0 for 2 on rape allegations.

Just a few years after humiliating themselves over the Duke lacrosse case, it's nice to see the media weren't the least bit hesitant about leaping on another ludicrous rape claim. Perhaps liberals were slipped Rohypnol, and that's why they can't remember that not every woman claiming she was raped is always telling the truth.

CHAPTER SIXTEEN

Liberals and Science: Regulate Al Gore's Refrigerator

When it comes to "science," liberals are more comfortable with the social sciences. *My scientific method will show you how to pick up models!* All the Left's ideas about scientific progress always end up being a version of the old *New Yorker* cartoon showing a scientist standing in front of a chalkboard covered with a gigantic mathematical equation, in the middle of which these words appear: "then a miracle happens …" That's how Democrats plan to run cars on solar and wind power: "then a miracle happens."

Global warming couldn't exist without fabulously rich people and their low-wage servants. Environmentalists think they can live in a world of only Malibu and East Hampton—with no Trentons or Detroits. If you're having a conversation about global warming in Los Angeles or New York, within three sentences, it will be all about "beach erosion."

It's a real knife in the back for rich liberals to imagine that the dentist from upper Montclair, who lives a block from the beach and has no ocean view—*HIM*, with that hideous house of his—is now going have beachfront property with the best view.

Poor nerdy scientists are constantly discovering they're not allowed to have an opinion on global warming. It's no good to say, "I'm sorry, but this is where facts lead me." Much better to just back away slowly and explain, "It's not my field. Apparently it's Scarlett Johansson's field."

The platonic ideal of a Liberal Who Cares is a sobbing high school girl, wailing that "THERE MAY NOT EVEN BE A PLANET SOON!" Our junior scientists have to be careful to not read anything. And to be passionate. It's also important to cite the "Union of Concerned Scientists" frequently and refuse to believe that its members are "scientists" in fields that have as much to do with climate science as acting. At least it shows a lot of courage for a person in Hollywood to take on global warming. The entirety of Hollywood politics consists of AIDS, global warming, gay marriage, and banning plastic shopping bags.

No matter how hip and world-weary they are, your true liberal zealot will always get heart-attack serious about one subject: global warming. MSNBC's Chris Hayes is the classic example. In the summer of 2013, Hayes did an entire segment on the "extremist" attorney general of Virginia, Ken Cuccinelli, then running for governor. Hayes accused Cuccinelli of waging "a witch hunt of intimidation, persecution, and bullying against one of the top climate scientists in the country, a man who happened to be teaching at the University of Virginia." On and on, Hayes railed at the attorney general for trying "to destroy and discredit one of the most prominent people in the scientific community[, a] scientist who is warning us what is happening to our earth,… global warming."

At no point did Hayes mention that this "most prominent" person, Michael Mann, had been accused of fraud in the creation of his "hockey stick" graph. The prominent Michael Mann didn't mention it either. The graph purported to show that the Earth's temperature was perfectly flat for nine hundred years until the twentieth century when human activity heated the place up so much, it nearly broke the thermostats.

Emails then surfaced showing Mann had cooked the books. The most devastating one came from the director of the East Anglia University Climate Research Unit, the leading proponent of global warming hysteria, referring to Mann's "trick...to hide the decline [in global temperatures]." Another CRU email describes the manipulation of the data to get a "hockey stick" graph thus: "[W]e can have a proper result, but only by including a load of garbage!" (Am I just crazy from the heat or was Mann trying to deceive us?)

Inasmuch as Mann had been a professor at University of Virginia during the "trick" period of his career, Attorney General Cuccinelli had an obligation to investigate possible fraud against the taxpayers, much as he would have to investigate a government contractor accused of using "tricks" and "including a load of garbage" in his work. To describe Cuccinelli's investigation as a vicious attack on academic freedom without mentioning the scandal surrounding Mann's "hockey stick" graph would be like an angry report on a death sentence being imposed on a brave fighter pilot—without ever mentioning what Hermann Göring was on trial for.

Liberals like Hayes believe bullying is the essence of science. It's frustrating to them when crowd psychology doesn't work on other people the way it works on them. As with their political opinions and cultural tastes, their scientific opinions are based entirely on status anxiety. (*Every major scientist believes it! Everyone's voting for Obama! Surely you agree Beyoncé is the most gorgeous human who ever lived!*)

The only silver lining to these scientific fads is that back when Scarlett Johansson was furiously emailing Obama during the 2008 campaign, you have to know that every single email was about global warming.

The Coming Ass Age
March 21, 2007

No matter how much liberals try to dress up their nutty superstitions as "science," which only six-fingered lunatics could doubt, scratch any global warming "scientist" and you get a religious fanatic. These days, new religions are barely up and running before they seize upon all the worst aspects of the God-based religions.

First, there's the hypocrisy and corruption. At the 1992 Democratic Convention in New York, Al Gore said, "The central organizing principle of governments everywhere must be the environment." The environment would not, however, be the central organizing principle of Gore's own life.

The only place Al Gore conserves energy these days is on the treadmill. The last time I saw him on TV I thought, "That reminds me—we have to do something about saving the polar bears." Never mind his carbon footprint—have you seen the size of Al Gore's regular footprint lately? It's almost as deep as Janet Reno's.

But I digress. As has been widely reported, Gore's Tennessee mansion consumes twenty times the energy of the average home in the entire state. But it's OK, according to the priests of global warming. Gore has purchased "carbon offsets."

It took the Catholic Church hundreds of years to develop corrupt practices such as papal indulgences. The global warming religion has barely been around for twenty years, and it's already granting dispensations to pollute with papal indulgences called "carbon offsets."

Further proving that liberalism is a religion, its practitioners respond with the zeal of Torquemada to any dissent from the faith of global warming.

A few years ago, Danish statistician Bjorn Lomborg wrote a book titled *The Skeptical Environmentalist*, disputing the hysteria surrounding global warming and other environmentalist scares. Lomborg is a Greenpeace anti-war protester—or, as he is described on liberal websites, he is a "young, gay vegetarian Dane with tight T-shirts." His book was cited favorably in the *New York Times*.

But for questioning the "science" behind global warming, Lomborg was brought up on charges of "scientific misconduct" by Denmark's Inquisition Court, called the "Ministry of Science, Technology and Innovation." I take it Denmark's "Ministry of Truth" was booked that day.

The moment anyone diverges from official church doctrine on global warming, he is threatened with destruction. Environmentalists would burn heretics at the stake if they could figure out how to do it in a "carbon neutral" way.

Climatologist Dr. Timothy Ball is featured in the new documentary debunking global warming, titled *The Great Global Warming Swindle*. For this heresy, Ball has received hate mail with such messages as, "If you continue to speak out, you won't live to see further global warming."

I'm against political writers whining about their hate mail because it makes them sound like Paul Krugman. But that's political writers, who are supposed to be used to the hurly-burly of political passions.

Global warming is allegedly "science." It's hard to imagine Niels Bohr responding to Albert Einstein's letter questioning quantum mechanics with a statement like: "If you continue to speak out, you won't live to see further quantum mechanics." Come to think of it, one can't imagine the pope writing a letter to Jerry Falwell saying, "If you continue to speak out, you won't live to see further infallibility."

If this is how global warming devotees defend their beliefs, it may be a few tweaks short of "science." Scientific facts are not susceptible to liberal bullying—which, by the way, is precisely why liberals hate science.

A few years ago, the *New York Times* ran an article about the continuing furious debates among physicists about quantum mechanics, which differs from global warming in the sense that it is supported by physical evidence and it doesn't make you feel good inside to "do something" about quantum mechanics.

Though he helped develop the theory of quantum mechanics, Einstein immediately set to work attacking his own theory. MIT cosmologist Max Tegmark called the constant testing and arguing about quantum mechanics "a seventy-five-year war."

That's how a real scientific theory operates. That's even how a real religion operates. Only a false religion needs hate mail, threats, courts of inquisition, and Hollywood propaganda movies to sustain it.

A Glowing Report on Radiation
March 16, 2011

With the terrible earthquake and resulting tsunami that have devastated Japan, the only good news is that anyone exposed to excess radiation from the nuclear power plants is now probably much less likely to get cancer. This only seems counterintuitive because of media hysteria for the past twenty years trying to convince Americans that radiation at any dose is bad. There is, however, burgeoning evidence that excess radiation operates as a sort of cancer vaccine.

As the *New York Times* science section reported in 2001, an increasing number of scientists believe that at some level—much higher than the minimums set by the U.S. government—radiation is good for you.

"They theorize," the *Times* said, that "these doses protect against cancer by activating cells' natural defense mechanisms." Among the studies mentioned by the *Times* was one in Canada finding that tuberculosis patients subjected to multiple chest X-rays had much lower rates of breast cancer than the general population.

And there are lots more! A $10 million Department of Energy study from 1991 examined ten years of epidemiological research by the Johns Hopkins School of Public Health on 700,000 shipyard workers, some of whom had been exposed to ten times more radiation than the others from their work on the ships' nuclear reactors. The workers exposed to excess radiation had a 24 percent lower death rate and a 25 percent lower cancer mortality than the non-irradiated workers.

Isn't that just incredible? I mean, that the Department of Energy spent $10 million doing something useful? Amazing, right?

In 1983, a series of apartment buildings in Taiwan were accidentally constructed with massive amounts of cobalt-60, a radioactive substance. After sixteen years, the buildings' ten thousand occupants developed only five cases of cancer. The cancer rate for the same age group in the general Taiwanese population over that time period predicted 170 cancers. The people in those buildings had been exposed to radiation nearly five times the maximum "safe" level according to the U.S. government. But they ended up with a cancer rate 96 percent lower than the general population.

Bernard L. Cohen, a physics professor at the University of Pittsburgh, compared radon exposure and lung cancer rates in 1,729 counties covering 90 percent of the U.S. population. His study in the 1990s found far fewer cases of lung cancer in those counties with the highest amounts of radon—a correlation that could not be explained by smoking rates.

Tom Bethell, author of the *The Politically Incorrect Guide to Science*, has been writing for years about the beneficial effects of some radiation, or "hormesis." A few years ago, he reported on a group of scientists who concluded their conference on hormesis at the University of Massachusetts by repairing to a spa in Boulder, Montana, specifically in order to expose themselves to "excess" radiation. At the Free Enterprise Radon Health Mine in Boulder, people pay $5 to descend eighty-five feet into an old mining pit to be irradiated with more than four hundred times the EPA-recommended level of radon. In the summer, fifty people a day visit the mine hoping for relief from chronic pain and autoimmune disorders.

Amazingly, even the Soviet-engineered disaster at Chernobyl in 1986 can be directly blamed for the deaths of no more than the thirty-one people inside the plant who died in the explosion. Although news reports generally claimed a few thousand people died as a result of Chernobyl—far fewer than the tens of thousands initially predicted—that hasn't been confirmed by studies.

Indeed, after endless investigations, including by the United Nations, Manhattan Project veteran Theodore Rockwell summarized the reports to Bethell in 2002, saying, "They have not yet reported any deaths outside of the thirty who died in the plant." Even the thyroid cancers in people who lived near the reactor were attributed to low iodine in the Russian diet—and consequently had no effect on the cancer rate. Meanwhile, the animals around the Chernobyl reactor, who were not evacuated, are "thriving," according to scientists quoted in the April 28, 2002, *Sunday Times* (UK).

Dr. Dade W. Moeller, a radiation expert and professor emeritus at Harvard, told the *New York Times* that it's been hard to find excess cancers even from Hiroshima and Nagasaki, particularly because one-third of the population will get cancer anyway. There were about ninety thousand survivors of the atomic bombs in 1945, and, more than fifty years later, half of them were still alive. (Other scientists say there were seven hundred excess cancer deaths among the ninety thousand.)

Although it is hardly a settled scientific fact that excess radiation is a health benefit, there's certainly evidence that it decreases the risk of some cancers—and there are plenty of scientists willing to say so. But

Jenny McCarthy's vaccine theories get more press than Harvard physics professors' studies on the potential benefits of radiation. (Liberals refer to this as "the scientific method.")

I guess good radiation stories are not as exciting as news anchors warning of mutant humans and scary nuclear power plants—news anchors who, by the way, have injected small amounts of poison into their foreheads to stave off wrinkles. Which is to say: the general theory that small amounts of toxins can be healthy is widely accepted—except in the case of radiation.

Every day Americans pop multivitamins containing trace amount of zinc, magnesium, selenium, copper, manganese, chromium, molybdenum, nickel, and boron—all poisons. They get flu shots. They'll drink copious amounts of coffee specifically to ingest a poison: caffeine. (Back in the '70s, Professor Cohen offered to eat as much plutonium as Ralph Nader would eat caffeine—an offer Nader never accepted.)

But in the case of radiation, the media have convinced Americans that the minutest amount is always deadly. Although reporters love to issue sensationalized reports about the danger from Japan's nuclear reactors, remember that, so far, thousands have died only because of Mother Nature. And the survivors may outlive all of us over here in hermetically sealed, radiation-free America.

Liberals: They Blinded Us with Science
March 23, 2011

In response to my column last week about hormesis—the theory that some radiation can be beneficial to humans—liberals reacted with their usual open-minded examination of the facts. According to Noel Sheppard at NewsBusters, MSNBC's Ed Schultz devoted an entire segment to denouncing me. He called me toxic, accused me of spreading misinformation, and said I didn't care about science.

One thing Schultz did not do, however, was cite a single scientific study.

I cited three physicists by name as well as four studies supporting hormesis in my column. For the benefit of liberals scared of science, I even cited the *New York Times*. It tells you something that the most powerful repudiation of hormesis Schultz could produce was the fact that a series of government agencies have concluded—I quote—that "insufficient human data on hormesis exists." Well, in that case, I take it all ba—wait, no. That contradicts nothing I said in my column.

Liberals should take up their quarrel with the physicists cited by both me and the *New York Times*. I'm sure the Harvard physics department will be fascinated to discover that the Left's idea of the scientific method is to cling to their fears while hurling invective at anyone who cites evidence.

The fact that liberals chronically wet themselves over science wouldn't be half as annoying if they didn't go around boasting about their deep respect for science, especially compared to conservatives. Apparently this criticism is based on conservatives' skepticism about global warming—despite the findings of distinguished research scientists Dr. Alicia Silverstone and Dr. Woody Harrelson. (In my case, it's only because I'm still waiting for liberals' global cooling theory from the '70s to come true.)

The Left's idea of "science" is that we should all be riding bicycles and using the Clivus Multrum composting latrines instead of flush toilets to save a universe that's been around for billions of years. Anyone who dissents, they say—while adjusting their healing crystals for emphasis—is "afraid of science."

A review of the record, however, shows that time and again liberals have been willing to corrupt public policy and allow people to die in order to enforce the Luddite views of groups such as the Union of Concerned Scientists. (Original name: "Union of Concerned Activist Lawyers Who Took a Science Course in High School.") As I described in my book *Godless*, both the government and the entire mainstream media lied about AIDS in the '80s by scaring Americans into believing that heterosexuals were as much at risk for acquiring AIDS as gays and intravenous drug users. The science had to be lied about so no one's feelings got hurt.

In 1985, *Life* magazine's cover proclaimed: "NOW, NO ONE IS SAFE FROM AIDS." In 1987, *U.S. News & World Report* reported that AIDS was "finding fertile growth among heterosexuals." Also in 1987, Dr. Oprah Winfrey said that "research studies" predicted that "one in five heterosexuals could be dead from AIDS at the end of the next three years." In 1988, ABC's *20/20* claimed the CDC had discovered a shocking upsurge of heterosexual infections on college campuses. It struck no one as odd that twenty-eight of the thirty infections had occurred in men (all of whom had alphabetized spice racks and at least three cats, one named Blanche). Two years later, CNN broadcast the exact same 1988 study, proclaiming: "A new report from CDC indicates that AIDS is on the rise on college campuses."

A quarter-century later, and we're still waiting for the big heterosexual AIDS outbreak. But at least science achieved its primary purpose: AIDS was not stigmatized as a "gay disease." Scientific facts were ignored so that science would be nonjudgmental. That was more important than the truth.

Liberal activists also gave us the alar scare in the late '80s based on the studies of world renowned chemist and national treasure Meryl Streep. Alar is a perfectly safe substance that had been used on apples since 1968 both to ripen and preserve the fruit. It made fresh fruit more accessible by allowing fruit pickers to make one sweep through the apple grove, producing ripe, fresh fruit that could be distributed widely and cheaply.

But after hearing the blood-chilling testimony of Streep, hysterical soccer moms across America hopped in their Volvos, dashed to their children's schools and ripped the apples from the little ones' lunch boxes. "Delicious, McIntosh, and Granny Smith" were added to "Hitler, Stalin, and Mao" as names that will live in infamy.

The EPA proposed banning alar based on a study that involved pumping tens of thousands times more alar into rats than any human could possibly consume, and observing the results. The rats died—of poisoning, not tumors—but the EPA banned it anyway. Poor people went back to eating Twinkies instead of healthy fresh fruit. Meanwhile, the World Health Organization advised against an alar ban, and Europeans continued to eat fruit with alar in their nice warm houses powered by nuclear energy (halted in the U.S. thanks to the important work of Dr. Jackson Browne and Dr. Bonnie Raitt).

Other scientific theories developed in the laboratories of personal injury lawyers and TV networks included the Left's "cancer cluster" thesis in the '80s. The Centers for Disease Control investigated 108 alleged "cancer clusters" that had occurred between 1961 to 1983 and found no explanation for them other than coincidence—and a demonstrable proximity to someone with deep pockets. As Yale epidemiologist Michael Bracken explained: "Diseases don't fall evenly on every town like snow." Random chance will lead some areas to have higher, sometimes oddly higher, numbers of cancer.

But just to be safe, we all better stop driving cars, eating off of clean dishes, and using aerosol sprays.

Some of the other scientific studies and innovations that make liberals cry involve: vaccines, IQ, breast implants, and DDT. After decades of this nonsense, the *New York Times'* Paul Krugman has the audacity to brag that liberals believe the "truth should be determined by research, not revelation." Yes—provided the "research" is conducted by trial lawyers and Hollywood actresses, not actual scientists.

The Flash Mob Method of Scientific Inquiry
August 24, 2011

The definition of hell is being condescended to by idiots. It will probably be MSNBC's Chris Matthews and Contessa Brewer sneering at you for all of eternity for not believing in evolution.

Roughly one-third of my 2006 No. 1 *New York Times* bestseller, *Godless: The Church of Liberalism*, is an attack on liberals' creation myth, Darwinian evolution. I presented the arguments of all the luminaries in the field, from the retarded Richard Dawkins to the brilliant Francis Crick, and disputed them.

But apparently liberals didn't want to argue back. Despite Matthews's obsessive fixation on the topic, manifested by his constantly asking elected Republicans if they believe in evolution, in a one-hour interview with me on *Godless*—the very book that is chockablock with attacks on Darwinism—Matthews didn't ask me a single question about the subject. No liberal did. Matthews doesn't even know what Darwinian evolution is. (Nor has he undergone it.)

Just two years later, at a 2008 Republican presidential candidates' debate, Matthews asked for a show of hands of who believed in evolution. No discussion permitted! That might allow scientific facts, rather than schoolyard taunts, to escape into the world.

Evolution is the only subject that is discussed exclusively as a "Do you believe?" question with yes-or-no answers. How about conservative journalists start putting mics in front of liberal candidates and demanding, "Do you believe in the Bible—yes or no?," "Is an unborn baby human—yes or no?," and "Do you believe teenagers should have sex—yes or no?"

This is the flash mob method of scientific inquiry. Liberals quickly surround and humiliate anyone who disagrees with them. They are baffled when appeals to status (*"every major scientist believes it!"*) don't work on other people the way status works on them.

Now that Republican presidential candidate Rick Perry has said there are "gaps" in the theory of evolution—or "gas" as the *New York Times* originally reported, before issuing a correction—we're in for another round of fact-free mocking of fundamentalist nuts. In fact, however, it has not been advances in Christianity (which is pretty much settled), but in science that have completely discredited Darwin's theory.

This week, we will consider one small slice of the mountain of scientific evidence disproving this mystery religion from the Victorian age. Most devastating for the Darwiniacs were advances in microbiology since Darwin's time, revealing infinitely complex mechanisms requiring hundreds of parts working together at once—complex cellular structures, DNA, blood-clotting mechanisms, molecules, and the cell's tiny flagellum and cilium.

Darwin's theory was that life on Earth began with single-celled life forms, which by random mutation, sex, and death would pass on the desirable mutations. This process, over billions of years, would lead to the creation of new species. The (extremely generous) test Darwin set for his theory was this: "If it could be demonstrated that any complex organ existed which could not possibly have been formed by numerous, successive, slight modifications, my theory would absolutely break down."

Thanks to advances in microscopes, thousands of such complex mechanisms have been found since Darwin's day. He had to explain only simple devices, such as beaks and gills. If Darwin were able to come back today and peer through a modern microscope to see the inner workings of a cell, he would instantly abandon his own theory.

It is a mathematical impossibility, for example, that all thirty to forty parts of the cell's flagellum could all arise at once by random mutation. According to most scientists, such an occurrence is considered even less likely than John Edwards marrying Rielle Hunter, the "Ground Xero" of the impossible. Nor would any of those thirty to forty parts individually make an organism more fit to survive and reproduce, which, you will recall, is the lynchpin of the whole contraption. And that's just one part of the cell. There's also the cell's cilium, composed of hundreds of parts.

As Michael Behe, biochemist and author of *Darwin's Black Box*, explains, even a mechanism as simple as a three-part mousetrap requires all three parts to be working together at once to be at all useful. Otherwise, you don't get a mousetrap that catches half as many mice— and thus might win a survival-of-the-fittest competition—you don't get a mousetrap at all.

The more we have learned about molecules, cells, and DNA—a body of knowledge some refer to as "science"—the more preposterous Darwin's theory has become. DNA is, as Bill Gates says, "like a computer program, but far, far more advanced than any software we've ever created." (Plus DNA doesn't usually crash when you're right in the middle of reproducing.)

Evolution fanatics would rather not be called on to explain these complex mechanisms that Darwin himself said, if they existed, would disprove his theory. Instead they sneer about people who know the truth, claiming that to dispute evolution means you must believe man walked with dinosaurs. Galileo's persecutors probably had some good guffaws about him believing in Fred Flintstone.

This is why the brighter Darwinians end up sounding like Scientologists in order to cling to their mystery religion. Crick, winner of the Nobel Prize for his co-discovery of DNA, tried to explain the evident design in nature by hypothesizing that highly intelligent extraterrestrials sent living cells to Earth on an unmanned spaceship, a theory he set forth in his 1981 book, *Life Itself*.

Thus was God narrowly averted! But Crick's solution obviously begs the question: How did the highly intelligent extraterrestrials evolve?

Harvard population biologist Richard Lewontin said the Darwinians accept "unsubstantiated just-so stories" of evolution and ignore "the patent absurdity of some of its constructs" because they are committed to coming up with a theory that excludes God. "We cannot," Lewontin said, "allow a divine foot in the door."

Maybe if we called the Intelligent Designer "Louis Vuitton" to avoid frightening the Godphobics, they'd finally admit the truth: modern science has disproved Darwinian evolution.

CHAPTER SEVENTEEN

I Have a Savior, and His Name's Not Obama

L iberalism, our official state religion, is a doctrine with a specific set of tenets that can be discussed, just like other religions. Liberals deny, of course, that they are practicing a religion—otherwise, they'd lose their government funding. "Separation of church and state" means separation of YOUR church from the state, but total unity between their church and the state. Enforcing the state religion, in 1992, for example, the Supreme Court held that Reform rabbis were prohibited by the Constitution from saying brief prayers at high school graduations. Federal courts across the nation have swooped down on town squares to cart off their Ten Commandments monuments. Meanwhile, Al Gore's *Earth in the Balance* and various propagandistic books like *Heather Has Two Mommies* are mandatory in the public schools.

Indoctrination in the religion of "liberalism" will cause otherwise seemingly normal people to propose teaching children how to masturbate, allowing gays to marry, releasing murderers from prison, and teaching children that they share a common ancestor with the earthworm. (They haven't yet found the common ancestor…but like O. J., the search continues.)

Practitioners of liberalism write letters like this one to the *New York Times*. The writer was offended by an article that referred to the more elegant human jawline, compared to that of apes:

> *March 30, 2004*
> *Eye of the Beholder*
> *To the Editor:*
>
> *I was startled to read in "Less Jaw, Big Brain: Evolution Milestone Laid to Gene Flaw" (front page, March 25) your reference to "the more graceful human jaw, in contrast to apes' protruding jaw and facial ridges."*
>
> *This is uncalled for. Believe me, we don't look so pretty to chimpanzees either.*
>
> *CAROL JOCHNOWITZ*
> *New York, March 25, 2004*

Sadly, Carol did not include a photo.

The liberal cosmology is everything liberals say Christianity is, but isn't: down-the-line intolerant, with no room for compromise or trade-offs and aggressively evangelistic. Its adherents are terrified of facts and science because nature discriminates. They waged a campaign of lies against AIDS for not infecting the population equally. They were afraid of a book that told the truth about IQ (*The Bell Curve*). Christians have no fear of hearing facts about genetic differences in IQ because we don't think humans are special because they're smart. There may be some advantages to being intelligent, but a lot of liberals appear to have high IQs, so, really, what's the point?

Dressing for Distress: In Hoc Signo Vinces
October 25, 2001

I knew the events of September 11 were big, but I didn't really realize how big until I read in the *New York Times* that fashion was, "Taking a Back Seat to Unfolding Events." The *Times* also had a moving piece on the trials of people who lived near Ground Zero having to beat a quick retreat to Manhattan's finer hotels: "living in a hotel—particularly a high-design hotel—can both speed and complicate a return to normalcy."

But insolent staff and room service mishaps are not the only suffering in Gotham. *New York Times* headlines could barely convey the unspeakable horror of it all: "Style: O Fashion, Where Art Thou?," "New Look for Entertainment in a Terror-Conscious World," "Refugees at the Ritz," "After the Attacks: the Magazines—Editors Rush to Revise Long-Made Plans." There were innumerable wartime sacrifices made by many ordinary New Yorkers. "By putting up a courageous front, fashionable businesses and institutions—even a single style arbiter—can provide a service during tough times." Designers planned to give women "freedom to dress as they want." (Get it?)

In another story from the frontlines, the *Times* somberly reported that Manhattanites were feeling an urgent need to "connect primally."

Explaining that he "wanted something physical," Adam Lichtenstein, thirty-six, a film editor, offered more detail than readers necessarily wanted about his recent one-night stand. "She is someone I very openly refer to as my wartime liaison," he said.

In addition to meaningless sex and courageous fashion design, there was a more controversial balm helping some New Yorkers through their grief. It could not be discussed frankly in pages of the *Times*. This questionable topic would require the utmost brevity and delicacy.

The rescue workers found a cross standing in the rubble of Ground Zero.

It was discovered just a few days after the attack. While performing the soul-numbing work of pulling human bodies and body parts from the smoking wreckage, construction worker Frank Silecchia happened upon a perfectly symmetrical cross in the midst of the wreckage. It was standing straight, twenty feet high, surrounded by many smaller crosses. Silecchia stopped in his tracks and stood crying for twenty minutes. "When I first saw it, it took my heart," Silecchia said. "It helped me heal the burden of my despair, and gave me closure on the whole catastrophe."

Meanwhile, as one *Times* reporter recounted, other Manhattanites took refuge in belly dancers. "Finally the belly dancer came through, and maybe it was all that pressure that had built up this week, but when she beckoned, a lot of people at my table started running." Hard-hat Silecchia brought his fellow rescue workers to the site of the cross, and they have been making regular pilgrimages to the cross ever since. Many of the men call it a miracle. But for other New Yorkers, the *Times* reported, "Finding Solace Means Returning to Malls."

The daily horror of pulling human remains from the rubble has the rescue workers at the breaking point. Someone etched "God Bless Our

Fallen Brothers" on the cross. In other news, the *Newspaper of Record* reported, New Yorkers are part of a huge comeback in sewing! "People want to sew, create and get back to basics," one shop owner told the *Times*. Some of the city's darkest fears turned out to be needless hysteria: "At the Plaza Hotel, a Fifth Avenue landmark, fears that the famed Oak Room and Oyster Bar will close have dissipated." Also, fast food is "moving well."

The cross at Ground Zero was not simply the cross beams remaining from an existing building. It was formed out of beams from Building One plunging, splitting, and crashing into Building Six. "There's no symmetry to anything down there," the FBI chaplain said, "except those crosses." In another weird coincidence, as the coping-through-belly-dancing article described, a lot of New Yorkers are having sex. A woman named Miriam offered this insight in the pages of the *Times*: "I also like watching porno and that sort of thing. And I think [my boyfriend] finds that freeing."

The *Times* eventually mentioned the cross at Ground Zero in one small item on page B-12 more than three weeks after Silecchia found it. A Franciscan priest, Father Brian Jordan, blessed the cross with holy water in a ceremony attended by rescue workers, nuns, and priests. Bagpipes played "Amazing Grace." The workers sang "God Bless America." It was arguably an even bigger event than Adam Lichtenstein's one-night stand.

The one-night stand article was 1,755 words. The coping through sex article was 2,655 words. The knitting article was 1,134 words. Even the article on people finding solace in the malls was 752 words. The article on the cross was 423 words. While the *Times* impatiently waits for the ACLU to put an end to all this monkey business with the cross, the rescue workers continue their work, pulling human bodies from the wreckage and making the sign of the cross.

If You Can Find a Better Deal, Take It!
January 6, 2010

Someone mentioned Christianity on television recently and liberals reacted with their usual anger and blinking incomprehension.

On a Fox News panel discussing Tiger Woods, Brit Hume said, perfectly accurately: "The extent to which he can recover, it seems to me, depends on his faith. He is said to be a Buddhist. I don't think that faith offers the kind of forgiveness and redemption that is offered by the Christian faith. So, my message to Tiger would be, 'Tiger, turn to the Christian faith and you can make a total recovery and be a great example to the world.'"

Hume's words, being 100 percent factually correct, sent liberals into a tizzy of sputtering rage. This illustrated, once again liberals' amazing ignorance of Christianity. (It also illustrated Jesus's words: "How is it you do not understand me when I speak? It is because you cannot bear to listen to my words." John 8:43.) In the *Washington Post*, Tom Shales demanded that Hume apologize, saying he had "dissed about half a billion Buddhists on the planet."

Is Buddhism about forgiveness? Because, if so, Buddhists had better start demanding apologies from every book, magazine article, and blog posting ever written on the subject, which claims Buddhists don't believe in God but try to become their own gods.

Does anyone think Tiger's problem was that he didn't think of himself as a god? Not even after that final putt in the Arnold Palmer Invitational last year?

In light of Shales's warning Hume about "what people are saying" about him, I hope Hume's a Christian. At least he knows what

Christianity is, unlike Shales and every other liberal. Given the reaction to his remarks, apparently one has to be a regular New Testament scholar to have a passing familiarity with the basic gist of Christianity.

On MSNBC, David Shuster invoked the "separation of church and television" (a phrase that *also* doesn't appear in the Constitution), bitterly complaining that Hume had brought up Christianity "out-of-the-blue" on "a political talk show." Yes, why would Hume mention religion while discussing a public figure who had fallen from grace and was in need of forgiveness? Boy, talk about coming out of left field! (If liberals really want to keep people from hearing about God, they should give Him his own show on MSNBC.)

What religion—what topic—induces this sort of babbling idiocy?

Most perplexing was columnist Dan Savage's indignant accusation that Hume was claiming that Christianity "offers the best deal—it gives you the get-out-of-adultery-free card that other religions just can't." In fact, that's exactly what Christianity does. (I know it seems strange that a self-described atheist and "radical sex advice columnist faggot" like Savage would miss the central point of Christianity, but there it is.)

It's the best deal going. God sent his only son to get the crap beaten out of him, die for our sins, and rise from the dead. If you believe that, you're in. Your sins are washed away from you—sins even worse than adultery!—because of the cross. "He canceled the record of the charges against us and took it away by nailing it to the cross." Colossians 2:14. Surely you remember the cross, liberals—the symbol banned by ACLU lawsuits from public property throughout the land?

Christianity is simultaneously the easiest religion in the world and the hardest religion in the world. In the no-frills, economy-class version, you don't need a church, a teacher, candles, incense, special food, or clothing; you don't need to pass a test or prove yourself in any way. All you'll need is a Bible (in order to grasp the amazing deal you're getting) and probably a water baptism, though even that's disputed. You can be washing the dishes or walking your dog or just sitting there minding your business hating Susan Sarandon when, suddenly, you accept that God sent his only son to die for your sins and rise from the dead. That's it. You're in!

"Because, if you confess with your mouth that Jesus is Lord and believe in your heart that God raised him from the dead, you will be saved." Romans 10:9. If you do that, every rotten, sinful thing you've ever done is gone from you. You're every bit as much a Christian as the pope or Billy Graham.

No fine print, no "your mileage may vary," no blackout dates. God ought to do a TV spot: *I'm God Almighty, and if you can find a better deal than the one I'm offering, take it.*

The Gospel makes this point approximately one thousand times. Here are a few examples at random:

- "For God so loved the world, that he gave his only Son, that whoever believes in him should not perish but have eternal life." John 3:16.
- "For by grace you have been saved through faith. And this is not your own doing; it is the gift of God." Ephesians 2:8.
- "For the wages of sin is death, but the free gift of God is eternal life in Christ Jesus our Lord." Romans 6:23.

In a boiling rage, liberals constantly accuse Christians of being "judgmental."

No, we're relieved. Christianity is also the hardest religion in the world because, if you believe Christ died for your sins and rose from the dead, you have no choice but to give your life entirely over to Him. No more sexual promiscuity, no lying, no cheating, no stealing, no killing inconvenient old people or unborn babies, no doing what all the other kids do. And no more caring what the world thinks of you—because, as Jesus warned in a prophecy constantly proved by liberals: the world will hate you.

With Christianity, your sins are forgiven, the slate is wiped clean, and your eternal life is guaranteed through nothing you did yourself, even though you don't deserve it. It's the best deal in the universe.

Beliefnet Interview—Church Militant: Ann Coulter on God, Faith, and Liberals
July 2006

Q: Will most liberals go to hell or heaven?

A: I really can't improve on Jesus's words: "Make every effort to enter through the narrow door, because many, I tell you, will try to enter and will not be able to."

Q: You title your book *Godless*—are all liberals atheists?

A: No, but it increases the odds.

Q: What portion of liberals would you say are religious in the more conventional sense of the word: Christians, Jews, Muslims, Buddhists, even Wiccans?

A: Hmmm, so you consider Wiccans "religious . . . in the conventional sense"? That would definitely get liberals' numbers up! I'd have no way of knowing, but make no mistake: Liberals are everywhere, in every religion, denomination, and spiritual practice—especially Wiccans!

Q: We've done some polls here at Beliefnet, and a surprising number of Democrats at least say they are religious. Some 61 percent say they pray daily and 72 percent attend worship services once a month or more. How would you explain that?

A: Just curious: What percentage of them know which Testament the Book of Job is in?

Q: When you say that most liberals don't believe in God, what is your evidence? After all, according to a Fox News poll last year 92 percent of Americans believe in God. And nearly half of Americans voted Democratic in the 2004 election.

A: First let me say that I think it's terrific to hear a journalist citing a Fox News poll as authoritative evidence and would like to encourage this development.

I don't say "most liberals don't believe in God"; I say liberalism is a godless religion. Some liberals don't understand the underlying religious dogma and principles of liberalism—if they did, they would flee the building.

Q: You write on p. 3 of *Godless*: "Liberalism is a comprehensive belief system denying the Christian belief in man's immortal soul." Yet our Beliefnet polls show that 58.7% of Democrats believe in life after death. Doesn't that disprove your statement?

A: No, I think it proves it—58.7% of all Democrats? That's pathetic. Also, you forgot to ask them the follow-up question: Is that because you hope to come back as a snail darter?

Q: You cite opposition to the death penalty as a key tenet of the Church of Liberalism. Yet Pope John Paul II stated that the death penalty should be rarely, if ever, applied: only "in cases of absolute necessity."

How do you square this with your assertions (on p. 23) that "adoration of violent criminals" and "admiration of dangerous criminals" are the main factors behind opposition to the death penalty?

A: I agree with the pope. I also believe that it is an "absolute necessity" to execute cold-blooded murderers, rapists, and child molesters. As your own question indicates, opposition to the death penalty is not a "key tenet" of even Catholicism. That would be a difficult position to maintain inasmuch as God himself commanded the Israelites to go to certain cities and kill every living thing. If memory serves, the pope was also opposed to abortion. Liberals are not. How would you explain opposition to the death penalty for heinous murderers, but not for innocent children?

Q: Now, I know I'm going to sound like Ed McMahon feeding straight lines to Johnny Carson, but on p. 5, you say that the Episcopal Church is "barely even a church." Why?

A: Because it's become increasingly difficult to distinguish the pronouncements of the Episcopal Church from the latest Madonna video.

Q: Are churches that don't agree with your politics or religious beliefs not really churches?

A: Correct: They're called "mosques."

Q: And don't many people whom you would classify as belonging to the Church of Liberalism define themselves as Christian or Jewish? Jim Wallis of *Sojourners* and Michael Lerner of *Tikkun* claim to be applying authentic Christian and Jewish theology to political and social questions. Are such people not really Christians or Jews?

A: Yes, the percentage of liberals who define themselves as practicing Christians or Jews goes up in direct proportion to their proximity to elective office. I cannot speak to individual cases, only God knows who is truly following Him, but claiming to be Jewish or Christian doesn't immunize one from bad ideologies. Some slaveholders claimed to be Christians, too. Howard Dean, Bill and Hillary Clinton, Teddy Kennedy, and John Kerry all belong to a church that believes it's okay to stick a fork in a baby's head. To the extent one is practicing liberalism, one is not practicing the religion of our Father.

Q: Is it possible to be a good Christian and sincerely believe, as Jim Wallis does, that a bigger welfare state and higher taxes to fund it is the best way in a complex modern society for us to fulfill our Gospel obligation to help the poor?

A: It's possible, but not likely. Confiscatory taxation enforced by threat of imprisonment is "stealing," a practice strongly frowned upon by our Creator. If all Christians and Jews tithed their income as the Bible commands, every poor person would be cared for, every naked person clothed, and every hungry person fed. Read Marvin Olasky's *The Tragedy of American Compassion* for further discussion of this.

Q: Now for the topic to which you devote four of your eleven chapters: evolution. You say that Darwin's theory of evolution is "about one notch above Scientology in scientific rigor" (p. 199). So what do you think really happened? Did God create the world in six days? Did he create each species separately? Did he set a chain of causation in motion? Did he "cause" evolution in the sense that all the species are related to each other but God guided their descent?

A: These are unanswerable questions—except the latter. God did not "cause" evolution because evolution doesn't exist. Thus for example, He also didn't "cause" unicorns. My faith and reason tell me that God created the world and I'm not particularly interested in the details. I'll find out when I meet my Maker.

Q: Can there be such a thing as "intelligent design" without a divine designer?

A: Yes—you should read my book! Cambridge astrophysicists Sir Fred Hoyle and Chandra Wickramasinghe, as well as Francis Crick, winner of the Nobel Prize for his co-discovery of DNA, didn't believe in God, but realized Darwin's theory was a crock. In order to explain the vast evidence of intelligence throughout the physical world while excluding God, they concocted theories about intelligence being transported from outer space to Earth on comets or spaceships. Of course, some might say that begs the question: Who's the intelligent designer in outer space? Karl Lagerfeld?

Q: Many arguments in favor of Darwinian evolution strike me as actually being arguments against the existence of God—that is, why would a creator create tapeworms, disease viruses, and other bad things? Why do you think such things exist in a world of intelligent design?

A: Your question is incomprehensible. I assume you are trying to ask me: "Why would God create tapeworms?"

My answer is: God also created mosquitoes, which I hate. But purple martins love mosquitoes and would probably all starve without them. It's kind of a "big picture" thing. Of course that doesn't explain why He created Michael Moore. For that, I have no explanation. My guess is that disease, pestilence, and Michael Moore are all perversions of the good that God created, a result of sin entering the world through Adam and Eve.

Q: While I agree with you that the "Jersey Girls" turned themselves into political opportunists, one of your statements about them does strike me as over the top: "I've never seen people enjoying their husbands' deaths so much" (p. 102). By contrast, you at least admit the genuine nature of Cindy Sheehan's grief even though you're pretty hard on her—and you haven't been criticized for what you said about her: Is there anything you've said about the 9/11 widows that you wish you hadn't said?

A: Well as long as you bring it up, I think Cindy Sheehan is enjoying the celebrity status her son's death afforded her, too. Thanks for pointing that out—I'll correct it in the paperback edition.

Q: On p. 176, you make fun of journalists who predicted that AIDS would become a heterosexual threat: "It's been twenty years, and we're still waiting for that heterosexual outbreak." While it's true that here in the U.S., AIDS is an overwhelmingly gay disease (about 80 percent), that's not so true worldwide, especially in sub-Saharan Africa, where more than 40 percent, perhaps up to 48 percent, of those with HIV are women, according to UN figures. What do you make of that?

A: Same lie, different continent—with the same evil consequence: millions of lives being sacrificed on the altar of political correctness. (Could we get back to Fox News polls and dispense with UN studies?) AIDS is overwhelmingly spread by anal intercourse and dirty needles. In the U.S., dirty needles come mostly from junkies, in Africa, dirty needles come from medical workers. See, e.g.:

Craig Timberg, "How AIDS in Africa Was Overstated," *Washington Post*, http://www.washingtonpost.com/wp-dyn/content/article/2006/04/05/AR2006040502517.html.

Michael Fumento, "Why Is HIV So Prevalent in Africa," http://www.fumento.com/disease/aids2005.html.

Michael Fumento, "The African heterosexual AIDS myth," http://www.townhall.com/columnists/GuestColumns/printFumento20050414.shtml.

Oh and by the way, those journalists I make fun of *were* talking about AIDS in the U.S. So the above information is merely for your edification.

Q: You say: "The core of environmentalism is that they hate mankind." But in February the National Association of Evangelicals, including such signers as Ted Haggard, James Dobson, and Chuck Colson, etc., issued a statement urging Christian stewardship of the environment, "creation care," and so forth. Are these people Godless liberals who hate mankind?

A: Of course not—but I'm beginning to suspect you are. As Dobson and Colson say: God asks us to be good stewards—a statement that presupposes we are stewards of the plants and the animals, they are not stewards of us, as liberals prefer. We are commanded to worship the Creator of the environment, not the environment. As Jesus said, we are of more value than many sparrows. Matthew 10:21.

Q: You say you're a Christian. Do you think Jesus would want you to be nicer to your political opponents?

A: Who knows? Maybe He'll say I was too tough or maybe He'll chastise me for not being tough enough on those who hate Him. Ask the money-changers in the temple how "nice" Jesus was. Maybe He'll say I needed more jokes or fewer adjectives. I'll just apologize for not getting it right and thank him for dying for my sins.

Q: Do you think it is persuasive to trudge out long-dead horses such as Willie Horton (1988) or Piltdown Man (1912) and flog them one more time? Does anyone, even on the left, seriously regard Willie Horton as a "martyr," as you call him? Tookie Williams, maybe, but Willie Horton? Does he really rate a chapter of his own?

A: The word you're searching for is "dredge," not "trudge." No: I included a pointless chapter just to take up space. Yes, of course it's important. The Willie Horton chapter illustrates how a religion untethered to the Creator exhibits all the bad aspects of religion—myth-making, self-righteousness, and preachiness—in defense of remorseless killers while casually sentencing the unborn to death.

Q: If the Church of Liberalism lets you do anything you want, why do you think the divorce rate is higher in red states than in the Godless blue states?

A: Assuming that's true, probably because marriage is more popular in the red states than in the blue states and because of all the blue-staters living in the red states.

Q: I found your book enormously entertaining, and I laughed out loud on practically every page. But when I finished, I asked myself: What was the point of this book? To drop hilarious one-liners? To outrage your political opponents? To comfort religious people feeling besieged by a secular culture? To make serious arguments—about what? What would you say the point of *Godless* is?

A: It is a clarion call, a flashing neon sign warning people that liberalism is the opposition party to God. (And by the way, I had the same reaction the first time I read the Bible: sure, it's fascinating and wise and full of important information, but what was the point of it exactly?)

Q: What does it mean to be a good Christian, and do you consider yourself to be a good Christian?

A: To believe with all your heart at every moment that God loved a wretch like you so much that he sent his only Son to die for your sins. Most of the time, I'm an extraordinarily good Christian.

Q: Tell me something about your own spiritual life. Do you attend church frequently? Do you pray, and whom and what do you pray for?

A: Yes and yes. I pretend to attend a giant church in New York City, where I pray for the souls of people who claim I've never been there. I pray for mercy and divine protection from God's enemies. When I'm in a jaunty mood, I pray for Him to smite liberals.

Q: Is it important to you as a woman to be standing up for positions that many people (especially liberals) think are unrepresentative of women: opposing abortion, favoring the death penalty, and so forth?

A: The answer to any question beginning "Is it important to you as a woman" is: no. It's important to me as a Christian and an American to take the positions I take, but I would hold the same positions if I were a man. And by the way, despite your nearly mystical fascination with polls in earlier questions, you have apparently not brushed up on the abortion polls if you think opposition to abortion is "unrepresentative of women." No matter who takes the poll or how the questions are asked, women almost always oppose abortion more than men do. Abortion is a convenience for men who want to be able to have sex with women without consequence. Women love and protect children. Godless men, like Herod in Jesus's time, the Pharaoh in Moses's time, and Bill Clinton in our time—target babies for destruction.

Q: As a woman, do you long for that source of great fulfillment for many women: a husband, a family? Or do you see your life's vocation as primarily in the public arena.

A: As a journalist, do you long to have a sense of decorum? Or do you see your life's vocation as primarily asking strangers utterly inappropriate personal questions?

Q: What's your favorite Bible verse, if you have one (besides "By their fruits you shall know them")?

A: I don't have a favorite, they're all pretty good. Some I like are:

So do not be afraid of them. There is nothing concealed that will not be disclosed, or hidden that will not be made known. What I tell you in the dark, speak in the daylight; what is whispered in your ear, proclaim from the roofs. Do not be afraid of those who kill the body but cannot kill the soul. Rather, be afraid of the One who can destroy both soul and body in hell.

—Matthew 10:26–28

Whoever acknowledges me before men, I will also acknowledge him before my Father in heaven. But whoever disowns me before men, I will disown him before my Father in heaven.

—Matthew 10:32–33

If the world hate you, ye know that it hated me before it hated you.

—John 15:18

CHAPTER EIGHTEEN

Not Far from the Tree

I don't really like talking about myself, so let me tell you about my parents. I always warned reporters who wanted to interview my mother that she was just going to tell them that I was a perfect little angel—and I could tell them that. An apparently very persuasive *Wall Street Journal* reporter got past me to interview my mother, in which she says, in essence, that I am a perfect little angel.

Wall Street Journal Interview with My Mother!*
October 2004

1) Q: What do you worry about when Ann is in the public eye?

A: *I don't worry, she looks incredibly beautiful, is well-spoken, knows just what to say. Not a single worry.*

---

* In October of 2004 my mother was interviewed for the *Wall Street Journal*, but it appears that the interview was never published.

Q: Your daughter obviously has strong opinions that upset some people. Do you ever give her advice about toning it down, reaching out to the other side?

A: *No.*

Q: Even if you admire her guts and her ability to say it straight, what input do you give her about delivery, her message, etc?

A: *I'm afraid it's past time for me to be effective. I sometimes tell her to dress more modestly, but I don't even do that much anymore. I'm extremely proud of her.*

2) Q: How do you like the book *How to Talk to a Liberal (If You Must)*?

A: *I think it's terrific, I can't put it down, I stay up late at night reading it.*

Q: Does it help you talk to liberals?

A: *I studiously avoid that.*

3) Q: When you see Ann on TV, do you ever critique her? What she says or what she wears?

A: *Occasionally, not what she says.*

Q: Have you given her any input that she has put into her books, speeches or media appearances? A good line?

A: *Yes, including recommending my favorite columns for the current book. Occasionally she listens to her mother.*

4) Q: At the University of Arizona last week, two men tried to throw a pie at Ann. Did you talk to her after that?

A: *I called her as soon as I could get in touch with her to see if she was all right.*

Q: Give her any advice? What were your concerns about that?

A: *I heard a lot of anger in her voice—justifiably—so my only advice was to remember that she is a Christian.*

5) Q: As election day approaches, I'm sure Ann has a very busy schedule. What have you told her about eating right, sleeping well, etc.?

A: *I always tell her to get plenty of sleep she'll need to rebuff these crazy things, eat well, and keep exercising. Unfortunately, she's past the time when I can determine her bedtime.*

Q: And if Bush loses, what might you say to console her?

A: *Let's go to Africa!… I'll need consoling of my own. It would be a tragedy if Kerry gets in.*

Luckily, we didn't have to go to Africa. My parents got to spend most of their remaining days on Earth in the blessed peacefulness of a Republican administration. Now, they root for America from heaven.

John Vincent Coulter
January 9, 2008

The longest baby ever born at the Albany, New York, hospital, at least as of May 5, 1926, who grew up to be my strapping father, passed away last Friday morning.

As Mother and I stood at Daddy's casket Monday morning, Mother repeated his joke to him, which he said on every wedding anniversary until a few years ago when Lewy Body Dementia prevented him from saying much at all: "fifty-four years, married to the wrong woman." And we laughed.

John Vincent Coulter was of the old school, a man of few words, the un-Oprah, no crying or wearing your heart on your sleeve, and reacting to moments of great sentiment with a joke. Or as we used to call them: men. When he was moping around the house once, missing my brother who had just gone back to college, he said, "Well, if you had cancer long enough, you'd miss it."

He'd indicate his feelings about my skirt length by saying, "You look nice, Hart, but you forgot to put on your skirt."

Of course, he did show strong emotion when the *New York Post* would run a photo of Teddy Kennedy saying the rosary. I can still see the look of disgust. I saw that face in *How to Read People like a Book* and it was NOT a good chapter.

Your parents are your whole world when you are a child. You only recognize what is unique about them when you get older and see how the rest of the world diverges from your standard of normality.

So it took me awhile to realize that by telling my friends that Father was an ex-FBI agent and a union-buster whose hobbies included rebuilding Volkswagens and shooting squirrels in our backyard, I was painting the image of a rough Eliot Ness type, rather than the cheerful, funny raconteur they would meet.

Besides being very funny, Father had an absolutely straight moral compass without ever being preachy or judgmental or even telling us in words. He just was good. He would return to a store if he was given too much change—and this was a man who was so "thrifty," as we Scots like to say, he told us he wanted to be buried in two cardboard boxes from the A&P rather than pay for a coffin.

When I was bombarded with arguments for baby-killing as a kid, I asked Father about the old chestnut involving a poverty-stricken, unwed teenage girl who gets pregnant. (This was before they added the "impregnated by her own father" part.) Father just said, "I don't care. If it's a life, it's a life." I'm still waiting to hear an effective counterargument.

Father hated puffery, pomposity, snobbery, fake friendliness, fake anything. Like Kitty's father in *Anna Karenina*, he could detect a substanceless suitor in a heartbeat. (They were probably the same ones who looked nervous when I told them Father was ex-FBI and liked to shoot squirrels in the backyard.)

He hated unions because of their corrupt leadership, ripping off the members for their own aggrandizement. But he had more respect for genuine working men than anyone I've ever known. He was, in short, the molecular opposite of John Edwards.

Father didn't care what popular opinion was: there was right and wrong. I don't recall his ever specifically talking about J. Edgar Hoover or Joe McCarthy, but we knew he thought the popular histories were bunk. That's why *Treason* was dedicated to him, the last book of mine he was able to read.

When Father returned from the war, he used the GI Bill to complete college and law school in three years. In order to get to law school quickly, he chose the easiest college major—a major that so impressed him, he told my oldest brother that if he ever took one single course in sociology, Father would cut off his tuition payments.

As a young FBI agent fresh out of law school, one of Father's first assignments was to investigate job applicants at a uranium enrichment plant, the only suitable land for which was apparently located on some property owned by the then vice president, Alben Barkley, in Paducah, Kentucky.

One day, a group of FBI agents saw the beautiful Nell Husbands Martin at lunch with her mother. They asked the waitress for her name and flipped a coin to see who could ask her out first. Father lost the coin toss, so he paid off the other agents. And that's how Nell became my mother.

Mother swore she'd never marry a drinker, a smoker, or a Catholic, and she got all three, reforming Father on all but the Catholicism. Even in foreign countries where none of us spoke the language, Father went to Mass every Sunday until the very end.

Of course, toward the end, he probably didn't even remember he was a Catholic. But on the bright side, he didn't remember that Teddy Kennedy was a Catholic, either.

Father spent most of his nine-year FBI career as a Red hunter in New York City. He never talked much about his FBI days. I learned that he worked on the Rudolf Abel case—the highest-ranking Soviet spy ever captured in U.S. history—during one of my brother's eulogies on Monday. But when Father read a paper I wrote at Cornell defending McCarthy and came across the name William Remington, he told me that had been his case.

Father mostly had contempt for Soviet spies. In addition to damaging information, such as military plans and nuclear secrets, the spies also collected massive amounts of utterly useless information on things like U.S. agricultural production. These were people who looked at a flush toilet like it was a spaceship.

He told me Soviet spies reveled in the whole cloak-and-dagger aspect of espionage. One spy gave weirdly specific details to a contact before their first meeting: he would have the *New York Herald Tribune* folded three times, tucked under his left elbow at a particular angle. When the spy walked into the hotel lobby for the rendezvous, Father nearly fell off his chair when the man with the *Herald Tribune* folded under his elbow just so... was also wearing a full-length fur coat. But he couldn't have told his contact: "I'll be the only white man in North America wearing a full-length fur coat."

In the early 1980s, as vice president and labor lawyer for Phelps Dodge copper company, Father broke a strike against the company, which culminated in the largest union decertification ever—at that time and perhaps still. President Reagan had broken the air traffic controllers' strike in 1981. But unions recognized that it was the breaking of the Phelps Dodge strike a few years later that landed the greater blow, as described in the book *Copper Crucible*.

There was massive violence by the strikers, including guns being fired into the homes of the mine employees who returned to work. Every day, Father walked with the strikebreakers through the picket line, (in my mind) brushing egg off his suit lapel. By 1986 it was over;

the mineworkers voted against the union, and Phelps Dodge was saved. For any liberals still reading, this is what's known as a "happy ending."

To Mother's lifelong consternation—until he had dementia and she could get him back by smothering him with hugs and kisses—Father wasn't demonstrative. But all he wanted was to be with Mother (and to work on his Volkswagens). They traveled the world together, went to DAR conventions together, engaged in Republican politics together, and went to the New York Philharmonic together—for three decades, their subscription seats were on the highest landing, or as we Scots call it, the "Music Lovers" level.

When Mother was in a rehabilitative facility briefly after surgery a few years ago and Father was not supposed to be driving, we were relieved that a snowstorm had knocked out the power to the garage door opener, so Daddy couldn't get to the car. It would just be a week and then Mother would be home. My brother came home to check on Father the first day of this arrangement to find that he had taken an ax to the side door of the garage, so he could drive to the rehab center and sit with Mother all day.

When she left him for five days last summer to go to a family reunion in Kentucky, at some point, Father, who hadn't been able to speak much anymore, looked up and asked his nurse, "Where is she?"

And last Friday morning at 2:00 he passed away, in his bedroom with Mother. The police and firemen told my brother that they kept trying to distract Mother to keep her away from the bedroom with Father's body, but she kept padding back to be close to him.

Now Daddy is with Joe McCarthy and Ronald Reagan. I hope they stop laughing about the Reds long enough to talk to God about smiting some liberals for me.

Nell Husbands Martin Coulter
April 22, 2009

A lot of people claim to be my No. 1 fan—God bless them—but my true No. 1 fan left this world last week. My mother quietly stopped breathing last Tuesday, as she slept peacefully, holding my hand. She was the biggest fan of all of us—Father, me, and my brothers, John and Jim.

After reading the eulogy column I wrote for Father last year—not to excess, probably only about 4,637 times—Mother realized to her chagrin that she wouldn't be able to read the eulogy column I'd be writing for her and started hinting that maybe I could rustle up a draft so she could take a peek.

But I couldn't do it until I had to.

The only thing Mother wanted to be sure my brothers and I included in her remembrances were her contributions to the Republican Party, the New Canaan Republican Town Committee, and the Daughters of the American Revolution. She was a direct descendant of at least a dozen patriots who served the cause of the American Revolution and traced her lineage on both sides of her family to Puritan nonconformists who came to America in 1633 seeking religious freedom on a ship led by Pastor Thomas Hooker. Or, as Homeland Security Chief Janet Napolitano would call them, "a dangerous right-wing extremist hate group."

Back in the Puritan days, Mother's female ancestors were brought up on charges for their heretical dressing styles (and then sassed the judge). During the Revolution, one female ancestor, Effie Ten Eyck Van Varick, contributed to the rebel cause by donating lead for bullets from the curtain weights in her home in what was, even then, traitorous, Loyalist Manhattan.

Mother's deep-seated political activism saved me on more than one occasion. At the 2004 Republican National Convention in New York, I was taking my parents to a lot of the parties and, at one of them, Herman Cain walked up to me and told me he was a big fan even though I probably didn't know who he was. Cain was the former president and CEO of Godfather's Pizza who was then running for the U.S. Senate from Georgia. I had seen him on Fox News's *Cavuto* a million times—but I couldn't remember his name for the life of me. Luckily for me, Mother was standing next to me and she piped in, "I know who you are—I donated to your campaign." Thank you, Mommy!

Mother probably contributed hundreds of thousands of dollars to various conservative outfits over the years—all in her little $20 checks—especially to any organization that claimed it was going to stop Hillary. In fact, if they mentioned Hillary in their letter, Mother sometimes made it $25.

My brothers and I always figured we'd have no inheritance, but there would be a lovely memorial to Oliver North somewhere.

Mother may have thought her most notable characteristic was her Republican activism, but, for the rest of us, it was her constant, unconditional love. She was a little love machine, spreading warmth and joy wherever she went. Every time she'd see me, even after just a few days' absence, she'd hug me as if I had been lost in the Himalayan Mountains for the past twenty years.

On Mother's birthday last year, I had a dinner party for her with Rush Limbaugh, Conrad Black, and my friends Peter and Angie. Mother was always delighted to be with people talking about politics—actually she told me that, lately, she was delighted to be around any conversations that didn't involve who had a doctor's appointment or who had died that day. So I let her stay up until 3:00 a.m. that night, well past her bedtime. Mother was so happy that after I had her all tucked in and the lights out, I heard her singing herself to sleep.

Even on the rare occasions when I'd be cross with her, she'd completely forget about it, and within ten seconds would be telling me what a wonderful, precious daughter I was. My brother Jimmy found out recently that she'd even forgotten that he had caused her to miss Reagan's first inauguration by getting in a car accident the night before we were leaving—and she never should have forgiven that.

Everyone wanted my mother to be his mother. (The "his" in that sentence is grammatically correct, and Mother would never let us forget it.) I'm sure everyone thinks he has the perfect mother, but we really did. Since I was a little girl, friends, relatives, and neighbors would bring their problems to Mother. She had a rare combination of being completely moral and completely nonjudgmental at the same time—the exact opposite of liberals who have absolutely no morals and yet are ferociously judgmental. You could tell Mother anything, get good counsel, and not end up feeling worse about yourself.

Several of Mother's New Canaan friends sent us notes last week, calling her a "gentle lady" and remarking that she never had an unkind word for anyone. As a family member, I can assure you that—much to our annoyance—she really did never have an unkind word for anyone. I mean, except Democrats, but not anyone she knew. Whenever the rest of us would be making fun of someone—trust me, always for good and sound reasons—Mother would somehow manage to muster up a defense of the miscreant. Father would always smile and say, "Your mother defends everyone."

She was, in fact, such a "gentle lady" that I had to go to her doctors' appointments and hospital visits with her and be her Mother Lion. If officious hospital administrators had told Mother to get off a gurney, go outside in the pouring rain, and stand on one foot for three hours before the doctor would see her, she'd thank them profusely and apologize for being such a bother.

She viewed her doctors' appointments as more about the doctor than herself, which is the other reason I'd have to go with her, to make sure we eventually got around to the business end of the appointment.

When she began her final decline last fall, she had to go to her Connecticut doctor without me to find out what was wrong. This was the first time she didn't seem to be getting better after a chemo treatment. So I had been worrying about her appointment all day, but when I called her that night, she immediately turned the subject to me and asked me how my book was going. I insisted on knowing if she had seen the doctor, and she perked up and brightly told me that, oh yes, she had seen him, he had all my books in his office, he was worried about Obama, too, and he has such beautiful children! One of them was excelling in some sport.

Before she launched into a spirited discussion of his children's extra-curricular activities and triumphs on the athletic field, I had to ask her, "Mommy, did the doctor happen to say anything about why you're feeling lousy?" It turned out, of course, that it was the ovarian cancer—as well as the massive amounts of poison she had been receiving to kill the cancer over the past five years. That was the beginning of the end.

Now I'll never be able to introduce my mother to friends and surprise them with her charming Southern accent.

And I'll never see my mother's beautiful face again, at least not for the next several decades here on Earth. I've been looking at her across the room in doctors' offices over the past few years, thinking to myself: there will come a point when you won't see that face again. Her angelic face always looked like home to me. My whole life, as soon as I'd see my mother's face I'd know I was safe, whether I was a little girl lost in a department store or a big girl with a problem, who needed her mother.

Thanks to the doctors at Memorial Sloan-Kettering and mother's fighting Kentucky spirit, we got to see that face much longer than anyone ever expected.

So now she's with Daddy and Jesus. Every single day since Daddy died last year, Mother would say how much she missed him and gaze at his photo, telling us what an amazing man he was and repeating his little expressions and jokes. Even though I miss her, I'm glad they're together again. I don't know about Jesus, but I think Daddy was getting impatient. Mommy was always running a little bit late.

Acknowledgements

nasmuch as some of these columns go back more than a decade, the list of people I've pestered to read material in this book is long. My circle of advisors, who get a barely-in-English draft column from me once a week, are (in the random order they appear on my group email): Jon Tukel, Miguel Estrada, Jay Mann, Gene Meyer, Jim Moody, Jeremy Rabkin, David Limbaugh, Dan Travers, Jon Caldara, Bill Armistead, Stephen Bujno, Ned Rice, Sandy Frank, Melanie Graham, Trish Baker, Robert Caplain, Merrill Kinstler, Marshall Sella, James Higgins, Mike Armstrong, Rodney Lee Conover, and Jim Hughes.

If you're thinking "it takes a village to write an Ann Coulter column," I should mention that these people work for a living and may never send me a single comment. For all I know, some of them have gone offline and joined Imam Omar Shahin in his search for the real perpetrators of the 9/11 attack. But the columns land in their inboxes and even if they only shoot back an observation once every few years, I am so grateful!

Here's a more specific breakdown, with official titles:

In addition to my actual editors at Universal Press Syndicate, Greg Melvin and Alan McDermott—who are aces!—Marshall Sella, Trish Baker, and Jim Moody are amazing friend-editors. I just wish Sella's employers would stop taking so much of his time. Trish Baker sees the big picture and will sometimes send back a column completely rearranged. No one can find tiny missing words or apostrophes like Jim Moody, and, if he ever missed one, Miguel Estrada would find it. (That's why I always say, "the Supreme Court's loss is my gain!")

Ned Rice, Rodney Conover, Mike Armstrong, and Sandy Frank are four of the funniest people I know, which comes in handy when I need an emergency joke or a zippy title. (Unfortunately, they are also among the funniest people Hollywood knows, so they're too busy working at actual jobs for my taste.) Robert Caplain is the master of titles so risqué, even *I* won't use them. But he always makes me laugh.

Mark Joseph is my consultant on Hollywood and on Christianity. (It's a highly specialized field.) Jeremy Rabkin and Miguel Estrada are my designated wet blankets, usually responding only when they take issue with something I've written—which is fantastic. James Higgins is my expert on Republican screw-ups, a vast and complex field. Jon Tukel is my criminal law and terrorism advisor; Jim Hughes is my invective stylist; and Younis Zubchevich is my counsel on Arabs, Muslims, and hating liberals. Bill Armistead is my firearms advisor—not so much for my writing, but for actual firearms.

If I allowed any of them to review this acknowledgements page, they'd probably disagree. But like everything else I write, it's mine, so I can say whatever I want.

I harassed most of these people—and more!—in choosing which columns to include. After I had brutally, painfully cut about 70 percent of them from the past decade, I started sending batches of columns to everyone I knew, asking, "Do I keep this one or that one?" It was like a never-ending, right-wing optometrist's exam.

I got an enormous amount of help in culling the columns, as well as in reading the new introductions, from Suzy Vassillov, David Friedman, Younis Zubchevich, Jim Hughes, Trish Baker, and Allan Ryskind. (I find that after spending years annoying one batch of friends, it's good to switch to new victims.) They generously read the new material and—since my first drafts are written primarily in Pig Latin—that wasn't an easy job. When we could cut no more, my Regnery editor, Elizabeth Kantor, did a terrific job performing the final amputations, as well as suggesting a nice reorganization of the chapters.

I couldn't include half of my favorite columns, but I tried to respond to popular demand. My brother John's favorite column is "Negroes With Guns," followed by every other column of mine about guns. My brother Jimmy's favorite column is the one contrasting the wimp-ass "torture" at Guantanamo to growing up with him. If you had forced my mother at gunpoint to pick a favorite column, it would be "In Hoc Signo Vinces." (Either that or Father's eulogy. Or the last one she read.) All those columns are in the book. I don't think my father ever told me he had a favorite column—he liked them all! But he'd be happy that I included a few mentions of Tailgunner Joe.

Speaking of liberals' "McCarthyism" myth, I will conclude by saying to anyone I've forgotten to mention here: at least you won't be denounced on the Senate floor by Senator Chuck Schumer for being thanked in an Ann Coulter book, as Bush nominee Miguel Estrada was in February 2003.

Index